Top business leaders and experts rave about *Creating WE*

"The right book for the challenging times we face in today's business environment. As many companies struggle with trying to sustain growth utilizing outdated programs, [Glaser's] book takes the reader from [her] description of the 'culture of toxicity' to thought-provoking concepts she mentions that allow people to 'tune in' and create ways to help companies grow stronger. . . ."

—**Rich Wilson,** *Director, Retail Sales East Region,*
Pepsi-Cola Company North America

"Judith E. Glaser's *Creating WE* is a virtual toolbox to build an effective and 'happy' organization where a business and its team players can succeed. She combines real case studies with easy-to-follow 'how-to techniques' that move the business owner/leader into action quickly. I started applying Glaser's tools to Women's Leadership Exchange from the get-go and am already seeing results. *Creating WE* is a 'must-read' for every business owner who is on the growth track. It's one of the most valuable business books I have read this year. . . ."

—**Leslie Grossman,** *President, B2Women;*
cofounder, Women's Leadership Exchange

"Judith Glaser hits on the single most important element in all of the discussions about leadership, culture, and transformation: She deals with the power of individual and co-creative leadership."

—**Jim Hoverman,** *President and CEO,*
Blue Chip Marketing Group; author of Summiting

"The key in business is the leader's ability to enable everyone to feel like they are part of a winning team—we know this mantra in our hearts, yet making it happen is much more difficult. *Creating WE* gives leaders a roadmap for shaping the DNA of their company—creating a culture of inspired leadership and ownership of the future. This is a seminal book on leadership that every executive must read!"

—**Judy George,** *CEO, Domain Home Fashions*

"*Creating WE* should be required reading for every 'C-suite' executive who has the courage to really embrace change."

—**Dick Singer,** *President, RDS; Associates Chair, TEC International*

"*Creating WE* is a terrific book. Judith Glaser develops a real-world approach to help companies see beyond their limitations and the constant crisis *du jour* to develop new attitudes for success. I'm a believer."

—**Alan Baral,** *COO, New Wave Entertainment*

Top business leaders and experts rave about *Creating WE*

"I found *Creating WE* practical and inspiring, complete with real 'here's what people were facing, and here's how they (and you) can create a different and better outcome' examples. [Glaser took] what are genuine challenges we all face to one degree or another and helped us see much better alternatives!"
—**Angela Scalpello,** *VP Human Resources, PRNewswire*

"In the fast-paced corporate world we live in, common sense is often forgotten— or simply ignored. Judith Glaser's *Creating WE* is full of common-sense thinking that invites the 'human' back to the corporate environment. The concept of 'WE' leadership can restore the humanity in our work and our homes."
—**Nancy Hunt,** *President, We Are Family Foundation*

"*Creating WE* puts you in the driver's seat as you steer your way through an array of practical situations and challenges that generate new ways of thinking about leadership and culture within an organization. A tremendous resource for leading the charge in creating a WE-centric organization."
—**Stan Juozaitis,** *Director, Sales/Systems Training, Unilever NA*

"I've spent twenty-plus years studying, teaching, and practicing how increased relationship connection, personal responsibility, and outcome-oriented language can positively transform corporate culture. This is a useful, powerful, and clearly written book that addresses these key organizational management and leadership competencies and how you can develop and apply them."
—**Robert White,** *CEO of ARC Worldwide;*
author of Leading an Extraordinary Life

"This is a book for skeptics of touchy-feely treatises on leadership that end up collecting dust on your bookshelf. *Creating WE* is a take-no-prisoners, example-filled look at the challenge of building healthy organizations from scratch or revamping corporate cultures, yet it is presented through stirring, heartfelt stories. And this is not just talk: Judith Glaser perfectly balances the 'why' of leadership with cogent and executable advice on how to take struggling organizations and turn them around."
—**Jon Entine,** *Fellow, American Enterprise Institute;*
Scholar-in-Residence, Miami University;
contributing author to Case Histories in Business Ethics:
The Virtues and Moral Decision-Making in Business

"Here is a brilliant step-by-step manual, in an easy conversational style, not just for businesses but for life itself. Separateness or connectivity is a pressing world issue; this inspirational book can have a global impact. Wow! Fantastic, Judith!"
—**Bronwen, Viscountess Astor**

Top business leaders and experts rave about *Creating WE*

"If you are a leader in any organization, for profit, not-for-profit, or government, you ought to read this book."
—**Lynn San Andres,** *Former President, NAWBO-NYC;*
Chapter President, Mason Alexander Group Ltd.

"*Creating WE* is an important book about whole systems transformation. Judith Glaser has written a practical book that helps individuals and organizations see the depth of interconnectedness in our world and in our lives. She provides an appreciative inquiry into the theory and techniques of building on our strengths and letting go of fear."
—**Marge Schiller, Ph.D.,** *President, Positive Change Corps*
(a global association serving schools and youth);
author of Appreciative Leaders: In the Eye of the Beholder

"For serious business and people organizations, Judith Glaser's *Creating WE* is, beyond a shadow of a doubt, a must-have book. It answers your 'Why,' 'How?' and 'So what?' questions about making things happen while demonstrating some exceptionally effective change strategies used in the real world. When you apply your specific learnings from this important book, you are likely to enjoy sharper focus, clarity of direction, and better use of your organization's power to achieve some amazingly sustainable organizational change."
—**Stephen Cotterell,** *Founder, Building Better Outcomes;*
Director, IPE International Publishers Limited

"This is one of the most useful and clearly written books on the leading edge of leadership and culture that I have read. The entire book is written with clarity, wisdom, and, not infrequently, with grace."
—**Cathi Raffaeli,** *President and CEO, Unext;*
President, Cardean University

"Judith Glaser has nailed it! *Creating WE* offers a compelling blueprint for the only kind of corporate dynamic that can work in today's world. A must-read for every corporate executive or business owner."
—**Gary Zammit,** *CEO, Clinilabs*

"A must-read for leaders and managers building businesses in this day and age. In a clear and engaging way, Judith Glaser gets to the essence of what is required to create a culture of collaboration—environments where people want to connect their hearts to their minds. Through stories, strategies, and solutions, *Creating WE* paves the way for companies of any size to soar to new heights."
—**Sharon P. Whiteley,** *President and CEO, ThirdAge Inc.*

Top business leaders and experts rave about *Creating WE*

"Judith Glaser has touched upon the heart and soul of that most elusive of qualities: inspired leadership. Read this book and embody the wisdom that lies within."

—**Stephen Balkam,** *CEO, Internet Content Rating Association*

"Judith Glaser crystallizes within the corporate environment that which separates success from failure; the team rules of engagement both within and without, focusing on the critical actions that separate losers from winners. A required read not only for those who aspire to climb the corporate ladder, but for life itself."

—**Arthur Lieberman,** *entrepreneur and litigator*

"Uncannily simple, yet profound in its revelations, *Creating WE* leaps from the business section—a life leadership journey, encompassing health, self and (family) enterprise—a truly great, mainstream read that also just happens to be a landmark business and leadership work. A must read!"

—**Brian Penry,** *Creative Ideation Expert*

"Just wanted to let you know I started reading your book when I got home and had a hard time putting it down."

—**Harold Feinleib,** *Chairman, Aperature*

"Somewhere between the 1960s and the 1980s, the We Generation became the Me Generation. Fortunately, the pendulum is swinging back, but with a new sophistication and pragmatism as Judith Glaser brilliantly documents in the world of work explaining why 'WE-thinking' is a key to success in personal and business terms. To borrow a phrase from Jamaica's Rasta culture, she 'overstands' the problem and points us in the win-win direction."

—**Danny Schechter,** *Editor,*
Mediachannel.org; author and filmmaker

"*Creating WE* is what leadership is all about. Judith Glaser's examples underscore the importance of investing in team building and working together for maximum organizational success."

—**Michael Frieze,** *CEO, Gordon Brothers Group*

"Judith Glaser is all about 'WE.' Now others can tap into Judith's wisdom and learn how to create and sustain miraculous transformation in their personal and professional lives."

—**Deb Jacobs,** *MSOD, President and CEO, Innolect Inc.*

creating we ™

Change I-Thinking to WE-Thinking

Build a Healthy, Thriving Organization

JUDITH E. GLASER

PLATINUM PRESS

AVON, MASSACHUSETTS

Creating WE™ is a trademark of Benchmark Communications, Inc.

Published by
Platinum Press, an imprint of Adams Media,
an F+W Publications Company
57 Littlefield Street, Avon, MA 02322. U.S.A.
www.adamsmedia.com

Platinum Press is a trademark of F+W Publications, Inc.

ISBN: 1-59337-268-X

Printed in the United States of America.

J I H G F E D C B A

Library of Congress Cataloging-in-Publication Data
Glaser, Judith E.
Creating WE / Judith E. Glaser.
p.   cm.
ISBN 1-59337-268-X
1. Corporate culture. 2. Organizational behavior. 3. Communication in organizations.
4. Interpersonal relations. 5. Leadership. I. Title.
HD58.7.G58 2005
658.3'145—dc22
2004022113

This publication is designed to provide accurate and authoritative information with regard to the subject matter covered. It is sold with the understanding that the publisher is not engaged in rendering legal, accounting, or other professional advice. If legal advice or other expert assistance is required, the services of a competent professional person should be sought.
—From a *Declaration of Principles* jointly adopted by a Committee of the American Bar Association and a Committee of Publishers and Associations

Many of the designations used by manufacturers and sellers to distinguish their product are claimed as trademarks. Where those designations appear in this book and Adams Media was aware of a trademark claim, the designations have been printed with initial capital letters.

Interior illustrations by Argosy.

This book is available at quantity discounts for bulk purchases.
For information, please call 1-800-872-5627.

Creating WE is dedicated to my husband, Richard D. Glaser. He opened my heart when it had closed, nourished my soul when it was barren, and gave me the courage to believe I could create a future of extraordinary possibilities with others. Rich taught me what it means to create WE in all aspects of my life. This book is dedicated to his never-ending love and affection.

Contents

The power of an organization is the capacity generated by relationships.

It's real energy that can only come into existence through relationships.

Power is energy. It needs to flow through the organization.

It can't be confined to functions or levels or hierarchy.

Positive or negative organizational energy is determined by the quality of relationships.

Those who relate through coercion, or in disregard of others, create negative energy.

Those who are open to others and who see others in their fullness create positive energy.

ADAPTED FROM
LEADERSHIP FROM THE NEW SCIENCES,
MARGARET WHEATLEY

The ability of teams to sustain their efforts
when times get tough is, to a large extent,
the result of the high standard
of interpersonal communication exchanged.

HOOP MORGAN III
THE FORTE INSTITUTE
2004

Acknowledgments

MANY OF US THINK we have books inside us, and we either find a
way to put the words to paper or we just dream about doing it. There
are a few people who I want to acknowledge who were pivotal in my
book-writing journey. First, to Judy Katz, my personal friend, who
is a genius at finding, developing, and promoting authors. Without
Judy, I would have lived only with my hopes and dreams of writing
a book. When my words were good enough, she introduced me to Al
Zuckerman, who became my agent. Al turned the task of finding the
right publisher into a Journey of Discovery. His never-ending belief in
me and this book, his diligence and incredible help with titling and
positioning with publishers gave me confidence that we would find the
best home for my book. His professionalism, wisdom, and foresight
were invaluable. To find the right home was his goal and so he did.

For all the horror stories I've heard about books getting bought
and then forgotten, my experience with the Adams Media team
has taught me another way. When Scott Watrous, COO, and Gary
Krebs, Publishing Director, visited Al's New York offices seeking
new acquisitions for Adams Media, Al handed them *Creating WE*.
They both thought exactly the same thing—that not only was it perfect for Adams, but it also reflected Scott's philosophies of business
culture; he's been using "WE" all along and doing an awesome job!
Gary brought the manuscript back to Adams and assigned it to Kate
Epstein, who acquired it. From our first contact to the delivery of

the books to the bookstore, I have come to believe that I am "living a dream." Everyone at Adams Media took my project under their wings and shepherded it to completion. From editing my words to creating the cover, they gave this project more attention and hands-on support than I could have ever imagined.

Gary Krebs, my primary editor, lived with my manuscript day and night, through family vacations, and weekends as well as workdays. He is the most extraordinary editor I have ever worked with. From the moment he took on the project, he brought a new level of energy, insight, and talent. Gary's ability to guide and influence the content as well as the structure of the manuscript took the stories and gave them breadth, always providing feedback and suggestions in a positive and candid way. Gary was the magical alchemy behind the book. His extraordinary approach brought life to the concepts and lifted the guidelines and practical suggestions off the page, presenting them in full view to the reader.

Another person who needs special mention because of the incredible role she played in helping me understand how to move from ideas to books is Juli Huss. Juli was my writing coach and the angel on my shoulder watching over the process, and who in a thirty-day marathon, helped me turn seventeen pages into a book by putting my heart and soul in the writing process. She taught me my most important lessons: to honor my own wisdom and trust my instincts.

Next to Larry Butler, who became my developmental editor during the major editing of this work. Larry joined our book-publishing team to help me restructure and reshape the material into an everyday practical life guidebook. Larry's insight, humor with words, and incredible standard for getting it right made the editing partnership we created a joy to experience.

And now to those closest to me: My sister, Joan Heffler, whose treasured editorial comments set me on the right path. To my brother, Jon Entine, who never stopped being excited and supportive of my work. My husband Richard was my rock, and without him I would have given up. My son Jacob taught me to trust the next generation, for they know more than we do. He came up with the term "Leadershifts," which you'll read about in the book. To write this book, I had to learn to keep dreaming and hoping. My daughter Becky taught me to keep dreaming. Her inspirational poem, which you will find at the end of the book on page 336, sat on my desk reminding me that dreams do come true. Thanks, also, to my mother and father, who did the best they could with a "rebel child," and to my stepmother Millie, who accepted me the way I was. To my grandmother Anna, who opened me to wonder, and Sara, Arthur, and Carole Glaser, my biggest supporters. And to Doreen Steg, who took me under her wings when I was in graduate school and launched me clearly on my path of intellectual curiosity.

The writing of this book was a labor of love and the contributions of so many people who gave their time, their experience, and most of all, their support. Special thanks to Myrna Popper for suggesting I write a book in 1996 when we met at a workshop. Thanks to my Goddess Group (authors and media professionals) who met every month to inspire and support each other: Laura Norman; Judy Kuriansky (Dr. Judy); and Judith Orloff, M.D.; Shelley Ackerman; Joanne Roberts; Joan Horton; Kathy Brady; Kathy Bishop; Candida Royalle; Myreah Moore; and Judy Grafe. And a special, special thanks to Goddesses LaurieSue Brockway, Barbara Biziou, and Wendy Sarashon who are amazingly fabulous women authors and friends who, over the past eight years, gave me courage to stay the course in spite of the pushback I was getting about my ideas.

A special thanks to Herb Addison, Tom Gorman, Mike Snell, Peter Cutler, Lindsay Pollack, Heidi Williamson, Tony Esposito, and David Griffith from Adams House, Helen Rees, Doris Michaels, Meredith Bernstein, and Arielle Ford who guided me forward into the publishing world. Special thanks to Lester Colodny, Bob Donovan, Lisa Goldstein, and Christine Lewis-Varley, who read manuscripts and gave me feedback when it was needed most. And special thanks to Ken Shelton, publisher of *Executive Excellence* magazine, and Florence Stone of American Management Association, who selected "Vital Instincts" and "WE-centric Leadership" as lead stories in 2004 special editions on leadership. Thanks to Joann Lublin from the *Wall Street Journal*, with whom I shared thought leadership on workplace issues.

Special thanks to a few people who have challenged my thinking and taught me to trust my insights: Jose Acevedo and Bob Fuller and Michelle Boos-Stone, and Lucy Nelson, whose friendship and wisdom inspired us all farther along the arc of innovation and insight; all are colleagues, co-creating partners, and lifelong friends, who continue to inspire this work. And to Franklin Rubenstein, Ph.D., who helped me see how to make the complex simple.

Special thanks to my treasured business associates who have worked with me over the past twenty-three years to make sure I stayed on course: Hoop Morgan III from Forte, Deanna Brown, Dr. Lynda Klau, Wendy Kaufman, Yael Zofi, Linda Buggy, Jamie Goddard, Bryan Mattimore, Ben Dattner, Marc Gaccionne, Jim Hoverman, Nancy Snell, Geoff Grenert, and Todd Applebaum, who fueled my mind and helped us create WE. To a writing partner, Barbara Glacel, Ph.D. Special thanks to my speaking coach Jean Gatz, and to Brian Penry, an incredible graphics designer and art director who always makes words create music on the page.

To write this book, friends helped as I worked at finding the right words and the right stories. Thanks to Donna Flagg, who introduced me to a great writing coach; to Marilyn Horowitz, Jan Goldstoff, and Evie, who provided spiritual love and friendship along the journey.

My friends commented on my manuscript, and their insights added so much: to Susan Sachs of Hayden Resources and Shelly Sachs who kept me in good humor through the process; to Jon Barb, Jeremy Nash, Mark Hall, Ellen Goldstein, Kathie Duff-Wilson, Kathryn Switzer, Roger Robinson, Leslie Jaffee, George Anderheggen, Jan Balkam, Miriam Nelson-Gillette, Steve and Bari Rosman, Diane Downey, Anne and Burt DelVillano, Cindy and John Tortoricci, Catherine Samose, Cathi and John Raffaeli, Lee and Nancy Keet, David Lemberg, Karen Pinkman, Marnie McBryde, Heather and Gerardo Valez, Glen Mercanti, Amy and Gary Nenner, Bobbie Little, Laura Day, Susanne and Richard Atkins, Susan Leis, Nikki Petty, Sylvia and Alan Neigher, Beverly and Arthur Lieberman, Gary and Kristin Zammit, Rick Steirwalt, Lauren and Bob Cohen, Roy and Linda Jacobsen, Deborah Dumaine and Mark Hochman, Margot Raven, Sue and Tony Revis, Shirley and Jim Roberto, Michele and Tony Grimsditch, Joan and Michael Gray, and Judy and Harold Feinleib. Special thanks to my friends and neighbors Tera and Michael Morris, whose constant support, wisdom, and insights into the publishing maze gave me hope that my book would find the right home.

Thanks to some extraordinary consultants: Jim Kouzes; Instructional Systems Association, Earl Rose, David Berlew, and Alex Moore; Robert White; Lou Peluso from Industrial Revolutions, Inc.; the DBM (Drake Beam Morin) team of incredible coaches, regional managers, and sales managers; Paul Connolly from Performance Programs; Nancy Parsons, president of CDR, Steve Gilliland, CEO of Performance Plus; and the whole Innolect team, especially Kittie Watson and Deb Jacobs for their friendship and collegial "pushback."

To my nonprofit colleagues who work to create a bigger WE in the world: Nile Rodgers and Nancy Hunt of We Are Family Foundation; Stephen Balkam of State of the World Address; and Danny Schechter of Media Channel and Global Vision. To my colleagues from WITH (Women in Transition Helping and Healing) and my cofounders of the Executive Women's Business Forum, Paula Weiner, Judy Harrison, and Leslie Benning, along with the other sixty women who meet regularly to stimulate each other's growth and professional development.

Thanks to Steve Sadov, former CEO of Clairol, who gave me the opportunity to learn and practice the best wisdom on communication strategy with his organization, and to Carl Freund, who worked as my development partner and taught me the value of a commitment to Category Leadership. A special thanks to Valerie Held and Nick Amadori from UST, and Boehringer Ingelheim executives, who allowed me to test my ideas with them. And special thanks to Hanneke Frese at Citibank, who was willing to challenge our own best thinking for the next best level.

To Mary Wang, president of DKNY, who never stopped believing in this work, and who, over a decade, made leadership development our mutual priority, and to her support and diligence in reading chapters and drafts over the years to let me know when I was losing my focus or intellectualizing words. To Michael Frieze, CEO of Gordon Brothers, who read my first major proposal and helped me stay focused on Vital Instincts and language so I could see the real wisdom of my work. To my friend and respected colleague, Angela Ahrendts of Liz Claiborne, who told me over and over again to stay focused on instincts and culture, giving me courage to proudly stand tall at times I felt alone. To Tom Kabat, from PWC, who read me the underlinings of his favorite passages so I knew which words resonated most.

Special thanks to the many clients who continue to allow me into their lives to test out the concepts in this book and develop them further—without their commitment, these would have only been words on a page: to the former Donna Karan presidents George Ackerman, Anna Bakst, Linda Beauchamp, Jane Terker, Sonia Caproni, Betty Ende, and Steve Ruzow, who made our work both exciting and challenging; to Stan Juozaitis from Uniliver and Lipton; to Rich Reardon from Union Carbide, and Carol Wood of Champion International, who trusted the process and became part of it; Paul Carluicci from News America Marketing who believed in partnering from the get-go; to Mike Buckman, CEO, and Nancy Pavey from WorldTravel BTI, to Dianna Keith, Barry Andersen, and Stratton Sclavos, CEO of VeriSign, who enabled us to push the leadership envelope one more time. To Sandy Garrett, of National Council of Jewish Women; Lynn San Andres of National Association for Women Business Owners (NAWBO-NYC); Mike Pilnik of Columbia House, Greg Flores of Reed Elsevier; Mark Bruckner, Phil Sleeman and Mila Baker of Pfizer Inc.; Sean O'Neil of Novartis; and Angela Scofield of PRNewswire.

And most of all, to my treasured clients who, both during the writing and experimenting with new ideas, kept their doors open and continued to invite me back to play: most significantly Alan Baral, Allen Haines, and Paul Apel of New Wave Entertainment; Kyle Rudy, Dan Nockels, Ethel Wragg, and Felice Schulaner from Coach Inc., who enabled us to teach and coach the next generation of leaders; Bob Lutz (now vice chairman of GM) and Craig Muhlhauser, CEO of Exide Technologies, who enabled us to test out the work at a global level, and to Donna Karan who, in an industry that changes faster than street lights, provided me a way to get my Ph.D. in human behavior and culture transformation.

Preface

The more original a discovery,
the more obvious it seems afterwards.

ARTHUR KOESTLER, WRITER

Creating WE It sounds like such a high-blown concept. If you're picking this book off the shelf and are unfamiliar with my business philosophies, you may be wondering who I am and how I arrived at this grandiose-sounding idea.

Creating WE has grown out of my work over the past twenty years with hundreds of executives from dozens of well-known companies around the globe—clients who were willing to experiment with new ways of thinking, to "test-drive" refreshing new beliefs and behaviors about how to create healthy, productive, and thriving companies. Clients who were willing to be on the cutting edge, to push the envelope, to challenge norms. I could not have written this book without them.

I've been consulting to *Fortune* 500 companies for over twenty years and been invited to work with incredible executives from companies such as Pfizer Inc., Clairol, Coach Inc., Lipton, Newscorp, and Citibank, who have thrown open their doors, shared their deepest concerns—their insecurities as well as their proudest moments.

My clients have taught me what I know today. They've pushed me to think beyond the conventional wisdom. They've asked me to help them grow. And, in doing so, they've made it hard for me to accept the status quo.

This book is inspired by my clients and my husband—and both have made sure I don't sleep at night. They have conspired to keep me awake thinking about how to expand their horizons, their opportunities, and their futures. Awake or asleep, I've been working on this book.

In the Beginning

One weekend morning, my husband and I decided to start working early. We share a home office, and often start our days early when we can do some of our best thinking together. Early for us is about 4:30 A.M. On this very special morning we saw the sun come up. We heard the birds chirp, and we talked about how our work connected. Why we had this conversation on this day is something we will never know. What we do know is that it happened, and, at that moment, we realized that we were both put on Earth to work on the same challenge.

Rich, the president of an early-stage pharmaceutical company, is discovering a new cure for cancer. It is a disruptive technology—in nontechnical-sounding terms, a technology that is so new and different from anything that has come before that it challenges how people view the solution to the problem. In this case, Rich's cancer research would radically change the way people think about how to cure cancer. Meanwhile, my life's work has involved finding new ways to help executives create healthy organizations. Rich is pursuing transformation at the cellular level; I am pursuing transformation at the individual and organizational level. The two were bound to connect, and, during this early-morning dialogue, they did.

My original theory was anchored to Vital Instincts, a concept I created to shift our thinking from territoriality to partnering—a shift that I felt would have a transformative impact on how we think, behave, and work together. The essence of the theory is that all human beings have an innate knowledge and wisdom about what partnering looks like. We have—wired into our systems—the instructions for how to partner. The basis of this instruction manual is that we are all connected, even though it may not seem to be the case. We already have the knowledge for how to build community, how to grow, and how to ensure that we expand our potential. These are our Vital Instincts.

And, because of these Vital Instincts, we also know that when our connections are disrupted or broken, we move from feeling okay to not feeling okay. We become afraid and we turn to defensive behaviors to protect ourselves, our families, and our communities.

We know intuitively what it feels like to be accepted, connected, trusted—a friend—and what it feels like to be rejected, judged, and outside the clan. When we feel disconnected and afraid, we project the word *enemy* onto the other person. In other words, knowing where we stand with others is hard-wired into our genes. Being connected as a friend creates health; being unconnected as a foe creates an unhealthy state.

So, on that very important morning, my husband and I made our first discovery. We realized that the work Rich was doing with his new approach to curing cancer and the work I was doing on helping cultures change and grow and become healthy were mirror images of each other. What was happening at the DNA level in cells could explain what was happening at the organizational level; they were all intimately connected. This was a profound moment and something we will both remember for the rest of our lives.

Rich's contribution to my thinking was enormous. His new company, Biomega, was discovering how to cure cancer not by injecting poison into the system, but by reminding the system how to be healthy and normal. His team's approach assumed that cells already know how to be healthy, yet sometimes they forget—particularly if they are under attack. When the stress and pressure of life outside starts to mount, when we think about how overwhelming life becomes when we feel so alone, when the toxins around us infect our health, our immune systems cannot handle it and we get sick. So, if we could remind cells how to be normal, they would be able to default to that healthy state because it's already hard-wired into the system. The reminder, it turns out, is a simple peptide which, when injected into cancer cells grown in culture, has the miraculous ability to reinstruct the cells at the DNA level to act again as healthy cells.

As I reflect further on the amazing synchronicity between my husband's cancer research and my work with organizations, I realize that, for me, the story is even bigger: It is a linking event that ties together my past, my present, and my future.

My Past

A month after Rich and I were married, my mother died of cancer after struggling for twelve years with a melanoma that traveled into her lymph system and ultimately spread throughout her body. We were not allowed to talk about her cancer. Back then, cancer was a taboo topic. We watched her go through round after round of chemo, underground drugs, and shame. We lived with painful memories about fights with cancer, fear of cancer, and the impact it has not just on the person with the disease but also on those who are connected to the patient.

My Present

On September 11, 2001, at the same time the World Trade Center was under attack, I was diagnosed with a rapidly growing form of breast cancer. This time, I had my own fears, pains, and challenges to deal with. But I chose not to retreat into silence as my mother had, but rather to connect and share my experience with those around me. I was about to break a fundamental pattern, one that gave me a new perspective on health and disease—my own and others. I reached out to all my friends and family and shared my experience, drew strength from them, and overcame my fear of this horrible disease.

In 2001, Rich's cancer research was just beginning, and he had newly become the CEO of Biomega. His job was to structure the company, help define the research, get investors, build alliances, and find investor support. His job was to ensure the patent rights for the product and advance the research.

Today, in 2005, they have made great progress in purifying the compound—the peptide—yet are still a few years away from getting the drug approved and on the market. This process takes time and money. It takes finding larger drug companies to either sponsor or invest in the research. I wish that his product had been on the market when I was diagnosed with breast cancer, but it was not.

Today, I'm in great health. Yes, I did undergo traditional chemo and radiation with all the toxic side effects. I lost my hair and bought wigs for all occasions. My body and bones were weakened quite seriously and for months I found getting out of bed almost too painful to describe. I developed what doctors call "chemo brain." I could not decide what to wear, eat, or think. I lost passion and direction and was not sure if I would ever work again. Some people give up working after cancer, or change jobs because they feel they cannot possibly return to their earlier levels of energy. I did not quit.

My Future

As I came out of my bout with cancer, I realized that this was a pivotal event in my life. I was not sure how, yet I knew I was going to see life in a new way—not because I had cancer, but because I was able to see how my understanding cancer would change my life.

Cancer cells are not like normal cells. They are alone; they are isolationists disconnected from the larger organism. They are territorial, growing all over the other cells. Cancer cells draw the energy and health out of healthy cells, and they protect themselves from harm in a way that enables them to live as though they were not connected to the larger system in which they are contained.

The relationship between Rich's work on cancer and my work on organizations created a fusion of new insights that would drive our respective efforts in new, exciting directions. I knew that pinpointing the connections between healthy cells and healthy organizations was a far deeper and broader endeavor than the work I had been doing. As I began to see and understand these connections, a crystal-clear arc was created that suddenly made new sense of my past, gave it new meaning, and enabled me to grow again. I was learning the very things I always taught my clients—to revisit the past to draw out new lessons for the future. I was about to take my own medicine.

Turning Pain into Growth

The Dalai Lama believes that the mind and heart are in some form of balance. Sometimes we may grow up and ignore the compassion and heart and focus only on the brain, thus losing the balance. That is when disasters and unwelcome things happen.

All my life I've been fascinated by the connection between heart and mind, logic and compassion, fact and fiction. These words seem so separate on the surface, yet I was drawn—as my life's work—to challenge the notion of *separateness* in everything.

As an undergraduate at Temple University, I pursued interdisciplinary studies such as anthropology and archeology, looking for answers to questions about how we bond and connect, how we create culture, and how we change culture. These incredibly fascinating courses exposed me to the lifestyles of both old—6,000-year-old Neolithic cultures—and new cultures. I studied how communities form, cultures develop, and human beings evolve socially. My studies in physiology, psychology, sociology, and general semantics all added depth and breadth to my questions about separateness and connectivity, fitting in and not fitting in, about pushing the envelope and challenging the status quo versus living in compliance with current rules and norms.

After finishing up my undergraduate work, I was fortunate to be awarded a research fellowship in human behavior and development from Drexel University. I was their first graduate fellow, and was given tremendous freedom in the courses I took. In that spirit, I spent a semester at Harvard at the Bales School of Social Relations, where I studied organization behavior—one of the most influential programs of my educational career. My sponsoring professor, Dr. Doreen Steg, also allowed me to take courses at the University of Pennsylvania, where I studied systems thinking and patterns of consumer behavior. While seemingly unconnected, both were pivotal in giving me a broader perspective on understanding the powerful link between behavior and impact in larger systems. In the late 1970s and early 1980s, I went back to school again and this time it was at Fairfield University, where I studied corporate and political communication. I was taking more courses to broaden my thinking about global communications, external communications, power, and influence. At Fairfield, I also studied video production and learned to use media as a tool for helping executives express their authentic voice, to help organizations "tell their story" and to reach broader audiences with critical messages. I was now coming face-to-face with the work I would come to love most of all—the world of business leadership. In looking back, I can now see the path I was on. Program after program gave me new thinking tools for sorting through the concepts about power and influence, leadership and productivity, innovation and transformation.

My drive to work with leaders and organizations, cultures and teams has stemmed from four things: my need to understand my upbringing; the lack of connectivity, caring, and support I witnessed firsthand in companies; the balance and tension that exists between health and disease; and the often tragic effect that unhealthy thinking has on our lives, our relationships—and our organizations.

My clients have always provided me with a working laboratory to experiment with new ideas on how to enable culture change and grow leaders; it has become my life's mission to help executives create leaps into their future potential.

By naming my company Benchmark Communications, I was affirming my mission: to work with CEOs and their teams to set new standards of excellence, even as they face new challenges in a world of moving targets. I would help them focus on building strong brands, inspiring leaders, and raising the cultural IQ. This mission enabled me to see how some leaders were able to create healthy cultures in the pursuit of their next level of success and soar personally, professionally, and organizationally. Those who did not focus on creating healthy cultures tolerated levels of what I call *cultural toxicity*, a situation that undermines the hopes, dreams, and aspirations of all involved.

While many people in my field were focusing on "fixing what was broken" in companies, I found myself exploring what was working and how to create health. I discovered that when I guided clients on how to "remember what they already knew" about creating environments poised for success, these executives miraculously remembered how to be Vital Leaders—and the business results that followed were astounding. Working with such esteemed companies and executives at Novartis, Revlon, Pfizer Inc., Siemens, Lipton, and PricewaterhouseCoopers, I came to realize that the principles I was learning cut across industry segments and geographic differences.

The principles seemed simple, and I started to codify them into Key Benchmarks for Success. First, I began to take note of why companies and executives fail:

- Lack of shared focus, shared purpose, and/or shared vision.
- Lack of enterprise-wide communication.
- Lack of organizational ambition and a strategic approach for getting there.
- Lack of respect for others within the organization.
- Failure to tap resources and inner talent, creativity, and responsibility.
- Failure to break down walls ("silos") between divisions.
- Lack of team cohesion and failure to develop team agreements, rules of engagement, and decision-making processes.
- Failure to focus outside and see the customer.
- Lack of hope and spirit; a punishing environment.

The end result? A company culture that expresses an I-centric fingerprint: a company riddled with internal politics, with silos and territoriality, and a company with an internal focus where pleasing the boss is more important than pleasing the customer. In sum, it's a non-WE-centric company.

Shortly thereafter, I proceeded to create a list detailing how executives and companies succeed:

- Ability to have healthy conversations that build a sense of common purpose and assert a strong leadership voice and laser-sharp focus on the work to be done.
- Ability to clarify organizational ambition and create a strategic focus that encourages employees to step out of their Comfort Zones and take action in the face of ambiguity.
- Ability to leave behind the toxic, emotional baggage of the past and to tap into new resources and underused talents by encouraging creativity and responsibility.
- Ability to exchange knowledge and wisdom between groups.
- Ability to have Vital Conversations that challenge all parties in creative ways.
- Ability to create and live by team agreements, rules of engagement, and a clear decision-making process.
- Ability to redefine challenging circumstances in creative ways, to tell new stories with an external focus that connect with the needs of customers, exploit and shape future trends, and reposition business for category leadership.
- Ability to focus on the positives, celebrate success, grow from failure, and build hope and spirit into the organizational DNA; to repeatedly create and achieve critical milestones of success.
- And, most importantly, ability to find one's voice and be fearless in creating a "WE-centric organization" that fosters an attitude of "we are in this together."

Transformation Through Conversation

As my associates and I worked with companies to create healthy conversations among leaders and their employees, among companies and their clients, and among colleagues, we began to see incredible breakthroughs—both in the changes that took place and in the speed with which companies were able to make these changes and shift directions. Many of these companies went from being on the verge of giving up to taking leadership positions in their industries.

In the mid-1980s, I wrote a business dictionary for Random House. In this project, I had to come up with 3,500 new business terms and define them. From this project I learned the importance of the meanings of words in shaping our thinking. The dictionary project has had a profound influence on all my client work, as well as on the writing of this book. It's caused me to realize the power of focusing on language, redefining words, and powerful conversations as transformational triggers.

One of the big "word shifts" for me came in the early 1980s when I began to use the word *transformation* instead of *change management* to explain what my associates and I were seeing take place in the work we were doing. We would witness a transformation that defied logic and always took less time than expected. We were not managing change. We were witnessing a transformation—the concepts are very different, and we had to understand why. One client, Mary Wang—the president of DKNY—expressed the results we were seeing in a way much better than I could:

"You and Jose accomplished in weeks what other consultants could not deliver in months. Your approach to solving organizational problems and helping us to focus on corporate goals is unique—no one works as you do. The way that you structured our two-day off-site meeting gave us tremendous focus, inspiration, and guidance. We were able to accomplish a number of major tasks toward future company strategies, and we did this together, as a management team. We feel that most managers came out of these sessions with a better understanding of what needs to be done overall (big picture) and their specific role within it (supply chain). Many associates were able to 'Let Go' of their past feelings and inhibitions, in order to move toward a better future. Thanks again for the enlightening experience."

The wisdom behind *Creating WE* began to emerge as a result of my work with our clients and out of their trust in the process of learning we were all experiencing together. The principle behind what we were seeing and experiencing seemed to be simple: We are all connected. Even though the umbilical cord is cut at birth, our emotions and energy remain connected. We are connected through our families, organizations, and communities. We are connected through the beliefs we hold about the world. We are connected at the heart and at the head. When these connections are broken at work, what was a healthy, growth-oriented culture turns unhealthy and every member of the organization—every cell of the human organism—suffers.

Creating Healthy Cultures

Growth, the very essence of change and transformation, is about pushing back what is—and making room for what can be. The dynamic tension between what is and what can be pervades the environments in which we work and live every day.

Healthy relationships operate from mutual support and concern for others. When we engage with others to remove barriers to growth and development, we miraculously feel more inspired and full of life. Healthy cultures, organizations, and families build rituals into their everyday lives that encourage growth and mutual success.

As we reflected on the work we were doing in companies, the conditions for health and lack of health in companies, organizations, and teams became apparent. When a culture felt territorial, or toxic, there were signs that we could now clearly identify. For example, in unhealthy cultures:

- Colleagues fail to communicate about challenges until it's almost too late—they therefore fail to get the assistance from other colleagues to turn things around.
- Colleagues lack sensitivity toward one another—they react territorially, blame others for problems, and produce unhealthy, toxic environments.
- Colleagues turn inward or become egocentric, creating positive beliefs about themselves and negative beliefs and

assumptions about others, thereby turning their environment into one of fear and reactivity.

On the other hand, when a company and culture were healthy, we would see the opposite set of behaviors showing up among colleagues. For example, in healthy cultures:

- Colleagues send out signals when they are in trouble—they therefore gain the help of others when they are in need of guidance.
- Colleagues have incredible sensitivity toward one another— and therefore work side by side to mutually support one another's growth.
- Colleagues do not allow themselves to turn inward, to become overly egocentric, or to fixate on past successes, all of which only serves to sap them of energy for growth. Instead, they learn from the past, let it go, and focus on embracing a future in which they can depend on one another.

What This Book Is All About

By the time you finish reading this book, you will have a whole new sensitivity for the words you use and the conversations you have with others. You will realize that words will either cause us to bond and trust more fully and think of others as friends and colleagues, or they will cause us to break rapport and think of others as enemies. By the time you are finished reading this book, you will see the connection between language and health and know how to create healthy organizations through the conversational "rituals" that you establish.

By the time you finish reading this book, you will have a storehouse of very prescriptive things to do, or not do, to sustain a healthy organization. You will be able to see the impact of change, and you will learn how to design organizational rituals that enable people to embrace and navigate change in healthy ways, and prevent those rituals that become toxic over time.

Creating WE is a positive, uplifting book about growth and transformation. The book helps you balance the dynamic tensions that must exist in order to create a WE-centric, healthy culture. The book will help you, the reader, tap your inner wisdom about what *WE*—the organization as a whole—needs to do to grow, transform, and thrive. The book is not about what is broken; it's about remembering what we all intuitively know about human nature—that we can only grow and thrive when we have concern for others in the organization.

We spend more time at work than anywhere else, and our workplace can become our best learning laboratory. As you read the stories in each chapter in this book, you will relate to them because they are universal experiences that we all face in our workplaces every day. If you take out the names of the people you will read about, and insert your own name or the names of colleagues you work with, you will see your workplace dramas unfolding right in front of your eyes, only this time as you read you will also find new ways to approach the dramas and challenges. You will find new strategies and tools for ensuring greater success.

In all the stories, the leaders or main characters face some type of challenge and need to make leadership decisions. How they decide to handle the situation and how they behave will have a huge ripple effect on relationships, teams, and the organization as a whole. As you read the stories you will begin to see how the leaders' sensitivity, focus on engaging others, and ability to see the larger enterprise affect everyone with whom they come in contact. Some decisions create growth; others stifle growth. Each story offers teachable moments— lessons and guidelines—from which you can learn how to become a more WE-centric leader with positive impact and influence. Finally, each chapter is filled with solutions, strategies, and takeaways that you can apply right away as you shape your Leadership Journey. Enjoy the ride!

Introduction

Feelings of worth can flourish only in an atmosphere where individual differences are appreciated, mistakes are tolerated, communication is open, and rules are flexible—the kind of atmosphere that is found in a nurturing family.

VIRGINIA SATIR, LINGUIST AND ANTHROPOLOGIST

EVERY PERSON HAS INSTINCTS FOR GREATNESS. We instinctively want to do well, to contribute, and to be included on the winning team. No one needs to teach us to have these desires; they are built into our DNA.

Yet many organizations often become toxic environments filled with politics, power, and control, arrogance, and competing egos. They develop into unwelcoming places with invisible street signs that say "Don't go there," "You can't do this," "You don't know that," "Save face," "Blame," and "Protect."

Allowing ourselves to get sucked into territoriality can lead to cycles of behavior that erode relationships and take energy away from being productive, healthy, high-performing individuals, teams, and organizations. When we are stuck in territoriality, protecting what we have and fearing loss, we are living at a low level of effectiveness, which ensures we will never achieve our greatest aspirations.

In the face of negativity, positional power struggles, and self-limiting beliefs, our courage and ambition shrivel up and die. Companies lose their spirit, and mediocrity becomes a way of life. Often, without seeing it until the pattern becomes a death spiral, we put out the very flame needed to thrive.

Growing Pains

For example, a small software and information management company that marketed its products to health care insurance companies was experiencing growing pains. One of three companies providing products to manage Medicare claims, they were not the market leader but were highly respected and often chosen as a low-cost provider. Clients and the industry respected them. Radical government cutbacks in Medicare subsidies created great pressure on the company.

Over time, this situation got even more serious. Insurance clients stalled on signing contracts for the next year's business and the company's partners argued, blaming each other for indecision and lack of growth. Employees saw that their two leaders were unable to sort out their business strategy, and, rather than find solutions, were enmeshed in personal conflicts.

The partners' personality clashes were public—they were out in the open and all too apparent. One partner, Jennifer, united the rest of the team behind her position. She openly heralded her distrust of her partner who she believed was focused on selling the company rather than weathering the current crisis. The downturn in the market and unpredictability of new business made their ability, as a management team, even more crucial. The main questions were, could they hire people to keep their current business, and could they count on a steady cash flow?

Richard, the other partner, was trying to sell the company. His rationale was that if a larger firm purchased it, there would be capital available to fund their growth. Fully aware of the economic challenge, Richard was not planning to hide the truth of the situation from a potential buyer. He knew that any good buyer would do the proper due diligence before making the purchase. Yet Jennifer believed that Richard intended to falsify the situation. The chasm between the partners widened. Jennifer succeeded in branding Richard as a dishonest person, and that perception tarnished how others saw him.

The business was in trouble. Some of their largest clients, already committed to future business, were putting their contracts on hold at a time when developing new business would be harder because of the government's regulation changes.

In this difficult environment, blame ran rampant. Richard was blamed for not committing to the current business. He felt frustrated because of what he saw as the shortsightedness of the team. People argued for their own positions and blamed each other for not taking action. People called the situation a business failure.

Communication was unhealthy, with people blaming anyone they could find to avoid being the target for failure, talking behind one another's backs, and complaining about one another. Richard, meanwhile, was frustrated and felt very alone in his effort to create awareness about where the company really stood. Jennifer felt alone, and the employees felt abandoned. Soon, Jennifer and Richard got into partnership arguments that blew up so much she left the company saying, "I'm better off starting a new company than trying to change this one."

Horror Stories

In spite of horror stories like the previous one, we optimistically continue to join up with hope and faith that this time we will find the organizational culture of our dreams. We go to work with an expectation that this time it will be different. We work in a new company in the hope that—whether we are joining a partnership, team, or complex organization—we will be welcomed into a well-functioning, healthy environment that is so compelling and human that we will find nourishment there and thrive. This expectation—and the deep disappointment that comes when it is not realized—is, in fact, an echo of our own individual wholeness. We know instinctively that a healthy human being needs to be part of a healthy human community. This sense of health—the recoiling from all that is toxic in human relationships—is the fundamental touchstone we need to hold in our consciousness at every moment of our organizational lives.

Evolving WE from Individuals to Organizations

We need to understand that the conditions necessary for creating healthy organizations are, in fact, the same conditions necessary for creating healthy individuals. We need to test and examine our beliefs about the balance between personal independence and the collective good—what I need in the context of what WE need. And we need to learn how to stand comfortably and confidently on that edge.

We can accomplish this if we look to our basic human biology—our DNA and our hard-wired Vital Instincts—and understand the impact they have on our behavior and on those around us.

There is, in fact, no *I*—only *WE*. Deep down we are not individuals, but rather collectivities, billions of cells working in concert, networked together in an exquisite equilibrium via a common genetic code buried in each and every cell. But this amazing, self-healing system operates unconsciously within each of us: When it fails, disease results. When it works, we all learn, grow, and nourish one another and live in a state of health. What keeps it working are our Vital Instincts for mutual success.

Triggering Vital Instincts

Cancer is an unhealthy state that depletes life energy from a system. The secret to reinstructing a cancer cell to become a healthy cell again and thus recharging it with fresh energy is driven by three Vital Principles: learning, growing, and nourishing. As you will learn in this book, when we create environments that trigger our Vital Partnering Instincts, we are able to change toxic organizational cultures back to healthy cultures and toxic relationships back to healthy ones. These three simple principles that govern the behavior of every cell in our bodies hold the power to break the code on culture change.

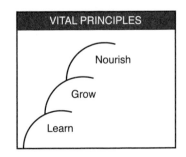

Learning Principle

When the body is healthy, the immune system works at all times to protect it, immediately identifying and attacking any threat to the body's health. The immune system actually learns about new threats and creates the flags to alert the system. These flags arise from cells, directing the immune system to know where and how to target their action and to marshal the internal resources to restore health. When cancer forms inside our bodies, normal cells lose these immune system flags. They lose the capacity to learn about new dangers and fail to pass this important information along to other cells.

The Learning Principle only functions effectively if it is constantly on alert and every cell is able to recognize a common threat or challenge. In other words, there needs to be total transparency throughout the body as to what constitutes potentially harmful toxins. Think of it as the ever-changing body of knowledge that each cell must learn. Any loss of vigilance or transparency can result in harm to the organism as a whole. Resources need to be marshaled quickly in the face of a challenge to organizational health.

Translated into organizational terms, this same wisdom suggests that we learn how to make any challenge to the health and success of the enterprise completely visible to one another. The organization, starting with its leaders, must identify and acknowledge the challenges so that the company can strategize to handle them collectively.

It is equally as important that we—both individually and collectively—monitor the health of our business culture, organization, teams, and one-on-one relationships. Everyone in the organization must have the power to raise a flag if he or she needs help handling challenges, whether they arise from within the organization (conflicts) or from outside in the form of competitive challenges or negative feedback from customers. We need to look at challenges not as threats, but as opportunities to learn. Each of us must be empowered to be part of the team, to watch and listen for challenges and respond to them. Each of us must become alert to challenges and listen in new ways to one another so that we add to the collective ability of the organization to respond quickly and proactively. With this level of awareness in place, we can better recognize how to respond by drawing on the wisdom of the whole organization.

Growing Principle

When cancer grows, cells lose their sensitivity to one another and rampantly grow anywhere they can. They invade the body and grow into tumors that can block the normal functioning of organs and the systems designed to sustain health. The Growing Principle, in other words, is about sensitivity to the boundaries and growth needs of each and every cell—an awareness of the needs of each cell to express itself and grow, and to do so in the context of the overall needs of the organism as a whole.

Translated into organizational terms, this means creating a feedback-rich culture that enables individuals to establish healthy relationships with their neighbors and colleagues. In a feedback-rich culture, a new level of awareness and sensitivity emerges so that we "don't grow all over each other." Rather than creating environments full of territoriality and competition, we learn how to build robust environments that foster respect, understanding, and mutual support. The skills of giving and receiving feedback—of being comfortable having courageous and sometimes difficult conversations—become a skill set shared by everyone.

Nourishing Principle

Cancer cells multiply by creating their own growth factors. They build their own vascular system (known as angiogenesis) that supplies oxygen and nutrients to the cancer cells, enabling them to grow at a rapid rate. They become self-sustaining and encapsulated from the rest of the system, drawing out nutrients from inside the system for their own sustenance. Healthy cells, on the other hand, need nutrients from the outside. They engage with one another to bring energy-producing nutrients into the body.

Translated into organizational terms, the Nourishing Principle requires that we recognize when we are attached to past successes and are stuck in old patterns that sap the nutrients out of the system—

nutrients such as fresh ideas to grow the business, Best Practices to improve operations, and positive feedback and encouragement to inspire high levels of performance. In a healthy culture, people are focused outward on the customer, on the marketplace, and on outside influences to inspire new ways of thinking. In a healthy culture, we see colleagues engaged with one another, focused on creating the future together, and collaborating and synergizing with one another to grow on a personal and organizational level.

When we become aware of the key nutrients for partnering, which are learning, growing, and nourishing, we are better equipped to seek them out and embed them into our culture as healthy practices.

Recognizing that we all have Vital Instincts is the first step in understanding how to create positive, healthy environments for learning, growth, and nourishment to become a way of life. When we master these principles of learning, growing, and nourishing, we ward off the toxicity that limits life and health. These principles remind us of the life-giving wisdom we all know at the instinctual level. That's why I call them Vital Instincts.

The Forces Working Against Creating WE

There are numerous societal pressures that undermine the creation of healthy, WE-centric workplaces. We see this when Lone Ranger–style leaders are celebrated in the media. We see it in so-called "reality TV" programming that encourages humiliation and exclusion.

But our own biology tells us that, while it is essential for each cell to express itself uniquely, it can only protect itself from harm if it does so without harming the organism as a whole. As valuable as individual expression is, intuitively we understand that we can promote personal gratification and individual action only so far before we break the bonds of community, loyalty, and mutual concern that are vital at all levels of human interaction.

Individuals, like the cells that comprise them, are able to absorb nourishment and grow without compromising and limiting the growth of the larger communities to which they belong. At our deepest cellular level WE-centrism must happen—or we fall ill and die.

The Power of WE Is Very Strong

Even in our I-dominant society, the WE instinct is so strong it expresses itself anyway. Consider adolescent behavior. Just one look at teenage fashions and fads is enough to make the case that what is so ardently pursued as individual expression is actually an extreme expression of WE. Ironically, teens try to be rebellious and nonconformist against authority (their parents) by dressing like one another. And we need only consider gang behavior to see that the need to belong and express a shared sense of community is so instinctive and essential for human beings that it will find an outlet—even if it is destructive to society as a whole.

We need to learn how to tap our Vital Instincts in a conscious, positive way, so that we create WE in our organizational lives. If we don't, more and more of our enterprises will fail and we as individuals and as a society will be diminished, unfulfilled, and vulnerable to harm.

Leadership at the Edge

Creating WE is based on the premise that each of us plays a role in setting a tone that determines interpersonal engagement at every level of the organization. How we, as corporate citizens, behave creates an atmosphere that surrounds the organization, creating the unspoken guideposts for what good citizenship looks like.

Our interactions with others trigger instinctual responses. A territorial atmosphere triggers Territorial Instincts and we act defensively to protect what is ours. An inclusive and supportive atmosphere triggers Vital Instincts and we reach out to partner with others.

Let's say we know in our heads what good interactions look like. We believe inside that we want to be inclusive and supportive of colleagues. We've read all the latest books on teamwork and we know how to be strong in the face of challenge, to be driven in the face of ambiguity, and to be team builders in the face of chaos. We're able to express our personal vision of what a great workplace looks like. In fact, we know it so well we can even give keynote speeches about it. We know we can say it—but why can't we do it every day?

In business today, we are experiencing unprecedented rates of change. When we come face-to-face with challenges we have not seen before, we sometimes react without the finesse of the type of manager we would like to be. The future is uncertain and what made us successful in the past will not work today. I refer to these outer limits of our Comfort Zone as *the edge*. Under such stress and threat, we react with self-protective behaviors. At the edge—our moments of greatest challenge—we often feel that we are losing control and are unable to see resolutions to problems or a clear path to success.

We arrive at the edge when we face difficult decisions, when our resources are few, when we feel depleted, incompetent, and insecure—but are afraid to let others in to help. At the edge, consciously or unconsciously, we often default to hard-wired patterns of behavior that divert us from tapping into our Vital Instincts for partnering, and instead, we become absorbed in protective, sometimes sabotaging behaviors. When we are at the edge, we have a choice. We can turn away from others and try to handle the challenge on our own, or we can turn to others for help.

Old-style leaders and managers believe they should have all the answers and their people expect solutions to come from the top. New-style leaders and managers don't believe they have all the answers, but they engage people in coming up with them. I call this WE-centric leadership. WE-centric leaders realize that WE is the power that fuels corporate growth. They know they don't need to know all the answers, and they also know that in the face of unprecedented change, inclusive behaviors radically shift the power dynamics toward partnering and positively influence productivity and quality in a company.

WE-centric leaders tune in to what happens when people feel disconnected, rejected, and alone. They know that rebellion and resistance and conflict are often signs that the bonds of trust are broken, resulting in separateness and silos. Knowing we do our best work when we feel connected, WE-centric leaders create ways for us to work synergistically. They create a positive change in how work gets done, engaging their colleagues to create extraordinary results.

Whether you are a manager at any level in a large or small business, or an employee with a high level of responsibility, you have the power to connect to the rest of your company and respond to the challenges in the business world today. By following the principles of *Creating WE,* you will be able to work with your team to respond and adapt to the ever-changing nature of the marketplace, share new ideas and innovative ways of performing tasks, and help drive your team to a successful future.

How This Book Is Organized

Creating WE is a book about assuring, restoring, and maintaining health in our organizations. It is about how to create a mindfulness that enables and strengthens WE at the same time recognizing and preventing the obstacles that keep us from achieving it. This book is organized around the challenges to organizational health: the factors and conditions that threaten to destroy the healthy WE in favor of an illusory, self-defeating I; the forces that distort a constructive, whole WE enterprise into a corrosive US/THEM. It addresses the habits of mind that transform an US/THEM, narrowly focused mindset into a value-added, inclusive WE that builds alliances within and beyond the organization's boundaries and forges opportunities for growth and reward.

Each chapter highlights one of these universal challenges, illustrating the set of issues and related opportunities with examples drawn from today's headlines and from my twenty-year consulting practice. Throughout each chapter, I'll provide you with tips on prevention, Best Practices to aspire to, and exercises and tools that you can use to address and overcome these challenges—whatever your role within the organization. Many chapters conclude with a matrix highlighting the Vital Choices you need to consider to inspire your leadership journey.

The Triad of Believing, Learning, and Being

Taken together, the chapters of this book present a methodology for *Creating WE* that consists of three major entry points into a creative process. That is, *Creating WE* consists of three parts: Believing WE, Learning WE, and Being WE—a triad that is represented in the following:

Believing WE

Part 1, "Believing WE," is about changing attitudes or beliefs about organizations and the ways one is supposed to behave in them. It covers the following challenges:

I'm Giving Orders—and You're Not Listening!—
The Challenge of Authority

Traditionally, "boss" means *I have power over you.* Positional power sets into place a hierarchy of authority driven by fear and intimidation when at its worst. The challenges to Creating WE can arise during the smallest yet most meaningful forms of human exchange: the relationship between leaders and their direct reports. We're all familiar with the "boss" who, out of some misguided sense of authority, barks orders to "subordinates," expecting a prompt, effective response. This chapter explores how each party to the exchange can help instill an understanding of how engagement and partnering—even between boss and direct reports—can better serve the organization and create WE.

My Turf, Your Turf—The Challenge of Territoriality

Our brain is hard-wired for survival. We have evolved from animals, and all animals have this hard-wiring. When we feel threatened, physically or psychologically, we react. It is "informed" by the reptilian brain, the amygdala, and our need to protect our gene pool and our species from harm. In this chapter you learn about these deep-seated instincts and how to move up to higher-level responses by shifting your frame of reference from foe to friend—it's a mindset shift that powerfully creates WE. The shift is from "my success" to "our success."

It Must Be Your Fault . . . —The Challenge of Self-Interest

US versus *THEM* language emerges when we feel that *we* are doing our job and *they* are not. It happens among peers, bosses and direct reports, and even with customers. To create WE, we need to recognize how to work together to establish mutual accountability, shared responsibility, and mutually agreed-upon results. Sometimes instead of partnering, the "old-boy network" shows up and we get into blaming behaviors. The reality is that there is no substitute for mutual accountability. Creating WE is everyone's business. We need to look in the mirror, we need to address what is standing in the way, we need to get real, and we need to see how we affect one another. The model for success is intention and impact, and when we see how this works, we mutually turn it around.

Learning WE

Part 2, "Learning WE," is about adopting new habits of mind and behaviors and learning new skills (and unlearning old ones). It covers the following:

Hello, Can You Hear Me?—Understanding the Culture

People hate conflict. We hate getting into arguments. Some companies take great pride in being known as a consensus culture. On the surface, this means that we all agree. Below the surface, it means we can't speak up. Leaders have learned to seek consensus and alignment. Yet in many cultures, *consensus* and *alignment* are code words for "you can't speak up." The underlying message is that it's better to *Shut Up Than Speak Up*. When we attain that perfect state of alignment, we often lose the very voices that can take us forward into new places—the voices that contain the new ideas, the new wisdom, and the new inventions for the future. In this chapter we focus on how to create environments in which people *can* speak up, challenge the status quo, and open the space for transforming an unhealthy culture into a healthy one.

But That's How It's Always Been Done!—Embracing the Possibilities

Once we get into routines, we feel comfortable. From comfort comes confidence. Yet in the world of moving targets (ourselves included), we need to learn to be open to change. Sometimes we don't change because change means taking risks. We don't like to fail, and we protect ourselves from looking bad. Not changing protects us. It makes us feel smart because we repeat what we know, and we think we know it all. We perpetuate the illusion of knowingness. When leaders change strategic direction—on paper and in their minds, they have the further challenge of creating change in the company. Rather than hold to the comfort and stability of the past—which is an illusion—we need to embrace opportunities for the future, which means breaking through our Comfort Zones and working together to bring new changes and ideas into the workplace.

Are We Really on the Same Team?—Opening the Space

As long as we feel we are gaining, not losing, we will play as WE. The fear is always that someone will get more. The fear is always: I'll trust you and you'll stab me in the back. Most of us value being considered a partner. Living together interdependently requires a skill set that is one of our least developed. This set of skills and practices is so vital that in their absence, good leaders turn bad, good executives become ineffective, and good colleagues morph into adversaries. The skill of opening up to others and of creating the emotional space for others to open up to one another requires trust. Trust is the most precious of the golden threads. Without it, there can be no WE. When we open up WE to include partners outside of our conventional thinking, we encompass stakeholders and allies beyond the traditional boundaries of the enterprise—including vendors, customers, and donors. We expand the way we work and how we generate value. After all these years, we are starting to see how shifting boundaries—throwing the net wider—is a way to achieve alliances in a new way. This chapter speaks to how to create conversational spaces for a bigger WE to emerge.

Get Over It!—Shaping the Conversations

Everything happens through conversations. A seemingly simple act such as talking with a colleague—a small momentary exchange of words in a hallway—has the ability to alter someone's life permanently. Conversations carry meaning—and meaning is embedded in the listener even more than in the speaker. We communicate with each other through conversations. Conversations have the ability to trigger emotional reactions. The words we use in our conversations are rarely neutral. Words have histories informed by years of use. Each time another experience overlays another meaning, it all gets collected somewhere in our brain to be activated during conversations. Understanding how we project meaning into our conversations will enable us to connect with others and, in so doing, Let Go of much of the self-talk that diverts us from Creating WE. In this chapter we will focus on how to shape and craft releasing conversations through a variety of processes, the most important of which is the ability to change history, change memories, release, and Let Go.

Friend or Foe?—Transforming the Culture

This chapter focuses on understanding storytelling. Stories are embedded in conversations. The stories you tell can infuse relationships, teams, and organizations with new energy and direction—or, they can create territoriality. Storytelling, like language itself, comes naturally to human beings. It's how we share with others what we are seeing, feeling, and sensing. Storytelling is our view of reality. Typically, storytelling starts as an I-centric capability that enables us to communicate and often defend our point of view. In organizational life, storytelling shapes the way we view the world individually and collectively. It can have positive or negative consequences for the health of the enterprise. This chapter will help you break old storytelling habits and learn new ways to use this essential human skill to make over your relationship with the teams you lead. This chapter will help you tell a new organizational story—one that transforms silo thinking into pride in enterprise-wide performance.

Being WE

Part 3, "Being WE," shows how to face stressful situations in real time and express WE-consciousness through actions in the moment. Here, the challenges are the following:

If They Don't Care, I Don't Care!—Working in Concert

Human beings want to be included and appreciated. When we are not included, we feel left out and we reject the system that excludes us. We then turn to others to create our clan and are connected once again. We need connection to feel safe, loved, validated, and healthy. In Creating WE, we need to value the contributions of others; we need to learn how to include, not exclude them. The "old-boy network" mentality is not healthy when its intention is to exclude those who don't fit in. It *is* healthy when it's about including, embracing, appreciating, and valuing. When these nutrients are missing, employees feel outside the system and they resist the direction the company is heading. They spend more time complaining to others than contributing, and they are perceived as resistors. This chapter focuses on understanding the Arc of Engagement and how to truly work in concert to create a culture of inclusion and appreciation.

They Said It Couldn't Be Done!—Sustaining WE

The success of any enterprise is marked by how well it achieves what it sets out to do in the world, not merely how well it copes with changes that occur around it. Transformation is an inherent part of growth. Being WE—even in the face of challenges—can be daunting, given how much people seek to maintain a sense of safety that comes with a seemingly unchanging environment. There are few more dislocating challenges initiated by companies than a merger or acquisition. When two companies become one, or when a company is acquired, there is rarely if ever a simple 1 + 1 = a bigger 1. There are always separate cultures, separate norms, separate ways of doing things. Usually the small company is eaten by the larger and loses its identity. Usually, lots of people leave and with that loss goes much of the wisdom and human energy for creating the new entity. What is left is often a demoralized culture, riddled with the fear of how the new parents will treat them—friend or foe. The new entity needs to be shaped and crafted. As a leader or colleague in the middle of such a transition, you need to realize the choices you have and how your acts of leadership can powerfully change the outcomes for all involved. In this chapter you will see clear moments of decision where a leader needed to choose to act from a WE perspective to create the best possible outcomes for everyone, and how that WE-centric choice created a powerful ripple effect out into the world.

Afterword: Standing at the Edge of a New Beginning

As we learn the skills for Creating WE and we practice them every day, we will hit challenges that throw us back into our familiar protective behaviors. We are only human and with that comes the incredibly powerful DNA that has enabled us to survive and grow into the profound human beings we are today. Being WE requires that we continually remind ourselves of our Partnering Instincts. We need to remember the new skills that keep us vital and alive and healthy. Every day we need to practice these skills and bring ourselves back into that healthy state of ongoing transformation. This chapter deals with a final set of how-to's for Being WE—reminders of how to stay on the journey of health, wealth, and prosperity; how to focus attention on the energy-creating dynamics of Creating WE. In this chapter we see how, by focusing on creating together, we all can learn, grow, and nourish one another by becoming the best WE-centric leaders we can be.

There are many paths to creating a WE-centric culture. You can move sequentially from changing beliefs to learning new skills consistent with these beliefs and then to applying these skills to the particular circumstances you face. In other words, you can move from Believing, to Learning, to Being WE. But you can also move in reverse and still succeed. In the process of coping with stressful situations, for example, you can learn new skills and, in doing so, find yourself changing your ingrained beliefs. By "Being WE" you come to "Believe in WE." In the end, all three facets of the triad are essential to the process of Creating WE. Where you enter that process is up to you, as long as they meet the requirements of your real-world situation.

Creating WE is first about learning to transform ourselves, and through this process, we come to see our company and culture in a new way. When we become WE-centric leaders, we can no longer allow our cultures to be riddled with politics, power, and dysfunction; we instead become catalytic forces in transforming organizational disease into organizational health. The secrets to creating healthy cultures are transferable and when practiced have an extraordinary power to restore health and growth to individuals, teams, organizations, and, yes, even the global human community.

I want to take a moment to remind you that the stories in this book are real. Perhaps I've taken the liberty to embellish a few to make a point or expand on the details of an important dynamic; however, in most cases I stayed as faithful to the truth as I could—life in its most incredible way is our best teacher. When I've included the real names of executives or companies, they provided permission. In the cases where my client or I chose not to include real names, I provided a "stand-in." Some of my clients have been so supportive of sharing these stories that they have joined me on the speaking circuit to share them. Even in cases where executives were facing harsh feedback from their employees, they have wanted to share the lessons they learned with others.

Now, you are about to embark on the most fulfilling journey of all—the journey to WE. WE begins with creating a state of mind inside yourself, like a touchstone you can refer to every day to remind yourself how to bring back conversations when they slide off-center, to remind yourself how to turn breakdowns into breakthroughs, and to remind yourself how to *be* the change you want to create in the world. These are such simple principles that you can practice every day. And the more you practice them, the easier they are to activate even in the face of difficult challenges. When the market dynamics change and you are faced with challenges bigger than you feel you can face alone, rather than retreat, turn to others to help you work it out. You alone don't need to come prepared with all the answers. Instead, create them with others . . . Create WE, and along the way, enjoy the ride!

Part One

Believing WE

1.

I'm Giving Orders—
and You're Not Listening!

The Challenge of Authority

The deepest principle of human nature is to be appreciated.
WILLIAM JAMES, PSYCHOLOGIST AND PHILOSOPHER

Too often the message we communicate to one another about leadership is that to be successful you have to be powerful, and that to win you have to be dominant. In doing so, we confuse power with force and leadership with dominance.

The Vital Instincts that help us maintain health in ourselves and in our organizations are often undercut by erroneous and conflicting beliefs about authority, leadership, dominance, power, and winning. We too often accept many of our beliefs about these important concepts as "conventional wisdom" without questioning them. The problem is, these beliefs are not necessarily true—and, worse, they may be corrosive to healthy individuals and to healthy enterprises.

One of the most corrosive is the belief that authority is the same as leadership. In reality, this hierarchical, chain-of-command notion of leadership is a major contributor to organizational dysfunction. Too often, when we think of leadership, we envision the tough boss, the intimidating executive. Out of a desire to simply survive, we may even envision ourselves assuming a position of submission to such "leaders."

Abandoning these toxic beliefs can be the first step in your journey to Creating WE.

An Authority Figure Falls

Exide, a large 118-year-old company in the battery business, grew by global acquisition. While its U.S. headquarters are in Princeton, New Jersey, Exide had offices around the world. Each country had its own manager and a full staff of people with functional responsibilities. Both the North American and European sectors of the company had a chief executive officer and each CEO met with his "direct reports" (country managers) once a year.

The country managers were very proud of their businesses. It was as though each was a "king" ruling over his domain. Employees felt loyal to their respective country managers. The organization was very hierarchical and the leadership style was command-and-control.

If we were able to look down at the company from a satellite and see how the leaders interacted, we would see damaging dynamics at play. Countries competed for the same customers. Operational costs were extremely high. Countries produced their own products and branded them with unique marks. There was tenacious loyalty on a local level that created an ego-driven turf war with little loyalty to the parent company.

The CEO of Exide, Art Hawkins, was an extreme autocrat. He rarely held meetings with his senior team and never conferred with the European team. He did not delegate decisions to anyone. He moved from meeting to meeting, deciding what he wanted while being verbally abusive to people he didn't like. He'd make decisions and then suddenly change his mind in midstream.

Employees were incredibly fearful of Hawkins. Yet, he was extremely charismatic. While autocratic, he was charming and able to draw people into his closed circle. Getting into the "old boys network" was a sign that you'd arrived at the gates of senior leadership.

Meek people learned to be tough by watching him, and he had many followers. To feed his beastly ego, Hawkins spilled his arrogance everywhere, and there were people who found this enchanting. When he was nice to people, they treasured the moment, waiting for the next time they could please him and be praised. He was very much like a controlling and abusive parent.

Never did this powerful CEO show the slightest concern about the havoc he created as he micromanaged the company from the top down. Despite Hawkins's expertise and genius, his I-centric, autocratic style prevented him from seeing that he was the problem. In fact, he would have fired anyone who suggested that his oppressive style of leadership was the organization's fatal flaw.

People left the company. Those who stayed either tried to create a wall around themselves or took this difficult business situation as a challenge. The company became a hornet's nest of divisiveness. In public, Hawkins was aggressive and intimidating, creating a fear-based culture. But that's not all. In addition to the havoc he was creating in the company, unhealthy thinking and in some cases unethical behavior became acceptable. The sickness spread like a deadly virus throughout the company. Because the head of the company allowed and advocated unethical activities, many felt it was okay practice and followed suit. In private, there were secretive activities taking place behind closed doors and only a select few were included. Unbeknownst to most employees, the CEO had been brewing one of the largest consumer scams in history—one that continued undetected by an unsuspecting public for years.

It's difficult to fire a CEO, even when he demonstrates the most destructive behaviors. Fortunately, Exide's board found cause to fire him along with some of his top team when they discovered the horrendous business deals that later became public knowledge, á la Enron.

In December 2002, the *Associated Press* announced that Art Hawkins, "the former chief executive of Exide Technologies, once the nation's biggest automotive-battery maker, has been sentenced to 10 years in prison for his part in a scheme to sell defective batteries to Sears, Roebuck & Co. in the 1990s." Art's conduct along with Exide's former president, Douglas N. Pearson, and the Sears executives involved caused damage to Exide's reputation. It was this series of events that Bob Lutz stepped into, and the one that tested his leadership stamina.

Enter—a True Leader

When Bob Lutz signed up to join the company as the new CEO of Exide Technologies, he was unaware of the scope of the business problems he would find and just how sick the company had become, including a minefield of legal and ethical issues.

Bob was highly experienced and very well respected in the industry, having been the vice chairman of Chrysler in his most recent position. Now, as the CEO of Exide, he was about to drive a major transformation and find ways to heal the company. A seasoned, savvy executive, he knew how to handle himself in the toughest situations. However, he had no idea of the extent of the mess he had inherited until he started his job at Exide and began to uncover how things had been done. From the first day, he knew he needed to create a huge shift in Exide's culture, which had been driven by power and control, turf wars, and silos. He also knew he needed to bring his top team together to discuss strategy. He believed the company needed to focus on one brand and to transform itself from a collection of country-led fiefdoms into a single, customer-centric enterprise. Bob chose to work with a group of consultants, and I was among the team that was selected.

The first year he was in his new position, we helped Bob create an inclusive engagement strategy for bringing the senior team together to have the tough conversations they needed to have to create a strong brand and competitive customer-centric focus. We set up a series of meetings with senior management globally, and, for the first time in the history of the company, senior executives all came together to address the state of the business. The executives learned how to put the tough issues on the table. They learned how to debate and discuss decisions, and how to research together when they did not have enough information. For the first time they operated as a learning community.

After the larger meetings, the key executives went home and shared what they were learning with their direct reports. They involved their staff members in research on key issues that the company needed to face to become a strong brand. Some of these decisions were extremely difficult. For example, the organization needed to rethink its most basic operations, from purchasing supplies to sharing resources to interacting with customers. All of these changes needed to occur outside the country structure, while still honoring cultural diversity. The transformation was enormous.

Changes like these can spark deep-seated fears. Most often, we fear we will be the ones to lose our jobs or be demoted, or will find we have a new boss whose lack of sensitivity or leadership makes our lives miserable. When a new boss arrives on the scene, he or she brings a whole new way of working—new strategies, new relationships, new ideas for how he or she wants to run the business. With our old boss, we may have a power role, and with the new boss, we may have little influence. New bosses initiate processes that we may not agree with, and, when this happens, we know we're heading into potential land mines of conflict. When changes occur, most of us instinctively turn to our protective, I-centric fear-based thinking. This is an automatic response. Learning to interrupt this pattern opens up many wonderful alternatives for everyone.

In Exide's case, some employees chose to leave the company before the changes were set in motion. Others felt they might not get good positions and lobbied with their bosses to be assured a place. Bob and his senior team openly explained the changes and engaged the organization in reaching for the best solutions. Bob did not play "alpha dog" and make all the decisions himself. He did not exclude people for fear that conflicting points of view might be difficult to manage. He intuitively knew the way through the tough decisions was to ask the people involved in the decisions to be on the team that figured them out. This was a collaborative, rather than a manipulative, strategy.

Bob knew that as CEO he needed to set the context for change. He knew he needed to create an atmosphere of collaboration and trust—something that had not been there with his predecessor. Bob knew he had to help the company think about its mission and purpose.

He then had to think about the business in a way that would unite, rather than separate, the whole global team. Bob also knew he wanted people to collaborate, to share Best Practices, and to learn what world-class companies do—and then become one.

He wanted his people to think of themselves as leaders—to learn to challenge authority if it meant finding better solutions. Bob was the opposite of the previous CEO. He launched the company into a major transformation by setting the tone for collaboration. Whenever he saw people being territorial or replicating the toxic DNA, he would step in and demonstrate, through his own behavior, how to create an environment of health. Bob was open and transparent about his intentions, and therefore was able to reduce the fear that creates reactive behaviors, the fear that tells us we are going to lose something. He made collaboration the primary rule of engagement. In doing so, he facilitated the team's ability to find the answers to its toughest business challenges.

Engagement and Partnering Create Growth

Bob Lutz knew so well that the business of transformation and business growth is about flexibility and change. He knew that an authoritarian, command-and-control style of leadership does not cultivate learning, growing, or nourishing—it creates compliance. He knew that open and healthy conversations were needed to shift the culture, and he led the way.

Companies can't change without people changing their beliefs—and they change their beliefs through conversation. Bob was the consummate communicator. He was articulate, visionary, and, most of all, lived the values he wanted to help create. He created change by being the change.

Companies become toxic when the three most important principles for health are missing in the environment:

- **Enterprise Communication:** In unhealthy organisms, the immune system is not communicating with the individual cells. There are communication disconnects everywhere; cells are growing in their own directions, sapping the system's focus and strength. In healthy organisms, each part of the whole understands what health looks like and the signals are communicated, clear, and shared. At Exide, the previous CEO was the driver of everything. Some would say he micromanaged every major decision and made himself the center of the Exide universe. There was no larger strategic dialogue taking place, division to division, working to define the needs of the customer.

- **Sensitivity:** In unhealthy cultures, internal competition defines the landscape. As in unhealthy organisms, where there is a lack of sensitivity of one "cell" to another, unhealthy environments suffer from the same dynamics. From this lack of sensitivity, territoriality appears. There is great competition inside the organization as each division drives for greater use of resources and greater recognition and importance. At Exide under the previous CEO, each country was competing against the other.

- **Creating the Future:** Healthy cells turn outward for nourishment, rather than sapping the organism. Unhealthy cells take root in the system, drawing out nutrients and depleting the overall strength of the organism. Through the arrogance of the old Exide regime, there was no new thinking about how to grow the business—they were anchored in past success. There was no new thinking about how to strengthen the brand or invent new products. The company leaders were arrogant, living in their past success, and blind to the realities of the business.

  Bob Lutz understood how to create a healthy culture, and he wanted his whole team to be part of creating health by focusing on the following principles.

- **Vision, Values, Mission, and Purpose:** In his first six months with the company, Bob launched into a companywide project called "Recharging Exide." The senior team created the first draft of what became known as the VVMP (Vision, Values, Mission, and Purpose). Then over the next six months, there were major VVMP meetings run in different countries with the next level of executive who reported to the top team. These meetings took place throughout the world. We even translated the materials into five different languages so that there was no barrier to understanding.

Following the larger meetings, the senior leaders went back home and had a chance to vet the draft with their direct reports, to make changes, and send them back up the line. There was a larger strategic dialogue taking place inside the company and a commitment to align around common goals.

■ **Awareness and Sensitivity:** In healthy cultures, there is a learned and practiced sensitivity of one human being to another. From this sensitivity, grows an internal respect for the value each person brings. Bob created an environment where people could bring their talents to the table. He sought to develop his team and put the best people he could in critical positions. Bob and his team launched into challenging conversations about resources and how to best deploy them. He reorganized the company to be customer-centric, reducing the competition from one territory to another.

■ **Focusing on the Future:** Bob did not allow complacency or self-centeredness. He focused his top leaders on strengthening the brand. He launched key projects to figure out how to shape the business moving forward. New thinking and new approaches to reaching the key customers emerged. New product ideas began to flourish. He awakened the sleeping giant to the realities of the business. He called this process Recharging Exide.

Leadership from the Inside Out

Transformation starts with people thinking differently. We can change a process if it's not right. We can change a product line or service. But company transformation, which is really all about culture change, must begin with shifts that take place inside human beings—the leaders of the company. Transformation must start with something that causes leaders to think, see, feel, and act in new ways. For a company to change, people need to change from the inside first.

Change starts from inside and radiates out. The deepest change we can make is in our belief about who we are. Remember the book *Real Men Don't Eat Quiche*, by Bruce Feirstein? When we see ourselves as classic "real men" or "real women," there are things we won't do, because if we do them, we are not "macho" anymore. To reach our next level of leadership, we need to get over that way of thinking, because real leaders do have hearts and souls, soft spots and feelings. Consider the story of Arlene.

Believing Toughness Is Leadership

In the late 1980s, when Arlene signed on as general manager/president of a division of Revlon, the cosmetics manufacturing company, she was directed by the top brass to turn the division around. A physically imposing woman, Arlene had spent her life in retail and rose to the top thanks to her commanding style. She was known as someone who could "get the job done." Not only did she have years of experience in cosmetics, she also had years of experience as a manager. She fired people who didn't immediately perform. If you got on her bad side, you were out, with no further consideration. She was unforgiving of mistakes and mediocrity. Her "tough as nails" style was precisely why she was hired to take over the faltering division.

The division was in the red. The previous president had failed to understand the business and couldn't get people to support her and grow it. Arlene was determined to turn the business around. This would be her last big job, and she wanted to go out with a bang.

In order to accomplish this and ensure the results she promised the board, she knew she had to have the right people on her team. This was proving to be a difficult task; Arlene's rough personality was creating lots of tension among her management team. Within the first four months of her executive leadership, she became convinced that her direct reports were the main problem. Not only did she feel she couldn't trust them, she believed that they lacked talent. Rather than draw upon her managers' knowledge and wisdom during meetings, Arlene broadcast signals, through innuendo, that she was displeased with them.

In particular, Arlene expressed great concern over Bob, the executive vice president of finance. She thought he was weak and wanted an assessment as to whether or not to fire him.

Bob was a quiet guy. He sat, listened, and didn't present ideas until he had a clear point of view. Arlene was an aggressive extrovert who wanted people to help her think things through in new ways by presenting counterarguments. Whenever Bob pushed back and challenged her, she pushed back on him. This was just her style, but Bob saw her style as confrontational aggression, not "pushback." He recoiled, which made him look weak to his new boss. To her, he came across as someone who would acquiesce rather than be a good business partner.

Despite her tough demeanor, Arlene did not have all the answers, and she knew it. She wanted to get other people into the game, but when she did, her forbidding exterior shut them down. Only the toughest executives stood a chance with her. Lucy, who headed human resources and with whom I worked closely, was one of those people. I coached Lucy, and Lucy coached Arlene about her leadership style. Sometimes we both coached Arlene. In the beginning, regardless of our efforts, it was to no avail.

Early on, Arlene conducted an assessment in which she uncovered that the corporate team was not happy with the field management team—the people who were actually running Revlon's 131 stores. Arlene referred to the field as "one big animal" she couldn't control or work with. She expected her head of technology to fix the field communication problems, but he couldn't get the people in the field to learn the new systems. Employees were resisting and fighting management.

Arlene made it clear who her favorites were. Employees who were not yet aligned wanted to associate themselves with the people she favored so they could be part of the "in-crowd." People would show their allegiance to the senior management team by demonstrating support of its ideas at key meetings. Some people learned to just shut up so as not to be associated with "the other team."

People were becoming territorial and fearful of Arlene, the leader. Arlene's top team began to act out, exhibiting fight-flight-avoid behaviors toward one another. Anxious about appearing to take sides, some people tried to lie low.

As fear increased, performance dropped. Team members were vying for power and trying to prove who was smartest at the expense of the others. It became apparent that Sales didn't get along with Marketing, and Operations didn't get along with the people in the field. Communication was at its lowest, information was hoarded rather than shared, the company lacked direction—and no one was focused on the customer.

Expressing the Vital WE

Arlene, like all of us when we feel threatened, was responding from her survival *I* instincts, rather than a *WE* perspective. The division was in dire trouble—it was losing money and people weren't pulling together. As a leader in this high-pressure situation, Arlene believed it was *her* job to turn things around—and restore the organization to health.

This heroic sense of personal mission was causing her to act like an I-centric leader. She felt she alone was going to drive change. In doing so she was disconnecting from her senior team, was judging them rather than thinking about how to draw on their strengths, and was creating a followership mentality. In short, her own I-centric behaviors would end up catalyzing more toxic behaviors within the organization, such as internal competition, self-interest, and attachment to the past.

Her heroic sense of personal mission created blind spots that she was unable to overcome. Arlene believed in the conventional wisdom of leader as heroic savior, as authority figure with all the answers. Were she to sustain that stance, she would trigger a cascade of resentment in the organization—resentment toward her, resentment toward her strategies. Few of her direct reports assumed they could be open and share their feelings about her to her face. Instead, they turned to each other and out of protection, they created subcultures of fear.

Rather than causing them to protect their own territory, the Vital Leader engages colleagues in learning new signals everyone can share and use to intercept the impending danger, and engages them to work together to create new strategies for success. Would it be possible for someone like Arlene, with such a strong DNA for authority and heroics, to make a transformation? Would it be possible for her to see the light and learn to override her territorial instincts and realize that it is the leader's job to inspire everyone to learn new skills of collaboration and to monitor the health of the whole organization?

Arlene's belief in *I*—a belief so encouraged and rewarded in our individualistic society—needed to change in order for her to work in concert with others and create the conditions for company growth. Before she could transform the organization, she needed to change her own beliefs. Organizational transformation begins with people. More specifically, it begins inside every employee—both leaders and colleagues. It begins with something that causes each of us to think, see, feel, and act in new ways. For a company to change, everyone across the organization needs to change. Change starts from inside and radiates out. The deepest change we can make is in our belief about who we are.

Arlene Begins Her Leadership Journey

Arlene began to grow frustrated with her lack of results as a leader at Revlon. In my early meetings with Arlene, she was incredibly unreceptive to coaching; she wanted me to focus on "fixing her people." She changed her mind when she hit a low and saw no other way out. Arlene wanted to grow the business, yet her approach didn't match the task at hand. Lucy, her head of human resources, was pivotal in the process. Lucy and I suggested creating an experience for the senior executive team that would elevate everyone's thinking outside of their existing territoriality. We proposed an off-site meeting, and Arlene jumped at the idea. At first, however, Arlene wanted to use the off-site meeting as a way for her to assess her people and get rid of the "weak ones."

With Lucy's support—and recognizing that the real issues were about leadership and power—Arlene agreed to tackle the larger issue of culture first. Lucy was incredibly innovative, and proposed we create an *experience* of anticipation, so that by the time people came to the meeting they would be in a state of curiosity. We created an audiotape that contained an invitation to the company's top twenty-five executives to participate in a "Learning Journey" into what it takes to build a strong work culture and community.

Arlene was initially skeptical about our methods; she just wanted the poor performers to go away. A few years prior to this project, I had flown to Disney with another client, where we were one of the first outsiders to study the Disney culture. We learned a lot and brought back Best Practices about how to create incredible unity, collaboration, and innovation. Lucy got excited about the idea of applying this new wisdom to Revlon's culture. We explained to Arlene how Disney had created a culture in which everyone was part of the customer experience. Arlene liked that analogy, but she was still skeptical about bringing her team up to that level. Instead, she thought of the off-site meeting as a way to gain insight into her staff members and their capabilities.

Off-sites like the one she was planning are riddled with challenges. The thought of being face-to-face with people who aren't communicating effectively is threatening. Lucy used the "Learning Journey" audiotape to help people get past their trepidation and asked each person to list the top things he or she wanted to focus on to make the meeting a success. All twenty-five employees put "improving communication" as their number-one issue.

We held Arlene's team meeting in an office complex next to a warehouse, where team-building activities could take place. The meeting agenda covered Who We Are Now, Who We Will Become, the State of the Business, and Where We Go from Here. The team viewed two videos: one of a company with a great culture, and one of a company that was failing with a horrible, I-centric culture. They discussed how they were similar to and different from each one.

We put the group through a series of experiential team-learning and other trust- and rapport-building activities. Some activities brought sales and management together as one team. Everyone worked on creating ideas for field promotions, and everyone worked on solving technology problems. By the end of the first day, all participants were eagerly contributing new ideas. It quickly became clear that a shift had taken place—away from Arlene and her agenda of being the center of the company and the only one responsible for solving its problems and sparking growth, toward a team-centric leadership style.

After the meeting was over, Arlene took Lucy aside for a talk. She humbly confided that before the meeting she had been prepared to fire her head of technology and operations. She was disappointed in his work and felt he was not right for her team. At the meeting, she saw a new person emerge, one who showed he was strong-willed and direct, yet empathetic. These were qualities she had wanted to see in him, but never did until that day. His newfound leadership confidence had caused a breakthrough, and the shift in him altered Arlene's perception of him. He learned to push back without fear— and trust flooded the team.

A Collective Commitment to Shape Reality

Following the off-site meeting, people began to work together in totally new ways. The split between the field and management disappeared. The sense that *we are all in this together* was felt by everyone. People went out of their way to show what they could do. Arlene stopped being critical and antagonistic.

From that point on, every Monday from 10:00 until noon, the fifty-six leaders met in the warehouse. These meetings became a symbol of the new corporate culture—a community of engagement focused on growing the business. Yet that was not all: anyone who had an idea to share could come to the meeting. During those two hours, temps were hired to cover the phones back at the office, so even the receptionists could attend.

Arlene had learned how she needed to cultivate the contributors. She created a neutral, rewarding space for conversations to take place, and the team learned how to push back on each other in new ways. On one occasion, a secretary had the idea of starting an international division. Arlene gave her the go-ahead to show what she could do. Within two months, Arlene had the beginnings of an international division. The secretary was made vice president.

When the off-site meeting was first initiated, the company was in the red, with a projected twelve-month cycle to get into the black. As a result of the cultural shift and newfound open communication, the company was in the black within four months. This remarkable transformation at Revlon exemplifies how critical it is for a leader to implement change right from the top, starting with herself. And it all began with a shift from I to WE in the leader's own beliefs about what true leadership—not mere authority—means.

Imagine That You Are a New Leader

Imagine you just joined a new company in a new position, and you have been given the responsibility for achieving success. Your predecessor was unable to pull it off, so you have some extra pressure to deliver results. Imagine you accept this responsibility and start your job tomorrow.

While holding that thought, imagine the following situation, which I'll call Scenario 1. As you do your due diligence and make your assessment of the situation, you uncover concerns that you didn't see before. The talent seems to be light for the task ahead. You sense that the resource base is also light, and you realize that the job is bigger than you thought.

The business problems also seem bigger and you can't get your arms around them. You are new and believe you are supposed to be in charge of the situation. You decide not to share your fears and worries out of concern that others will think you are not capable of being a leader or are unable to handle the challenge. How would that decision impact the future success of the business?

As an alternative, let's look at Scenario 2. You come aboard, do your due diligence, and find problems are more difficult than you originally anticipated. You immediately bring your direct reports into your assessment, and with open and honest communication, you create an engagement process to build positive energy and focus. You include others in discovering new and exciting ways for building the business. In Scenario 2 you are more open and transparent with colleagues, you express your desire to create sustainable partnerships, and you are willing to coach and be coached to help yourself and others grow.

Leadership Choices

Whether you are a man or a woman, old or young, seasoned or new, you have leadership choices about how you want to engage with your organization from the moment you step into your new role.

In Scenario 1, you choose to hold your fears inside, but by doing that you broadcast to your colleagues that you are unapproachable. As a result, your concerns magnify and your fears amplify until they appear from the inside out as insurmountable. Without realizing it, you send out signals of secrecy, which cause other people to make up stories about what is going on inside your head. By not sharing what's on your mind, you set yourself apart from others—distancing yourself from the very colleagues you need to work with to overcome challenges that face everyone.

In Scenario 2, on the other hand, you know how to face your challenges by *including others* rather than *pushing them away*. You reflect on the challenges deeply and think about how to create the context for bringing them onboard with the challenges ahead.

Who Are You?

What kind of leader are you? How will you approach the job of moving your business forward? Will you be open or closed? Will you blame others for not having the talent you need, or will you engage others in finding ways for everyone to raise the bar and succeed?

What Kind of Leader Are You?

Power-over Leadership	*Power-with* Leadership
Exclusive	Inclusive
Being in control	Developing partnerships
Criticizing and judging others	Appreciating others
Punishing risk-taking	Encouraging risk-taking
Instilling fear	Instilling hope
Silo mentality	Encouraging sharing
Dictating	Developing
Compliant	Committed to higher purpose

Do you know who *you* are? Most of us know ourselves only from the inside out. We know how we want to be perceived and that we want to be acknowledged as a leader. We rarely see our dark side; we most often focus on our bright side. We know ourselves in terms of the values and beliefs we stand for—again, from the inside out.

Executive coaching has taught us that what is missing for many leaders is the view from the outside in—how we influence others and how they perceive us relative to the actions we take every day. Since *feelings* have been considered taboo for so long in the business world, we have pretended they do not exist. Yet, among the new leaders, feelings make a difference—a big difference. In fact, how we make others feel about our leadership is now a critical measure of our success or failure.

Leadership is not static. We are always maturing into our capabilities. It takes learning from experiences to grow. When we only hold one view of ourselves—and that view is from the inside out—we are living a one-dimensional experience of leadership.

When we become aware of how we affect others and the experience we create with them, we are living a three-dimensional experience of leadership—our view, other people's views, and, thirdly, the person we become from our synthesis of the rich feedback we absorb from both outside and inside views. It is through working within the gaps of perceptions that we trigger new growth in our leadership approach—and, fundamentally, our own identity.

Throughout this book I will advocate that you develop self-awareness and a keen sense of how you affect others now, and how that impact ripples into the future. Central to the story of leadership—in particular of becoming a WE-centric leader—is becoming comfortable with accepting feedback and experimenting with it to fully shape and craft the leader that you are able to become.

Regardless of the type of business you're in, as a leader you have power and influence. Learning how to use that power in positive ways is critical to your success. You can use your influence effectively to help the organization thrive and sustain success, or you can use it ineffectively—defaulting to an I-centric, authoritarian mode—and, in doing so, shrink the potential and aspirations of everyone you touch.

To be successful you need to reflect on how you want to lead and adjust your approach as artfully as you can. You will succeed by understanding your own leadership, and when your approach doesn't produce the results you desire, you must be willing and able to try something new to change it.

Unleash the Power of Co-creation

Arlene began as an authoritarian, I-centric leader. Her intimidating style had been reinforced throughout her career because people buckled when she dictated commands. Thus, her sense of positional power expanded and her ability to dominate became something she did not want to give up. She kept herself at a distance from the real needs of her management team and her organization because of her tenaciously held belief that "leaders need to be in control to drive results." As a result, Arlene's management team felt disconnected from her and the corporate goals.

Arlene's personal awakening and her commitment to become a more sharing, engaging, and transparent leader provided her and her team with a powerful transformational process for fostering engagement and community in the organization. Her shift from the leader as the center of the action to the company as the center transformed her organization.

Let's review the lessons of a WE-centric leader:

1. *Context of Community:* Give the whole team a chance to see the larger challenges facing the company, look at the business issues, and focus on what the organization needs to survive and thrive. Think of the organization as a community of people who depend on one another for mutual success.

2. *Agreement:* Help the team members find things they can agree on as they talk about the business issues, so they will emerge with successful decisions together.

3. *Reframe Conflict:* Give the team a chance to look at conflicts in a healthy way and come up with new and better decisions and perspectives.

4. *Teamwork:* Give the team a way to look at its team dynamics and improve them.

5. *Conversational Skills:* Teach the team new ways to communicate to turn breakdowns into breakthroughs.

Through this process, Arlene discovered a new way of thinking about her organization. She shifted from driving her agenda to establishing a community of people working together to achieve audacious results.

What Is Co-creating?

Arlene realized that WE-centric leadership was very different from I-centric leadership. WE-centric is more about *co-creating*. Co-creating is a word that emphasizes the importance of building collaboration inside an organization. It's bigger than collaboration—it is a mutual partnership for shaping and crafting the future. Many leaders do not realize that often their behaviors are not enabling the spirit of co-creating. Co-creating is a shared investment in creating the future. For a fundamental shift to occur in the organization, leaders need to embrace inclusion and mutuality. They need to recognize when they are encouraging competition rather than co-creation. This is the fundamental first step; without this, the others cannot follow.

Arlene had the courage to launch a Learning Journey, which helps leaders redefine what it means to lead a community, and opens eyes to how to create engagement opportunities (psychological space) for others to become leaders. The key ingredient is the wisdom of knowing how to foster engagement and partnership.

Co-creating is the WE-affirming style of leadership that brings colleagues together to create the culture they need for success.

Many leaders develop a reputation as "good communicators." But too often their communication is one-way rather than two-way. Co-creating is a dynamic process of engagement—an iterative dialogue about creating the future together, which we saw Bob Lutz do with his senior team and Arlene do with hers. Yes, it can be unsettling. As a leader, you may feel more vulnerable than you are used to, because you must allow yourself to be influenced and to be open to change. Yet, from this level of engagement is born the desire to transform and grow. Change starts with self-change. When we desire to change, we make change happen. Our energy for change influences others and the resulting partnership becomes transformational.

The New Leadership: Fellowship, Not Followership

Much of the literature on leadership portrays great leaders as heroes, people who have almost superhuman qualities. Not surprisingly, what we have learned about leadership has been based largely on the military model. We're all familiar with military stories and their themes of battles won and lost, powerful leaders, and blind followers. Leadership heroes have been politicians and historical war figures who, through sheer force of will, charisma, and influence, have led us toward great victories and versions of the Promised Land.

Many business leadership models over the past few decades were similarly drawn from studies of war and politics, painting glorious pictures of leaders charging into battle, fearlessly exhorting troops to follow them—regardless of the challenges ahead. This old paradigm of leadership is actually *followership*. Yes, followership can be a good thing sometimes. It is good when you are escaping from the enemy or need to get people across a busy street without an accident. It's good in a crisis when time is of the essence and you need people to follow rules to the letter. But there are side effects of the followership model when it is used as the primary means to gain alignment.

Followership is not good when we expect such lock-step allegiance to our point of view that we create alignment at the cost of real commitment, valuable contributions, or honest, robust dialogue. When people follow out of fear, we may create worse consequences than if they don't follow at all.

If you check your own beliefs about leadership, you will recognize that many of us grew up believing that the followership model captures the essence of good leadership. Turn around and, if people are behind you, you are a great leader. Yet, as we've seen in the stories in this chapter, this is only a small part of what is required for leaders to be effective. It is, in fact, just the opposite of the kind of leadership required for today's business world.

Although our organizational environments are typically hierarchical—the big boss at the top, the soldiers and worker bees at the bottom—businesses today are consciously evolving social systems away from authoritarian hierarchies. We are beginning to understand how to socialize, harmonize, and collaborate in ways that nullify some of the negative side effects of autocratic, hierarchical systems. We are urgently seeking systems and processes that enable colleagues to come together as equals, so that we can draw upon everyone's talents.

Are you an I-centric or a WE-centric leader? How do you show up at work? Your thoughts, behaviors, and attitudes influence others in profound ways. Reflect on who you are and how you come across at work. What aspirations do you have for your leadership?

Begin to act in new ways—as a partner, leader, and member of a community. Here are some steps you can take every day to foster partnering and co-creating:

1. Enable public dialogue and brainstorming about the business, and interrupt private dialogue about disappointments with people.
2. Go out of your way to make it easier for people to speak up and speak out about what is working, what is not, and what to do about it.
3. Encourage everyone to attend meetings together—from the janitorial staff to the CEO—to talk about how to create a business transformation.
4. Acknowledge where the company is heading, even if the company is in trouble. Rather than casting blame, ask for help. Value input.
5. Set new goals and engage the entire organization in sharing the risks and the benefits.
6. Define business challenges and open discussions for people to offer ideas and opinions about what to do.
7. Establish an accountability matrix, so colleagues can sign up for taking action. The accountability matrix enables you to have the team assign roles they will play on projects, such as who will be the leader or the accountable person, who will help with the project work, who will act as consultants with content expertise, and who needs to be informed.

Try This

When you are taking on a new role as leader, or heading up a new team, you explore the power of a Learning Journey to create WE. Follow these guidelines to help you launch the process:

- **Prework:** Communicate with participants in advance of the meeting to find out what issues they most want to discuss and what outcomes they desire. You can do this early discovery research through e-mails or through a Discovery Interview. Collect the themes so you can include them in the agenda for prioritization and discussion.

- **Invitation:** Send out an invitation that will create anticipation and excitement.

- **Agenda and Desired Outcomes:** In your agenda, include segments where you are raising a big question and having the group participate in addressing it: Who We Are Now, Who Do We Want to Become, What is the State of the Business, How Do We Want to Create the Future Together, and Where We Go from Here—Next Steps and Accountabilities.

- **Follow-up:** After a launch meeting, set up regular touch points for ongoing communication, updating, and innovation. Weekly meetings in the beginning solidify the team and create a sense that the group is reaching progressive milestones. Continue to ask big questions at the updating meetings so that the team gets into the new habit of collectively working on innovative solutions.

When leaders believe in WE, they behave in ways that cause others to also behave co-creatively. It's such a powerful shift that people often experience others and themselves as "born again." Personal and fundamental shifts in beliefs about leadership—from controlling to partnering—encourage others to offer their best ideas, their collaborative spirit, and their own openness to change.

WE-aving It All Together

A leader's work is internal work. The real change occurs in belief systems, how you envision your role as a leader and how you relate to your staff and colleagues. Do you find yourself feeling that the weight of the world is on your shoulders, or are you willing to create the space for an incredible new level of engagement and partnering in your business? Are you focusing outward on customers, learning what they need and want from your company, or are you focusing everyone on "meeting your needs"? When you create an enterprise of collaboration with the customer as the focus of attention, what had been your business becomes everyone's business—and you will have officially taken your first step in creating a healthy WE-centric environment.

Remember to Honor the Vital Principle of Learning

Leaders need to focus on making beliefs transparent—to share what's on their minds so everyone can focus collectively on the enterprise challenges and on pleasing the customer, rather than just on pleasing the boss.

True leadership that encourages fellowship not followership triggers the Vital Instinct of Partnering by substituting an enterprise agenda for the boss's agenda. The message you as leader are sending is that everyone shares the responsibility of learning and understanding what is best for the health of the enterprise and what is in the best interests of the customer. In this way, everyone learns when to signal others that there is a threat to the collective health of the organization and when there are opportunities for growth.

Vital Choices

Review the Vital Choices chart and identify where you spend most time. How do you show up at work? Are you a leader, or a boss? Are you I-centric or WE-centric? Monitor yourself every day. Come to recognize what beliefs you hold and the choices you make. Vital Leadership comes from recognizing your beliefs and the resulting choices you make, and most of all the impact these choices have on others. You can promote organizational health by making beliefs transparent around the seven principles shown in the Vital Choices list following.

Vital Choices

Are you more comfortable excluding others than including them? Are you more comfortable criticizing colleagues behind their back than giving them feedback face-to-face? Are you more comfortable not experimenting for fear of making mistakes, or are you willing to take risks? Do you prefer to hold on to important information, or are you willing to share with others to expand collective wisdom? Are you more comfortable telling people what to do, or are you willing to challenge them to think in new ways? What environment are you creating? Audit yourself.

Co-creating	I-centric — Protect	WE-centric — Partner
	Exclusive: *Power-over*	Inclusive: *Power-with*
The Context We Set	1. Only talk to those one level up; corner office; get my coffee	1. Senior executives discuss the strategy with employees
	2. Senior executives own the strategy; information kept close to the vest	2. Information about company's health, wealth, and business strategy shared with employees
	3. Using status to impress; keep the distance	3. Employees included in change process; involved, engaged, empowered
	4. Exclusion; closed doors	4. Inclusion, open-door policy
	5. Lack of respect	5. Respect abounds

Humanizing	I-centric — Protect	WE-centric — Partner
	Judging	Appreciating
The Relationships We Build	1. Critical; criticizing work; highly judgmental	1. Feedback; appreciating work; highly supportive
	2. Focus on "what you can't do"	2. Focus on "what you can do"
	3. Blame; finger-pointing	3. Accountability; responsibility
	4. Lack; not good enough	4. Strength; bring talent to bear
	5. Undervalued, underappreciated, and not trusted	5. Valued, appreciated, and trusted

(continued)

Vital Choices (continued)

	I-centric — Protect	WE-centric — Partner
Optimizing	**Limiting**	**Expanding**
The Dreams We Hold	1. Fear it won't work 2. Been there, done that 3. Too hard to get support; don't know how 4. Fear of mistakes 5. Don't get your hopes up	1. Believe it will work 2. Bring hope, dreams, and aspirations to work 3. Rally and attract support; know how to unite people 4. Learn from mistakes 5. Share hopes, dreams, and aspirations
	I-centric — Protect	**WE-centric — Partner**
Interacting	**Territorial; Scarcity**	**Share; Abundance**
The Actions We Take	1. Withholding; not sharing power or information 2. My territory; my power 3. Fear of giving too much freedom; restrict interactions 4. Don't cross the line 5. Don't get credit for sharing; don't share	1. Share power and information 2. Understand how to respect territory, to give and share 3. Give freedom for interactions 4. Open boundaries 5. Give credit for sharing; share
	I-centric — Protect	**WE-centric — Partner**
Catalyzing	**Persuading; Knowing**	**Generative; Wondering**
The Ideas We Evolve	1. Low risk-taking 2. Same is good 3. Our way or the highway 4. "Not invented here" syndrome 5. What is, is; don't fix it; it's not broken	1. Support risk-taking 2. Different is good 3. Experiment with new ways 4. Build scenarios 5. Break it!

(continued)

Vital Choices (continued)

	I-centric — Protect	WE-centric — Partner
Expressing	**Autocratic; Controlling**	**Developing; Encouraging**
The Words We Choose	1. Autocratic and dictatorial 2. I'm right; know-it-all 3. Own the airtime 4. Show what I know 5. Tell and sell	1. Direct and honest 2. Listen 3. Challenge others to grow 4. Share what I know; learn from others 5. Allow positive pushback
Synchronizing	**Compliance**	**Commitment**
The Purpose and Passion We Live	1. Disconnect 2. Punish/Failure 3. This is our way 4. Top down 5. Dogma	1. Connect 2. Reward success 3. Ongoing communication 4. Connect to a higher purpose 5. Spirit and passion
Integrity	**Double Standard**	**One Standard**
The Intention We Hold	Holding a separate standard for me than for you	Live with positive and pure intention

Are You Up for the Challenge?

What I am describing in this book is a new, inclusive *fellowship* model of leadership that builds a community of leaders, rather than a system of servitude to an authority figure.

As a business executive in this extraordinary time, you are part of a generation of leaders who live at the edge of this new business transformation. You are leaving the old world of command-and-control, authority-based leadership behind you. The new leadership in front of you consists of leaders who know how to master their internal drive for *power-over* others, and transform it into *power-with* others. New leaders change the way they communicate and the way work gets done; they help colleagues rise above conflict; and they understand how to create new and expansive possibilities. New leaders give us hope instead of fear, and turn competition into collaboration.

2.

My Turf, Your Turf

The Challenge of Territoriality

*Avoiding danger is no safer in the long run than outright
exposure. The fearful are caught as often as the bold.*

CONFUCIUS, CHINESE PHILOSOPHER

One of the great myths of organizational life is that territoriality
is inevitable—that people, particularly under stress, will naturally
retreat into their respective teams or departmental "silos," hunker
down, and adopt an unhealthy WE/THEY attitude. The toxic belief
that protecting one's turf is the norm and internal competition is
actually a good thing has caused much needless pain and kept many
individuals and companies from achieving their full potential.

Unhealthy internal competition erodes trust, breaks down relationships, and pits one group against another. This pattern can take
place in a one-on-one working relationship, within a team, across
divisions, and even with customers, as you will see in the following
story. Even those who believe they are WE-centric leaders can suffer
from a disconnect between what they think they are doing and what
they are actually doing—their intentions versus their impact. In the
spirit of "protecting the enterprise" or "the brand," some leaders may
actually be creating territoriality.

Champion or Despot?

Carol was the head of corporate communications for a major paper company. Her department was big and powerful, responsible for both external and internal communications. Carol had a direct line to the CEO and always had sufficient financial resources.

The department—and Carol—won many industry awards for the work they produced, from corporate brochures to internal communications programs. Their corporate newspaper was an industry standard. Carol worked with the top external graphics firms and had an attitude about it. She always had the CEO's ear and was politically connected. Some people disliked her because they perceived her to be arrogant and snobbish. Others wanted to be her friend to get access to the top. She was honest and direct. If you were not on her team, she would let you know.

Every few years Carol did an internal "customer survey" of the thirty-one divisions for whom she provided services. The survey was a short review of her department. As she prepared to send out that year's survey, she knew in her gut that there was a problem. Rather than work with Carol, some of the field offices were choosing to have their own outside graphics companies do their brochures, newsletters, and other branding materials.

Carol got to see some of the field communications brochures, which the local design companies created, and she was beside herself. Many of the outside vendors had taken liberties with the logo and brand imaging. Their work was not up to her standards, nor the standards of the company. *She* was the keeper of the brand and ultimately responsible for every piece of literature. She believed the field managers were taking excessive liberties with the brand; she could not allow this.

Carol needed to figure out how to address the problem and thought she could gain some insight into the situation through the survey. When the results came back, she saw that the problem was bigger than she realized. She contracted with our firm for a third-party set of face-to-face interviews with all thirty-one field managers. In effect, she was contracting for a "360-Degree Assessment" from her "customers." A 360-Degree Assessment is a way of gaining feedback about how others perceive you. Like a mirror that can see 360 degrees around you, this process enables you to know the impact you have on others, what's working and what's not, and suggests ideas for what you can do differently. A 360-Degree Assessment can be done anonymously through a Web site, like the one we have created for clients, or it can be done through an interview process. Carol contracted for my company to do interviews with her top internal clients—the executives who use her communication expertise for marketing communications projects like creating brochures for customers, and for internal communications projects, like internal newsletters and training programs.

The resulting interviews painted a clear picture of Carol as autocratic and dogmatic about how she wanted design and branding to play out in the company. This was her job and she took it seriously. But because of her arrogant leadership style, she communicated to the field that their opinions counted for very little.

For example, when one of these managers needed a brochure to sell a line of paper or a flyer to announce a local community event, she would bring the assignment to Creative Services, Carol's team, to fulfill the work. Carol's team approached the design process with her internal customers in a way that frustrated and alienated them. Rather than seeking insights about what they wanted and needed, Carol's team worked directly with a small group of outside graphic designers who would render many illustrations and graphics for each project. She failed to engage the senior executives in the company—her internal customers—in the project scoping, brainstorming, and detailing. Rather than talk with the divisional president of one of the paper divisions— the client she was servicing—or the head of sales for that division, she relied on the outside design firm for ideas. Carol didn't talk with her customer. She spent her time with the design firm coming up with all sorts of wonderful ideas; then Carol's team sifted through their many ideas and chose the *one* they wanted to present—all without conferring with her customer. The customer was outside the decision loop.

Carol thought she was being a consummate professional and was proud of the process she used for arriving at the best recommendations for her clients. Her field managers, on the other hand, found her and her design team to be dogmatic. Carol and her team felt so strongly about their designs that they appeared unresponsive to any feedback. Carol's customers felt she wasn't listening to them. She excluded them until the very end, when she presented her final recommendation. They felt she was not being collaborative.

In actuality, Carol was protecting her turf—the design world—and she didn't even realize the feelings of territoriality it was fostering throughout the organization.

Carol and her team set themselves apart from the other executives in the organization. She stopped listening to her customer, didn't accept feedback, and became insensitive to their wishes. After trying to gain her attention and failing, her customers turned to other design firms and formed the opinion that Carol's team was just too arrogant to work with. Carol's team was creating toxic relationships, causing separateness, and most of all, "rooting" themselves in their past successes. Their self-protective attitude made them impossible to work with. During the 360-Degree Assessment, we found that at first Carol's clients wanted to "vent" just to get their frustration off their chests. Then we guided them to provide great suggestions about what Carol's team could do differently. By focusing them on describing the future they wanted to create together, Carol would have a handle on what to do next.

Defending I or Creating WE

In the previous example, many field managers wanted to be more involved in the creative process. They wanted to feel like their input made a difference. They wanted to strategize with Carol and see options. This may seem like a small issue to have created such a significant problem, but it did. Her field managers were opting to work with outside design firms because they felt that the outsiders treated them with greater respect and gave them more opportunity to influence the final choice.

On hearing the feedback, Carol was initially angry and upset. She said that the field people didn't hold to the right standards and that was why they needed her. She referenced specific pieces of work they had created and pointed out how badly executed they were. She was very defensive and protective about her "process" of working with the field. She truly felt she was doing the right thing.

Carol believed she was bringing the best talent she could to the table and was able to guide her clients toward the best solutions. Despite these good intentions, her clients felt she had limited their participation, had excluded them from the most critical part of the process—sorting through options—and had determined that the field's voices didn't really count.

The Inside Scoop: The Triune Brain

In the decade of the '60s, Paul McLean, a neuroscientist, researched the brain and discovered it consisted of three levels, which he collectively termed the triune brain. He called the most primitive level the *reptilian brain* (for protection); the next level the limbic brain (for friend or foe?); and the third level, the most evolved, the neo-cortex (for problem solving, perspective, innovation).

The reptilian brain is believed to be the seat of our survival instincts, triggering the fight/flight reaction when we are in danger, enabling us to hunt for food and preventing us from becoming food. The reptilian brain protects us from harm to the body, and to the ego, and addresses these questions:

1. Can it hurt me? (Ego threats)
2. Can I acquire it? (Takeovers; mergers and acquisitions)
3. Can I dominate? (Perpetuate my clan, my culture, and my beliefs)

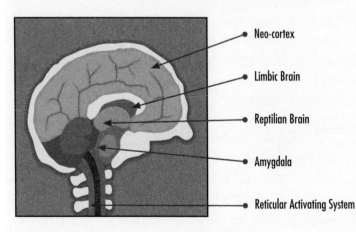

- Neo-cortex
- Limbic Brain
- Reptilian Brain
- Amygdala
- Reticular Activating System

Seeing Reality and Turning It Around

Carol finally saw something she hadn't seen before. She realized that her intention and her impact did not align. She thought she was doing something that would have a good influence on her client relationships, and instead it had a negative impact. She also realized she hadn't fostered a partnership with her clients, but rather had imposed her will on them. She was excluding them and, in doing so, was triggering a territorial response on their part. She was focusing on protecting her turf—the brand image—and they, in response, were focusing on protecting their respective territories and relationships with their own customers. Without meaning to, she was modeling I-centric behavior for the rest of the organization.

Carol was able to see this reality by using a 360-degree process with the intention of building new relationships with her colleagues. Following a debrief on this feedback-rich 360, and after some coaching on how to re-engage with her field managers, Carol was prepared to hold one-on-one meetings with them. She humbly, rather than defensively, addressed the feedback with each of them, listening and talking through how each wanted to work with her.

This feedback process took courage. Both Carol and her clients shared their insights and feelings in a transparent way, talking through how her earlier approach had alienated each one of them and why. The conversations went deep into the influence that her behavior had on each person. Carol responded to this feedback with great appreciation and openness.

By letting them know she was willing to be influenced and to alter her approach, she entered into a contract for ongoing feedback as they developed a new working relationship. Instead of adopting a *power-over* attitude that she might have felt entitled to because of her position as Brand Manager, Carol approached her clients with respect and a *power-with* mindset. She not only began to accept feedback, but she learned to thrive on it as well.

A few months after this project, Carol reported that her openness to establishing a feedback-rich relationship with her colleagues had caused them to view her in a new light. They came to value her as a strategic partner, calling her well in advance to work with them on larger business challenges they faced. Carol's team became known not just as the "graphics" team, but as the "communications strategy" team—an elevation in stature within the company that went far beyond Carol's expectations.

Linking Intention and Impact

As a leader in your organization, how do you engage employees in the process of getting work done? How do you interact with others to achieve corporate goals? Are you someone who must have power over others? Or are you someone who understands how to build a collaborative team? Do you know how to create a sense of commitment to the brand, to the company, and to everyone's mutual success? Are you I-centric or WE-centric? You can be your own coach and experiment with linking your intention and impact. The following box shows how.

Intention and Impact Exercise

Exercise Setup: Sometimes we have experiences that hit us hard and push us into defensive behaviors. When this happens, we can resort to acting out of fear or protection, developing behavior patterns to compensate—I call these *habit patterns*, or *postures*. When we're posturing, we negatively impact relationships, teams, and organizations—we create toxic reactions. We don't choose postures; they are our reactive responses to threat. We can, however, choose to release ourselves from them. Use the following questions to get in touch with your postures and to turn them around.

What Is Your Pattern? Turn It Around!

1. *Situation:* What is the situation? Where are you now?
2. *Intention:* What was your intention? What did you want to make happen?
3. *Expectations:* What were your expectations? What did you think others would do, and what did you think you would gain?

continued

continued

4. **Action:** What was your action?
5. **Result:** What did you get? What happened?
6. **Reaction:** What was your reaction (to getting what you wanted or not getting what you wanted)? How did the situation affect you? What did it mean to you?
7. **Pattern:** What was your pattern (your way) of handling the situation?
8. **Create:** What do you want to create? What questions can you ask to turn it around?
9. **Learn:** What did you learn? What wisdom did you access?

Ladder of Conclusions

At the heart of every interaction is a conversation that sets the ground rules of the relationship. When we are in conversation, we are doing more than sharing information and exchanging ideas. There is always a subtext in which we test our view of reality against our new experiences. This subtext will either prove what we know or raise issues about what we don't know. Most often, we are "making assumptions" in an attempt to find new data to prove old beliefs that assert we are right. Few people take the time to do research to prove they are wrong. As we engage in conversations, we confirm our beliefs, biases, and assumptions every step of the way. The Ladder of Conclusions is a graphic illustration of what goes on in our mind. When situations happen, we jump up the ladder to make interpretations. When we are in a protect mode, our interpretations pit one person against the other. Our interpretations are filled with beliefs and opinions that confirm our fears.

WE-centric leaders are tuned in to how their interpretation of reality can trigger territoriality, and they work consciously at choosing beliefs, words, and conversations that create WE. That is their job. If you want to be a WE-centric leader, if you want to create a unified culture, and if you want to build a community of colleagues who can work together as partners to achieve audacious goals, then you have to be the one to intercept the crashes. You have to be the one to set the tone. Then colleagues will sing with you. As you reflect

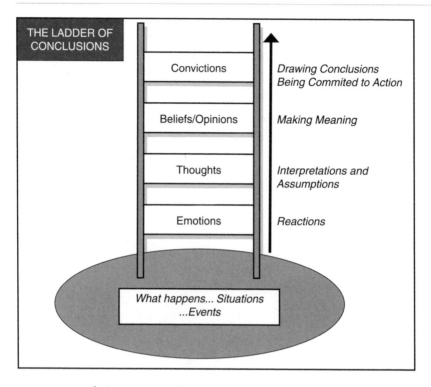

on your own behavior, you'll notice how you make assumptions and draw conclusions about others. Knowingly or unknowingly, you instinctively create meanings full of "territorialism." You must catch yourself in that moment, when you are at the edge of making wild assumptions, and bring yourself back to a neutral place where your interpretations can come from positive intention.

Uncovering Your Biases

Here's an exercise to help you use the Ladder of Conclusions to capture your own biases that may be influencing how you perceive your environment. With regard to any particular set of facts, ask yourself:

- What feelings am I holding that may be biasing me?
- What opinions am I holding that may be biasing me?
- What beliefs am I holding that may be biasing me?
- What convictions am I holding that may be biasing me?

Once you've captured your own biases, you can read the team space. You can read the tone of how people talk and what they say, and you can come up with a team "fingerprint" from which to make your interpretations and draw your conclusions. Because you read reality through a lens from the past, you will naturally sort things that look and feel familiar from those that look and feel different. Ask yourself:

- What may be creating a toxic environment?
- What may be triggering positive or negative spirals?
- What are my triggers?
- Notice what gets you going most.
- Notice what gets others going most.

Learning to be cognizant of when you are coming from an I-centric or WE-centric place requires clarity on how to separate fact from assumptions, to neutralize your thinking, to master how you create positive and transformational meaning out of experiences, in spite of the situation.

Appreciative Inquiry

Learning to manage the three critical dynamics for creating a WE-centric workplace is the key to success. First, you learn to manage your own reactions; second, you put your ego behind you; and third, you focus on the challenges facing the organization and build healthy relationships with others. Your ability to lead will increase exponentially, and you will enhance your ability to create inspiring environments where people work together for mutual growth and understanding.

Rather than finding yourself tangled up in conversations about blame and fear and frustrations about what is *not* happening at work, you establish a positive context for transformation by engaging people in ongoing and iterative conversations about what *has, can, and will* work to create a transformation. In doing so, you focus on what needs to happen to address the challenges facing the organization, and with that focus and commitment, you develop into the best company possible, as a WE. Rather than trying to fix the past, you focus on creating the future with others. It is an experience at once exhilarating, engaging, and profound.

When colleagues work in concert, they learn from each other and are more apt to develop the higher-level skills and wisdom needed to meet the organization's performance goals. When we connect, we learn how to turn breakdowns into breakthroughs—we become high performing. When leaders turn to others for advice, suggestions, feedback, and points of view, and value them, they create a community of colleagues who look forward to coming to work every day.

Dissolve Cultural Boundaries

Even though our communication technologies enable us to dissolve boundaries of space and time and interconnect us in exciting new ways, we are still faced with the same old human challenge: to dissolve cultural and psychological boundaries to build trust and to access the powerful people-resources we bring into our businesses.

WE-centric leaders know how to lift people out of fear, frustration, and anger, which cause people to *disengage* from each other. They know how to create a culture that enables colleagues to be *connected,* engaged, and involved in creating and living the values and vision of the company.

WE-centric leaders know that people become reactive when they feel disconnected. They understand that when people feel out of the loop, they project their anxiety onto others and blame others for what is missing in their lives. When we are rejected, we reject back.

Healthy Generative Culture	
I-centric Universe	WE-centric Universe
I am the center of the universe	We are the center of the universe
creates:	creates:
Territoriality and conflict	Creativity and growth
Lack of sensitivity	Sensitivity and mutual support
Indirect communication	Feedback-rich, vital communication

Hard-wiring the DNA of Organizational Life

As a leader, you have the ability to shape and craft the experiences people have at work by understanding how to reduce fear and inner focus and create environments that facilitate enhanced sensitivity, mutual support, vital communication, and engagement in the business strategy. When we live in toxic fear-based environments, we can become unhealthy in mind and spirit. We can react like cancer cells—like cells that stop communicating with the immune system that is designed to protect the whole body, cells that start to grow all over because they have lost their sensitivity to other cells, and cells that create roots and lock themselves in isolation, drawing nourishment from the body and weakening it. The parallel is striking. When we live in fear, we withdraw, build our Ladder of Conclusions, imagine others are out to get us, and react accordingly. We stop turning to others for help, and we stop taking feedback and advice from others. What happens at the cellular level happens at the organizational level.

Universal Fears and Universal Desires

Universal Fears:

- Being excluded . . . so we create "old-boy networks" and exclude others first.
- Being rejected . . . so we learn how to reject first.
- Being judged unfairly . . . so we criticize and blame others.
- Failing . . . so we avoid taking risks and making mistakes.
- Losing power . . . so we intimidate others to get power.
- Feeling stupid . . . so we either don't speak up or speak too much.
- Looking bad in front of others . . . so we save face.

Universal Desires:

- Be included on a winning team.
- Be appreciated and valued.
- Be successful.
- Learn, grow, and explore.
- Be creative and contribute.
- Have a leadership voice.
- Have meaning and purpose.

Fears and Desires in the Limbic Brain

The limbic brain surrounds the brain stem and manufactures hormones and other chemicals responsible for feelings, moods, and emotions, providing the capacity for nurturing, rearing young, creating communities, clans, and organizations. Inside the limbic brain is the amygdala, a small organ that has the ability to sense threats, helping protect our turf. Through more recent research, it's now believed that the amygdala is the emotional core of the brain. Its primary role is triggering the fear response, which it does through a series of changes in brain chemistry and hormones that put the body in a state of anxiety.

The limbic brain handles the following emotions:

- Anger
- Fear
- Sadness

When we perceive the world through a lens of fear, our egos drive us into habit patterns of protection, and without realizing it, we learn over time to incorporate defensive behavior patterns into our daily routines. Too often, we turn away from others when we are coming from protective behaviors, rather than turning to others for help in making vital changes in our lives.

In spite of the evolutionary leaps forward in brain capacity, giving us enormous untapped potential, our brains still contain organs hard-wired with guidance that reflects the multiple layers of evolution tightly packed into that small cavity in our heads. Each system speaks to the others. Each plays a role in driving behavior. And as you will see, we need to learn how the systems interplay as we learn to master our own human behavior.

Territoriality: Gauge Yourself

Organizations going through change are prone to have environments in which fear abounds. Fear, ambiguity, and uncertainty about the future often trigger "defensive behaviors." When we are frightened,

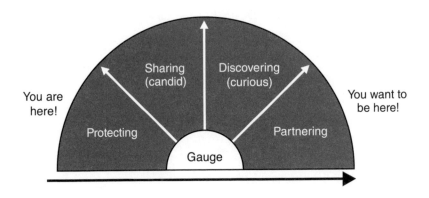

we recoil, avoid, freeze, acquiesce, and withdraw from engagement with others.

We become defensive when we feel we need to protect ourselves. In times of stress and ambiguity, when business is not performing as expected, or when self-doubt and doubt about others' abilities become a primary focal point, we can easily shut down and revert to defensive behaviors. These hard-wired response patterns can lead to negatively spiraling self-talk, adversarial interpretations of reality, and fault-finding conversations or just the opposite—overambitious

Minding Our Business

The neo-cortex is the most evolutionarily advanced part of the brain for learning, unlearning, and relearning. This part of the brain enables us to speak, think, create, problem-solve, and manage complex activities. This is our "vault," giving us a perspective of past, present, and future and the ability to design three-dimensional objects, calculate, forecast, and dream. It is our dream machine and our growth engine at work. The neo-cortex enables us to:

- Create game plans and strategies
- Innovate and pioneer
- Design what has never existed before
- Build alliance strategies
- Create large organizations and handle complexity and ambiguity

expectations, unrealistic aspirations, or overconfidence—all of which prevent us from accessing the strength and insight we need to turn things around.

Unleashing Humanity

There is no work more important for a leader than creating an environment where all team members can contribute their talent and potential. Potential is often invisible—yet to be discovered. It's not what we can easily see; it is born out of the healthy interactions of one person with another. As we interact, we trigger responses—that's what it means to be human.

Once you learn new strategies and techniques for rewiring your life, relationships, and workplace from those that are focused on fear to those that are focused on achieving outrageous results, your life and the lives of others who work with you will radically shift. When we live in a positive, inspiring, interdependent, catalytic, expressive workplace, we all share the power for turning a toxic culture into a healthy, WE-centric and inclusive workplace. From this new vantage point, you will begin to see how your own patterns change and along with that will come a whole new perspective about what is possible for you to create with others.

Try This

When colleagues work together to discover Best Practices in a company, they shift from focusing on the negative, refocusing on looking for the positive practices that help the organization grow to its fullest potential. Best Practices represent what is good and what is working in a company, and it defines what it means to be a world-class company that attracts customers. Sharing Best Practices is a way of elevating the skills and talent of everyone to a higher level. Here is something to experiment with that can change everyone's focus from loss to gain, from worst (internal conflict) to Best Practices.

How to create a Best Practices forum:

■ Bring a team together to discover and share Best Practices. For example, a team of sales executives, or a team of marketing executives.

■ Choose people who may all have different ways of working and may be able to raise the IQ for everyone.

■ It's possible that the colleagues have not worked well together or have been "labeled" as territorial. It's possible that they come from different parts of the company, with different ways of working. If the purpose is to create WE, then using a Best Practices framework can catalyze new levels of cooperation.

■ Ask all the members of the team to think of things they are currently doing that are having a positive impact or are creating business success.

■ Ask the team members to put together the following:
  • Descriptions of what they are working on.
  • Descriptions of the approaches they are taking.
  • Descriptions of the impact they are having on the client, or business result.
  • How to transfer this knowledge to others.

■ Each member of the team presents these Best Practices to the other colleagues.

■ The facilitator captures the key success principles: What is each person doing to create success?

■ Participants ask questions to clarify the Best Practices and to learn how to transfer them to other situations. The end result is that people feel heard, valued, and acknowledged.

WE-aving It All Together

Leadership skills are developed over time and across a company. The hardest part of leadership is that *everyone* wants to play an important role and wants recognition for his or her contributions. Sometimes a leader finds it difficult to manage the relationships, the competing demands and needs, and the apparent lack of resources—and so territoriality arises. Sometimes we lose our sensitivity to others. We become so enchanted with our own notoriety and entrenched in our own successes that we forget to honor others for their contributions.

Remember to Honor the Vital Principle of Growing

Leaders need to focus on creating a feedback-rich culture so that everyone is open to feedback on their ideas, on their behavior, and on how to create a vital environment. This way everyone grows.

As a leader, you can promote mutuality and counter tendencies toward territoriality and self-protective, silo thinking by tapping into the Vital Principle of Growing. You can encourage everyone to be sensitive to personal and group boundaries, while at the same time helping them to see how individual growth can best be achieved through expanding opportunities for growth of the enterprise as a whole.

Leader Behavior

Most often we turn to turf wars, to building silos and to stirring territoriality when we fear we are losing what we hold dear. Fear drives us into our I-centric behavior and we protect rather than partner. Health comes from creating environments that honor the seven universal desires we all have for being valued, for making contributions, for expressing ourselves:

- Audit yourself and see if you are creating environments that acknowledge the seven key universal desires.
- If you are not creating environments that encourage mutuality and support, are you open to feedback from peers and direct reports?
- Read the Seven Leader Behaviors chart on the next page and identify your areas of strength. Continue to do more of this because it creates healthy supportive environments.

Seven Leader Behaviors

For Sustaining Energy and Mutual Commitment
What is your engagement strategy for success?

Dimension	Universal Desire	Leader Behaviors
Connecting	TO BE INCLUDED ON A WINNING TEAM	Create inclusive environments that focus on interconnectedness and inclusion
Humanizing	TO BE APPRECIATED AND VALUED	Create environments that honor the uniqueness and diversity of people, that support open communication and feedback, and that respect the value of each individual
Optimizing	TO BE SUCCESSFUL	Create environments that are very dynamic and provide greater possibilities for people to strive for the impossible, to imagine the unimaginable, to dream the undreamable
Interacting	TO SHARE AND LEARN	Create environments full of learning and sharing of knowledge and wisdom
Catalyzing	TO CONTRIBUTE	Create environments that encourage innovation, creativity, and collaboration and the building of wisdom
Expressing	TO HAVE A RESPECTED LEADERSHIP VOICE	Create environments where voices are expressed, not suppressed, and that support leadership development, encourage risk-taking, and provide opportunities to take on leadership and team challenges
Synchronizing	TO HAVE PURPOSE AND MEANING	Create environments that honor the human spirit to achieve together and celebrate together and where mission and purpose drive the work

- Identify your developmental opportunities. These are leader behaviors that you have not been practicing—behaviors that create a supportive healthy environment.
- Create opportunities every day to experiment with the leader behaviors that you have not been practicing.
- Monitor your impact. Notice how you are able to reduce territoriality and increase positive energy and support.

Are You Up for the Challenge?

Sometimes creating a WE-centric environment may seem too challenging. Yet, by staying the course, you will reap the benefits. Over time you will see the much greater rewards that accrue from shifting to WE. By shifting from I-centric to WE-centric leadership, you will experience a wonderful ripple effect of positive outcomes that were not previously accessible. This initially takes place inside yourself, then your team, and throughout your organization, ultimately manifesting in the way clients and the world-at-large view your business.

At the interpersonal level, people will:
- Actually find you more interesting when you put them first.
- Listen to what you have to say with greater interest.
- Pay more attention to your needs.

At the team level, people will:
- Demonstrate greater capability when you believe in them.
- Appear smarter because you are giving them the encouragement to grow.
- Want to work hard for you because you respect them and have made them the center of your world.

At the organizational level, people will:

- Learn how to think about the larger business challenges, because employees are focused on the challenges rather than on compliance with your point of view.
- Learn to think about the organization as a whole rather than as silos, departments, or bosses to please.
- Learn how to come together as one culture, to focus on organizational challenges, to allow Best Practices to come to the surface, and to discover the power of WE.

At the customer level, your customers will:

- Feel loved, attended to, and loyal because they know you have their best interests at heart.
- Want to do business with you because you have created a good experience in making your relationship with them the most important thing in the world.
- Tell others about how good you are to them, which will send more business your way.

Since you have choices to make every step of the way, what will you choose? Will you choose to become a Vital Leader and trigger Vital Instincts—those that govern and guide our eternal growth and evolution—or will you choose to become a Fatal Leader and trigger those instincts that drive an organization into destructive territorial behaviors. The choice is yours—choose wisely!

3.

It Must Be Your Fault . . .

The Challenge of Self-Interest

*A man can fail many times, but he isn't a failure
until he begins to blame somebody else.*

JOHN BURROUGHS, NATURALIST

THE THIRD ESSENTIAL BELIEF that supports WE-centric leadership
is the belief that mutual success and accountability is both desirable
and possible. Only someone who takes an I-centric view believes that
authority is leadership, territoriality is inevitable, and self-interest is
the universal driver of success.

To create WE, we need to work together to establish mutual
accountability and shared responsibility. Sometimes, instead of partnering, we get into blaming. WE/THEY or US/THEM language
emerges when we feel that *we* are doing our job and *they* are not.
It happens among peers, between bosses and direct reports, and
even with customers. In the end, there is no substitute for mutual
accountability. Creating WE is in everyone's self-interest, whether
they initially realize it or not.

Do You Mean to Be Mean?

Few of us begin the day deciding we want to be tough on people. But at
times a riot breaks out and we feel we need to "get tough" (also known

as a "tit-for-tat" animal instinct). Human beings are reactive and language often triggers reactions. The words we choose can be swords for a fight or gifts for a celebration. We are either encouraging people or pushing them away. This all happens through conversations.

Learning how to monitor and manage the words we choose to create positive and rewarding outcomes—regardless of how challenging the circumstances—is vital to our success as leaders. Words have meaning to others far beyond what we intend. We may intend one thing and communicate another; very often meaning resides in the listener. More often than not, what we intend and what others "get" is not a perfect match. True power comes from understanding how we create and manage meaning in any situation.

How we interpret what is said to us determines how we look at people and at situations. If we are not careful, we can get caught in a morass of faulty interpretations and assumptions that may lead to adversarial relationships. On the other hand, if we are thoughtful, we can create interpretations that build strong, healthy relationships. What's most important is, when situations go south, do you know how to change the meaning and turn relationships around?

Stuff Happens

And so it was with Stephen, Chris, and David at Fifth Dimension, a young and fast-growing advertising and marketing company. Managing the growth of their company was harder than they expected. They had to decide on their objectives, how they wanted to grow, whom to hire, how much to pay each employee. Their success in the first five years took them by surprise. It gave them almost too many options, too many choices, and too many risks.

Fifth Dimension was a fast-paced, innovative company. Within just a few years, they went from a staff of 25 to 150. It was the first company of this size any of them had ever run. It was not as easy as any of them had thought it was going to be.

With rapid business growth and staff expansion, the company's culture changed from a place where colleagues knew each other by name and hung out together in the kitchen at breaks to an environment consisting of near-strangers with unfamiliar faces. Personal contact occurred less and less often. Soon clans and cliques formed, as people created smaller social groups to ward off feelings of isolation and alienation.

To make matters worse, each of the partners had his own idea about where he wanted to take the company. They did not always agree. In fact, many of their meetings ended in conflict and arguments. Individually and collectively they were frustrated, and each partner felt that none of the others was listening to his point of view. This impasse got worse as each created a story about what was happening.

Individually, the partners had a lot invested in the business and really wanted to see it succeed. They had reached a plateau, however, and were unsure of how to break through the growth barrier. The creative personalities of their staff and other issues challenged them so deeply that Stephen, Chris, and David realized the weight of the business was taking a toll on their emotional and physical well-being, as well as the company's well-being. The culture felt toxic, and going to work felt like a chore for everyone involved.

All three partners reacted defensively to each other, and often to their staff. Their I-centric, defensive behavior had three negative consequences in this environment: territoriality, fragmentation, and ineffective communication. Most challenging was that the organization split into silos. With people not communicating and problems all around them, the partners were baffled. At the deepest level, they did not understand the roles they played in creating this situation.

A Three-I Monster

Stephen, by nature, was a name-dropping social animal. He expected high standards from others, and when they didn't deliver, he was all over them, openly chastising them and pushing them to the "max." Some people loved his style because he was direct. Others were fearful, not knowing when he might fly off at them. Of the three leaders, he was the no-bullshit boss.

Chris was the teddy bear. He wanted everyone to love him. As a result, he was not able to give tough feedback to others even when they needed it. He cared so much about people's feelings that he was surprised when told he had hurt them in some way. In addition, although he often delegated work to employees, he couldn't keep his hands out of their areas. As he roamed around the offices, he would step in and get involved, often taking creative work in an entirely different direction. This caused consternation among the troops, since it isn't easy to tell the boss to stop meddling.

David, the third partner, was like the corporate coach. He loved to be everyone's confidant and, as a result, was often caught up in relationship conflicts. From his point of view, he was merely trying to help work things out. He may have been everyone's confidant, yet confidentiality was not one of his strong suits. Soon people lost trust in David and came to believe he was deliberately stirring the pot.

Disagreeing Disagreeably

The three partners shared a desire to grow the business, but had different ideas on how to do it. Chris wanted to build his postproduction division and put more money into technical resources. Stephen wanted to cultivate new clients and put resources into business development. David had ideas about growing several new divisions they had not previously considered. They argued about these strategies, and then the arguments became personal. Once this happened, it all went downhill.

At some point along the way, Stephen, Chris, and David began to view each other as adversaries. They became critical of one another's styles and blamed one another for the problems. Each began to point a finger at the other's failure to do his job, pull his weight, or turn the conflicts around. When problem employees from the production group complained that Stephen was growling at them and not appreciating their work, it got back to David who—as corporate coach—felt he had to mediate. This created even more acrimony among the partners.

Stylistically, they were very different people, which was ironic because, in good times, it was these very differences that made them such a great team. Confronted by new business challenges, however, they became insensitive and unappreciative of what each partner brought to the table. Stephen became more caustic and anxious. Chris became more affable on the surface. And David simply withdrew.

They also stopped having strategy meetings because these discussions went nowhere.

Sensing the partners' problems, employees saw a leadership vacuum and started to play one off against the other. When the creative group became upset with Chris for meddling in their studios, they complained to teammates who told other teammates. This finally got back to David, the corporate coach, who now felt he had to fix it. When he approached Chris about it, Chris flew off the handle and told him he was meddling. Then the other two partners banded together with complaints about David.

While the partners were caught up in their conflicts, the employees had no idea where the company was headed. They felt the partners were incapable of running the company, and so the staff went into "clanning" behavior to protect themselves. Everyone felt the climate of distrust—talk about a horrible environment to work in!

What Did the Leaders Expect?

Chris, David, and Stephen wanted everyone to feel good about coming to work every day. They wanted employees to work collaboratively and at the same time take pride in each other's contributions to the whole. They wanted colleagues to be excited and to challenge each other so that what a client received was the best work that Fifth Dimension could offer. They expected employees would take charge, work together, and figure things out collaboratively.

Instead, as they eventually realized, their environment had been taken over by politicking and unhealthy competition, with people looking for someone to blame when things went wrong and with everyone feeling that there were not enough resources to go around.

The environment became toxic and sick. Feelings of helplessness turned into blame and blame turned into "case-building." What was missing was a way for each individual to have a voice. There was no space for voices to be heard—so colleagues competed for attention.

Helplessness and powerlessness permeated Fifth Dimension, creating an unhealthy WE/THEY dynamic that forced people to pick sides for their own survival. At a time when they needed to bind together and meet the competition head-on, people began finding fault with each other. At a time when being connected was critical, they experienced deeper separation.

WE/THEY Thinking List

- "I win, you lose"
- Politicking and playing off partners, lack of respect for each other, lack of integrity, unhealthy competition among peers, and motivation by fear
- Resentful employees
- Jealousy among peers
- Lack of standards: Do just what it takes to get the job done, and no more; no urgency
- Looking for someone to blame, building of fiefdoms, and lack of loyalty
- Scarcity thinking (not enough to go around, therefore I'll take it all)

Blame Is in the "I" of the Beholder

In the beginning of my engagement with Fifth Dimension, I conducted my Discovery Interviews to learn, from each executive, how he viewed the business, his challenges, his hopes and aspirations. Even though they were partners, there was much they didn't share with one another in the beginning. It was my job to help them find ways to express their inner challenges with me and with one another, and to connect with one another on what they wanted Fifth Dimension to become.

Stephen, Chris, and David all spoke about their feelings, something they all needed to express. In his own mind, Stephen was struggling with how he felt. As he searched for the words to express his inner thoughts and frustrations, what showed up was anger and sometimes fear. Stephen believed he was a good provider and the problem at Fifth Dimension was that no one else was pulling his weight. In the privacy of his mind, he began weaving a story about who was falling short and who was not taking responsibility.

Meanwhile, Chris was doing the same thing. In his mind, the problems couldn't be *his* fault. He was a good leader, doing the best he could. It must be *someone else's* fault.

And David, in *his* own mind, was doing the same as his other partners.

A clear pattern had emerged. Stephen found fault with David's leadership of his team. Chris found fault with Stephen's anger with his team. David found fault with both of them. "Case-building" became the framework for interpreting reality. Management found fault with employees and employees with management, creating a cycle of mistrust that rippled throughout the company. Everyone seemed to be coming from a similar space: "I've cleaned up *my* act. How about yours?" No one could get past his own self-interest.

Fifth Dimension at the Crossroads

The executives could no longer deny what was at stake for Fifth Dimension. The management team was facing a critical challenge to the growth, even the survival of the company. It wasn't as if the business was failing. They were still operating successfully and making money. But the partners were not connecting about their hopes and dreams for the company. They were isolated from one another and from this isolation came territoriality. As a result, employees felt the disconnect. They weren't enjoying coming to work and could no longer see how the company would continue to grow. It was hard to focus on growth when territorial games were erupting everywhere. Employees were jockeying for the best projects, the partners were focusing on self-interest, and the environment was toxic.

Things had reached such a crisis point at Fifth Dimension that Stephen considered selling off his ownership share in the company and taking early retirement. The time had come to do something about it, but the partners were unclear as to how to begin. Stephen, David, and Chris could not accept that, having come so far together, they could not get things back on track.

What is needed under these toxic conditions is WE-centric leadership of the highest order—leadership that instills a renewed sense of mutual success, pride, and accountability—yet none of them were up to the task. It seemed insurmountable. After the Discovery Interviews we agreed a few next steps were in order. First, we talked about what the culture was like, and we talked about how they, as leaders, worked to create an environment for success.

As we talked, the leaders begin to take stock of what was going on in the company. At first, they rationalized that their current problems must have stemmed from a previous partner, now no longer with the company, whose style was extraordinarily autocratic. They wanted to believe that his negative impact lived on, like a ghost haunting the halls. The partners decided to speak with employees to find out how they felt about the culture. Yet, in most conversations they were unable to glean an insight into what was going on. Fear was compounding the problem. When the partners asked the employees their opinions, few were honest about what they were feeling. It's difficult to tell your boss, the person who pays your salary, you are unhappy. It's nearly impossible to tell your boss you feel that his or her style of leadership is too controlling or harsh. And how do you tell the truth when you're not even sure what the truth really is?

Courageous Conversations
Develop Power and Influence

When fear, power, and control dominate the organizational terrain as with Fifth Dimension, employees descend into territorial behavior. Morale is low, people feel dispassionate about work, and the energy for raising the bar against the competition disappears. How can organizations open up and build the capacity to create breakthroughs under such conditions?

Courageous Conversations

Be Intentional about Creating WE! *Shift from Suppressing to Expressing*

Employees	Management	Shift Focus
Employees feel excluded and see management as secretive, sometimes incapable of being leaders.	Management keeps strategy behind closed doors, afraid to share until it is complete, with all answers; there is a lack of honest communication.	HAVE CONVERSATIONS ABOUT MUTUAL CHALLENGES
Employees feel judged and critiqued, undervalued, underused, and disrespected.	Management is disappointed by performance, believes employees are incapable of delivering, and therefore criticize and judge.	HAVE CONVERSATIONS ABOUT SHARED ASSUMPTIONS
Employees fear making mistakes and often give up trying to test the waters.	Management wants people to experiment, yet when results are not there, pulls back support, instilling fear of repercussions and failure.	HAVE CONVERSATIONS ABOUT SHARED RISK-TAKING
Employees want to interact and learn from others, yet territoriality and silo mentality pervades.	Management wants a system they can manage, and keeping people in boundaries makes it all manageable and controllable; there is no process in place for Best Practice sharing.	HAVE CONVERSATIONS ABOUT SHARING BEST PRACTICES
Employees want to contribute, be creative, and give customers what they need; management is resistant.	Management wants stability; improving existing business means cutting costs, improving supply chain, reducing head count; there is a fear of investing in alternatives.	HAVE CONVERSATIONS ABOUT NEW ORGANIC APPROACHES
Employees want to have a voice, tell their stories, grow their point of view, and yet don't see how.	Management feels employees lack the courage of conviction, and need to be told what to do.	HAVE CONVERSATIONS ABOUT DEFINING NEW LEADERSHIP
Employees want to be part of a larger purpose; they feel management wants compliance and control.	Management wants to provide direction and focus in on the bottom line results, but everyone is going off in different directions; business is changing too fast.	HAVE CONVERSATIONS ABOUT CREATING COMMITMENT

A Time for Courageous Conversations

Fifth Dimension's leaders and employees had to learn how to create conversations that would address the issues head-on. It was a scary place to go. People have to move out of their Comfort Zones. It feels safer to be self-protective and withhold, or blame others rather than own the part each individual may be playing in the situation. To reach their own respective breakthroughs, the three partners first had to agree to open up and talk. They had to talk like they never had before—in ways that made them feel vulnerable and potentially open for attack. They had to address their greatest fears—the adversarial beliefs they imagined were in each other's minds—beliefs that were not necessarily in their minds or true, but all the more powerful and paralyzing because they were magnified by their imaginations. To get to the other side, they agreed to communicate in this new, open way despite the fears going in. They began a Vital Journey.

Creating a Vital Journey

The partners' immediate goal was to create a safe space in which they could talk openly with one another about the future of the company. This had never occurred before, and would set a new standard for open, accountable leadership communication in the company.

I worked with the partners to create the agenda. We agreed that we would shift our attention from focusing on problems from the past, to creating the future.

Our two-day agenda created the structure for the journey and included the following important facilitated conversations among the key leadership team:

- Creating the Future . . . What behaviors do we want to bring on our journey?
- Growing the Brand . . . What do we want to become?
- Growing the People . . . What do we value?
- Growing the Business . . . What does our customer value

■ Creating WE . . . How can we work together more effectively?
- How can teams work together?
- How can we coach and support each other?
- How do we involve the whole organization?

What Happens During a Vital Journey?

As the leadership at Fifth Dimension learned, a Vital Journey enables executives, teams, and employees to embrace the challenge of simultaneous and mutual personal and organizational growth. It is an experience that turns down the power and influence of Territorial Instincts and turns up the power and influence of Vital Instincts, opening up the minds of all involved so they can focus on creating the future together— "the impossible dream." A Vital Journey creates a time/space experience that bonds executives around current business challenges, heightens awareness of what it takes to win, and expands the team's capacity for the journey. They build journey maps together, form enterprise teams, and create a clear path to weather the storms as a cohesive team.

Step 1: Rewire

Vital Journeys are an opportunity to rewire the leadership mindset from *self-interest* to a focus on *mutual interest*. Participants become aware that their minds are like maps of the future and that their "wiring" determines the journey they will take. Exploring the patterns of their minds—their belief systems—and their behavior in a safe environment enables colleagues to make serious choices about how they will participate in the weeks and months to come.

Step 2: Revise

Vital Journeys focus on significant business issues and challenges. As the team members come to understand marketplace dynamics and competitive issues more clearly, they begin to learn what they need to do to win, and a sense of common ownership for the future emerges. There is something quite unique that happens to colleagues when they find themselves struggling in a crisis together. They depend on each other in new ways. They trust one another in new ways. They communicate with a different level of passion and expression. They are more intimate and more compassionate. Crises and challenges connect people in ways that don't generally occur when life is "business as usual." And, what is also important to know, is that people feel more alive when they are challenged to succeed. They grow more confident and take more risks. Vital Journeys provide a new, direct line of sight on an organization's challenges, opportunities, and customers. Often, for the first time, everyone sees internal and external reality the same way.

Step 3: Rebirth

Through designed interventions, a team of executives learns how to co-create their future by facing challenges in the present together in ways they have never done before. Everyone is a contributor irrespective of hierarchy and position and, through a highly targeted process, shapes the future of the business.

Vital Journeys are designed spaces for co-creation. They are orchestrated moments in time—sometimes launched in weeks and more often in months—where a discovered or co-created business challenge becomes the total focus of attention. As the intervention road map unfolds, it becomes a virtual space in which employees at all levels take part in powerful enterprise team experiences that enable everyone involved to discover how to help shape the organization's strategic future and intent.

Vital Journeys are not change-management programs—and they are not one-time events. They are life-changing experiences that recalibrate and reconnect human beings in conscious and unconscious ways, enabling them to create a new line of sight to their future. It's as though an invisible garment is woven around those involved, shifting the way work is done and the way people interact, creating ongoing organizational capacity for achieving extraordinary business results. It is a way to move from blaming others to having courageous conversations about creating the future together.

The process powerfully affects human dynamics—how people work through tough issues—and at the same time, it impacts business dynamics—how people create value in the marketplace. The process works for teams, for divisions, and for organizations. It works for virtual teams as well as teams who work face-to-face.

Vital Journeys are all about co-creating. Co-creation is about bringing together executive teams and employees to shape their future through conversations about what the future can become. It takes the "sweat equity" of employees at all levels to challenge what they know, recontextualize the organizational space, and expand their ability to arrive at a new perspective for the future. Long gone and out of favor is the autocratic "I tell you how to do it" style of management.

Yet, the challenge of shifting leadership behavior from a more autocratic style to a collaborative and innovative style is easier said than done. Senior executives who are working on being more democratic and participative in their style tend to notice they overdelegate, and then when they realize they've gone too far, they pull back and overdirect. The pendulum swings and overcompensates.

Co-creation, on the other hand, is outside of the delegate-and-direct paradigm. Leaders are encouraged to examine the role they play in the process of growing their executives. Executives are encouraged to be *boundary setters and expanders* rather than *tellers*. Executives are encouraged to see the big picture and focus on creating dialogue around what the organization can become, rather than on merely becoming the best at the game they are playing today.

Human beings are part of the problem *and* part of the solution. We *collectively* have the answer for how to "unglue" our past and create a better future. We *mutually* have the answers for how to make our organizations more effective and efficient and to make them a better place to work; solving the organization's problems as a solo-agent will not give us the rich answers that we can reach for and attain collectively.

While beliefs about "who we are" and "what we are capable of doing" individually exist inside our own minds, beliefs also exist inside us that govern how we view teams, how we view the organization, and how we interact in the organizational space.

Vital Journeys are a process for creating a new organizational space in which co-creation is an honored activity. When territorial instincts become the primary drivers of human behavior, we construct a view of the world that pits people against people, supports a win/lose strategy, and causes human beings to listen without compassion and trust. Vital Journeys are a process for breaking from the past—of getting rid of old belief systems that are mired in history, tainted with failures, surrounded by frustrations, and replacing them with new beliefs about extraordinary possibilities for the future. We all know that when we are able to Let Go of the past and discover new beliefs about the future filled with excitement and aspiration, we discover energy and vitality that was never there before. Vital Journeys create safe environments in which we can find new ways of communicating with one another—ways that reignite our Vital Instincts and allow new possibilities to emerge and transform our organization, our team, and our business reality.

Vital Journeys are reproducible, but no two are exactly alike. This is because they take on the personalities and complexities of the individuals involved. Akin to a psychodrama in the workplace, Vital Journeys enable the complexity of power struggles to take place on the same stage as the birthing of a new level of human awareness and sensitivity. And, behind the scenes, the mind-opening experience of a Vital Journey allows all those involved to see with new sight the power of behavior patterns motivated by power, fear, and control—which they previously enabled.

Once raised to consciousness, the territorial instincts are unseated and a new cultural consciousness emerges, *disallowing* a game-winning

Co-creation

When people join in co-creation, they leave behind the I-thought, and live inside the WE-thought. Co-creation creates a fundamental shift in how we speak to each other, how we honor each other's being, how we move and act and play together—a space that honors the human struggle we're in together. Co-creating is a prolific space that harvests the ingredients for personal change and seeds organizational growth beyond what any one person can imagine.

mentality in which winning means competing against one another. This consciousness disallows the power of control, when control means control by force of intimidation. Vital Journeys *disallow* the power of fear to invade human interaction, and, in doing so, ignite the possibility of "co-creating outrageous futures."

The Transformation of Fifth Dimension

Let's revisit Fifth Dimension to see how they made out on their Leadership Journey. How did Stephen, David, and Chris feel about the process?

David

"We spent seven weeks preparing for a retreat as a part of our leadership transformation. We asked each other questions, listened, and learned how we react to situations and how we react to each other. We discovered how we personally created the situations around us by how we interpreted and responded to challenges. We began to understand how different our interpretations are when we think about ourselves alone rather than about the impact we have on others. After our retreat, we arranged another retreat for our top twenty-five employees, away from the office and distractions. The only way that could be done was on a weekend. Friday came and we all left work early with the hope of getting extra rest before the long weekend. But we were so apprehensive we hardly slept."

Chris

"Saturday morning I drove from home to pick up David and Stephen. We drove together, which was smart. I had butterflies in my stomach like I haven't had since my first date with my wife—maybe since I was a kid. Stephen and I always had a good relationship, but it came with incredible baggage because of the history we had in those seven or eight years together. The three of us looked at each other and asked, 'What the hell are we getting ourselves into?'"

Stephen

"Going in, there was a lot of trepidation. Someone said they thought they were being sent away to a 'growth camp.' I think there were fears that if people didn't grow, they were going to be fired. No one was given a choice of participating or not. But if we said you could opt out, everyone would have. The real fear was that if they participated and failed, they would be out of a job. Weeks before we started this process, there were discussions about cutting overhead and redesigning the company. So there was a lot of fear and anxiety, not knowing the end result."

Chris

"The Journey, as our retreat was called, began with each of us talking about what the process meant to us. What got to me most were the looks on our people's faces. We cut past everyone's resistance by saying, 'We're here, we're open, we want to hear what you have to say.' They looked back at us as if they didn't believe it. I remember looking around the room as people started saying things, and then there was sort of a wellspring. It wasn't venting. We thought it would be venting, based on what we uncovered from the 360 process. I don't even know the words to use to explain what happened. It was like positive energy flowed. It wasn't about the facts. It was about feelings and about interactions at a very deep human level.

"I think the most important thing that I came away with, personally, was that I had a tendency to hurt people. But it was unintentional. The last thing I wanted to do was hurt someone with anything I said. I always had the best of intentions. I forgot what it's like to be an employee. The employee-employer relationship looks very different depending on which side you're on. We uncovered so many misunderstandings and situations where I had no idea of the impact I had on people."

Chris

"Before we embarked on our Journey, I would have compared us to a submarine, all submerged. But today there is a vital communication inside our organization. We can have discussions about things we would never discuss before. We talk about performing and not performing; we discuss conflicts that occur. We get through the discussions with honest communication. Groups are now redesigning themselves. They don't need us to do it. It's as though we've all got more to work with, and we're figuring out how to tap into the skills everyone has."

David

"Before the Journey, I thought it would turn into a bitch session, that we would come back and people would have attacked other people and created a whole new set of problems. It's amazing what actually happened. We've been in this for about a year now, and we've had the best year ever. Our business has transformed itself. We've created four new divisions based on newly discovered talents in our people. We're also seeing opportunities in a new light and discovering new ways of working robustly with our clients. We're winning projects we only dreamed of getting, and we're attracting the best people in the industry to our staff. Overall, we're seeing our business in a new way. What we created is beyond our imagination. It's amazing what we are now capable of doing when we work together this way!"

Stephen

"A lot of development took place that is continuing—this is a process that we can sustain. As new people join us and become part of our company, we bring them into an orientation so they can see who we are and what our culture is all about. As leaders, we moved from dictating to employees, to working with our employees to define the culture we wanted to create. Recently we had the opportunity to bring someone in at a high level who could get us lots of business. We didn't take him. He is a real threat-and-intimidation type of person, and we wanted to preserve what we were growing. We were not going to put up with people who will not fit in. We're about growth, personal and organizational. We want to take more market share in our industry and provide the highest-quality work environment we can. Hopefully, we'll continue to diversify with what we've already created. Since we began this process, we've launched a new production company, we're doing motion picture graphics, TV trailers—every day we're discovering new ways to expand the services we provide for our clients."

Chris

"What also happened was an opening of a dialogue of respect. Sure there's backsliding from time to time, but because there's more open communication we catch it right away, deal with it, and the issue is over. We always had great people here, but there were also plenty of old behaviors that were not working. Now we have an environment that is safe enough, friendly enough, and supportive enough to encompass many styles of behavior without anyone losing their identities.

"Before we began this process I had sleepless nights. Since we've had the process underway, I haven't had a sleepless night about my business. I don't feel scared to go away on vacation. I don't have the need to control everything I touch. I feel connected and in control in a good way.

"We weren't a company that was sinking. We were a company that was expanding, but we were doing it the hard way. Now, we've really created something special here, and we're all committed to keeping it this way!"

Beyond Self-Interest: A New Dimension of Mutuality

Chris, Stephen, and David learned that the world looks different depending on where you're standing. Coming from an adversarial space, people only see adversaries. Coming from an I-centric place, people only see self-interest. Coming from a place of cooperation and co-creation, however, people see trust and the prospect of mutual success. Mutuality is a belief acquired only through opening up to the possibility of shared hopes, dreams, ambitions, and, yes, fears and anxieties. If we intentionally adopt a WE-centric mindset, seeking ways of working together to create the kind of world we want to live in, we can create extraordinary things together. Fifth Dimension's executives realized that rather than changing others, they needed to transform how they viewed their environment. Rather than blaming others and finding fault, they realized that as leaders they set the tone for the organization. To lead at the edge, they had to address their own edges—where they attack, withdraw, or acquiesce. They had to push through their own discomfort. They had to engage in tough, and sometimes rough, discussions with others about what was really going on. But when they got through it, they had their prize—a mutuality breakthrough.

Today, Fifth Dimension has a new culture. Employees love working there now. Here are a few of their comments:

- "It's not like any other company in our business. People want to work here."
- "It's nonhierarchical."
- "You don't have to be a backstabber to get ahead."
- "We can wander all around the company and sit in on other meetings and learn."
- "I like being at work more than at home. I look forward to coming in every day."

The company has had several growth spurts. The leaders are leading and employees are growing. Employees are part of the business development team. People are rewarded for their ideas and contributions. People feel like they are a part of the results, and they give back 150 percent.

Stephen, Chris, and David continue to check their egos at the door and constantly monitor themselves for how they are doing as leaders. When one of them goes off track, the other partners provide rich feedback. They also know that when they backslide, they can do some emotional workouts and get themselves back on track.

Today the company is one of the most respected in their industry. They own their own building, which they designed with open, engaging workspaces. Employees drive business growth and development. There are opportunities everywhere to contribute. Employees have a say in shaping the culture—they have a voice that counts. Clients love them and they have loyal, growing relationships with every customer in their segment. There is a waiting list for people to join at every level and in every business unit they have evolved. They are a generative company and still growing.

Ending the Blame Game:
I'm Right; You're Wrong!

When your company is going through major changes like those faced by Fifth Dimension, there are no easy answers. You need to engage colleagues, to encourage them to innovate, strategize, and experiment. Often the early discussions determine the outcomes. If you are unable to find a safe way to talk with one another, to discuss alternatives and scenarios, then the challenges become even greater. You will foster conflict and a fatal spiral may begin.

Fifth Dimension's experience is not unlike that of many organizations coping with rapid growth, competitive challenges, mergers, acquisitions, or other disruptive circumstances. We are human beings and we succumb to the Blame Game because it's so much easier to look at someone else through a magnifying lens than to look at ourselves in the mirror. It's so much easier to blame than take responsibility for the role you may be playing in producing negative results. When our world is threatened but we know we're working really hard, when our intentions are good and yet the precarious situation persists, we often develop a pattern of finding fault in others. Consider the following statement: "If I'm doing my best in this situation, it must be someone else's fault." Have you ever said this to yourself at any point in your business career?

Should You Protect or Partner?

Fifth Dimension had hit a wall, yet finding a way to discuss the problem appeared to be out of reach. We are all wired with protective instincts to defend what is ours—instincts that take over when events threaten us and when we feel the need to protect our territory. When we believe we may lose something we value, these hard-wired instinctive systems erupt, sending us into fight, flight, or freeze postures.

If your organization is undergoing massive changes such as growth, reorganization, downsizing, or a merger, you may see these patterns at play. When these changes occur in environments where there is little or no open, direct, or honest communication, the blaming behavior ripples out into the organization, forming webs of negative conversations about "Who done it?" In some companies it feels like a witch hunt. These fears generate a cycle of negative thoughts and beliefs that harden into patterns of behavior.

Organizations that are not skilled in self-expression, straight talk, and speaking up are more prone to protective clanning, turf-building, blaming, and criticizing behaviors. Rather than confronting the problem head-on and coming together to work it out, our fears go underground, where they fester and build to outrageous proportions. This creates an even greater distance between "you" and "me," rather than strengthening our connection as partners. We become adversarial. We consume energy in protecting ourselves from potential danger. We channel energy into building walls instead of into working things out.

When we are feeling threatened, when we are fearful, when things are going wrong, we drain energy that we could focus on creatively shaping and crafting the future. When we are fearful and busy protecting what we have, we lower our capacity to innovate. We take the easy way out, and the easy way out is to blame others—put the spotlight on them rather than ourselves. Mutual accountability is an option, yet one often not chosen. However, once we choose to accept our place in the unfolding drama, we elevate our role to a key role. Once we choose to be part of creating the future, rather than blaming others for the past, we step into our powerful leadership role, and in doing so we enable others to step up too.

When threat occurs, we move into our protect behaviors. We separate from the outside world and we create a world inside. What is going on inside us? Where is our energy going? Why don't people just talk it out? When we are fearful, we turn inside; instead of focusing on growth and creating the future, we:

- **Withdraw and simmer inside:** Keep the emotion alive by telling ourselves stories and building a strong case against the other person and the situation. (This was David's approach before the Journey. Rather than asking the other partners to shape up, he simmered inside and kept it in.)
- **Attack verbally:** Accelerate the emotion to a higher level, attempting to intimidate the attacker. (In the beginning, Stephen was an outright intimidator.)
- **Acquiesce and get them back later:** Resentfully play along, allowing for time to build the attack strategy.
- **Retreat into apathy:** Just give in and stop caring. (This was Chris's style at first. He wanted to be universally liked, so he acted as if he were simply going along.)

The best choice, of course, is to learn the skills of self-expression: face the challenges and address the issues together; be *intentionally* direct; and create an environment for open and honest dialogue. This choice enables you to define the challenges together and create a sense of shared understanding and mutual ownership of the situation. In doing so, you also build bridges of support with others to create strategies for moving forward. You redefine self-interest into mutual interest.

When we feel helpless, we often turn around and find others to complain to, building a "case" about another person we believe is harming us. When we get angry and frightened, we activate ritualistic defensive routines. We protect our space and our lives and everyone feels as though they are pulling in opposite directions.

Stopping the Toxic Pattern: Case-Building

Do you recognize behavior patterns inside your organization that look like case-building? Do you ever feel as though you're living in a WE/THEY environment—one in which management and employees are not aligned around shared goals and people are blaming each other for the state they're in?

If you were an employee inside Fifth Dimension, how would you express yourself? Would you . . .

- Sit back, watch, and be glad you weren't being singled out. (avoid accountability)
- Complain to your colleagues about what a terrible workplace it is. (inspire third-party involvement)
- Talk with your boss about what you are experiencing. (open up to share the challenges with others)
- Initiate conversations to help surface the issues. (take a bolder stand to create better outcomes)
- Get your resume out on the street. (withdraw from the action)
- Do a combination of the above strategies.

If you were management, how would you express yourself? Would you . . .

- Complain to the other members of the team about how immature your employees are. (add to the toxic environment)
- Decide to get rid of people who just don't fit in. (make assumptions about employees that may not be true)
- Bring people together to talk about it. (open the space for healthy conversation)
- Decide to bring in some talent from the outside to "shake" everyone up. (expand the key players to bring in new thinking)
- Hire a consultant to "fix" the problem and make it go away. (an unrealistic illusion—the hero on the white horse)
- Do a combination of the above strategies.

Making Matters Worse: The Third Party

Rather than looking inside for what we we need to do to address the situation, we can turn it around and make it "their problem." In case-building we focus on others' weaknesses and deficits, pointing fingers and finding fault. Soon case-building involves complaining to a third party rather than speaking to the person we're having problems with. This person gets assigned the role of "working it out" for you.

Case-building and manipulating a third party to join in (which I refer to as triangulation) are not subtle. When we vent to another person to get things off our chest, we do it to feel better. The emotions quickly get passed along to the person we are confiding in or complaining to, and soon a web of relationships develops that is built around negative, judgmental fault-finding. When individuals in teams get drawn into case-building and third-party involvement, they are no longer a team. Holding on to negativity, judging, and fault-finding often lead to behavior patterns that splinter teams into factions and subgroups. We may not even recognize that we are doing it until the damage is done.

When any of these signs begin to emerge, you as leader or executive should be thinking about how to develop your organization's ability to create a new road map for the future.

Try This

Brainstorm these questions with your team as a guide to build your agenda:

- Creating the Future . . . What behaviors do we want to bring on our journey—our rules of engagement.
- Growing the Brand . . . What do we want to become?
- Growing the People . . . How do we create environments for learning, growing, and nourishing one another?
- Growing the Business . . . What does our customer value, and how can we deliver this value to them?
- Creating WE . . . How can we work together more effectively?
  - How can teams work together?
  - How can we coach and support one another?
  - How do we involve the whole organization?

WE-aving It All Together

When we believe that territoriality and self-interest drive the motivations of others, we often miss taking the most essential step to make it disappear. When we see in front of us the possibility of creating something great, something bigger and better than we have today, something that will expand the possibilities for all of us, then we are willing to Let Go of our territorial patterns and "go for the gold ring together."

When we can embrace our mutual interest, we can Let Go of our self-interest. When we feel that betting on the future is hitting the jackpot, then we will put our money in that machine. Your job, as a leader in Creating WE, is to create the environment for mutual growth and prosperity, like the partners at Fifth Dimension. In doing so, they discovered the third principle of healthy organizations.

Remember to Honor the Vital Principle of Nourishing

Leaders need to focus on creating the future with others, rather than on fixing the past. This way everyone is reaching out to learn about the customer, about the marketplace, and about what it will take to sustain his or her leadership role in the industry.

You can help your team and the organization as a whole resist the tendency to retreat into a belief that self-interest is all that matters by triggering the Partnering Instinct. When you can help them see and feel the rejuvenating power of focusing on the future, of sharing with one another fresh ideas and insights that will fuel the entire organization's growth and better serve customers, they will respond with WE—working together to distinguish the organization in the competitive marketplace.

When we fear we are losing something that we value, we become self-centric, focus on protecting what we have, and fail to focus outward on nourishing each other for the journey ahead. When we are fearful, we also develop habit patterns to protect ourselves from seeing that we are stepping back from the challenges ahead.

Fear drives us into our I-centric behavior and we protect rather than partner; we cover up rather than sharing the truth; we give in rather than going after solutions; we blame rather than sharing the blame; we hang on to the past, lose our voice, or take it to heart and retreat from moving forward. Health comes from creating environments that disallow deceptive behaviors and allow us to look in the mirror and see what we are all about, and then do something about it. Review the chart that follows and reflect on how you show up at work.

- Audit yourself and see if there are any habit patterns that may be familiar.
- If you are not creating environments that encourage mutual accountability, what can you do differently?
- Read the seven I-cenric habit patterns in the following table and identify your specific patterns that may not be serving your organization.
- Identify those patterns you are willing to challenge and work with as developmental opportunities.
- Create opportunities every day to experiment with the WE-centric patterns that you have not been practicing.
- Monitor your impact. Notice how, by shifting to WE-centric patterns, you are able to increase positive energy, focus your colleagues on creating the future, and enable greater leadership behaviors in everyone.

Are You Up for the Challenge?

To create a healthy culture, you need to recognize the nutrients you need for yourself and from others, and provide them so that you don't retreat back into yourself and become self-serving or I-centric. When you become aware of the key nutrients for growth and development, you are more equipped to release these nutrients into your culture and thrive on them. When you do this, you build robust, WE-centric environments full of incredible support, synergies, and expansive possibilities for everyone.

Transforming I-Centric Habit Patterns

How Are You Showing Up at Work?

Habit Patterns	Aspiration	WE-Centric Patterns
So, I'm the boss Fear of giving up power and control over others; believe you need to "tell" people what to do *IMPACT: You do it all; limit others' accountability; fail to access organizational genius*	*I wonder:* ➤ How can I be a leader, not a boss? HOW CAN I GAIN CONTROL BY GIVING UP CONTROL?	**COURAGE** • Opening the space for self-discovery, leadership, growth, and development to emerge • Transforms fear and control into the ability to access organizational wisdom and talent
I got a case on you Blame others for making mistakes; build cases and play off weaknesses; judgmental *IMPACT: Holding grudges; resting on your laurels, limiting growth; negative workplace*	*I wonder:* ➤ What negative feelings am I projecting onto you? WHO CAN I FORGIVE AND WHAT NEW EXPERIENCES CAN I CREATE?	**HONESTY** • Opening the space for growth in relationships through mutual appreciation • Transforming the tendency to be judgmental into appreciation of others' strengths and direct honest feedback
Giving in, giving up Fear of the future; resigned to less than what you really want; bailing out; hopeless; loss of will *IMPACT: Stagnation, loss of will, dissatisfaction, and frustration*	*I wonder:* ➤ In what way am I giving up my greatest dreams and aspirations? HOW CAN I OPEN THE SPACE FOR NEW PASSION, POSSIBILITIES, AND DREAMS?	**OPTIMISM** • Opening the space for dreams and aspirations for the future to emerge • Transformation of loss of will into accessing passion and fulfillment
Hanging on for dear life Fear of sharing; holding on to knowledge and past successes; carrying baggage *IMPACT: Destroys relationships; limits potential; limits personal power*	*I wonder:* ➤ What am I attached to; what do I need to Let Go of and embrace? HOW CAN I OPEN THE SPACE FOR SHARING WITH OTHERS?	**RESILIENCE** • Freeing yourself and others to release the past, and create the future • Transforming attachment to the past into desires for growth for the future

(continued)

Transforming I-Centric Habit Patterns (continued)

How Are You Showing Up at Work?

Habit Patterns	Aspiration	WE-Centric Patterns
Know it all Have all the answers; don't listen to others; overconfidence and hubris *IMPACT: Assumptions and inferences; closed-down space*	*I wonder:* ➤ How do I open my mental boundaries and expand my frame of reference? How can I uncover blind spots and learn what I don't know I don't know?	**EXPANSIVENESS** • Opening the space for learning, insight, and wisdom to emerge • Transformation of hubris and overconfidence into accessing wisdom
I lost my voice! Accept authority; follow Groupthink and status quo; unwilling to rock the boat; unsure of own voice *IMPACT: Mediocrity; loss of insight and inspiration*	*I wonder:* ➤ How do I communicate powerfully to expand the boundaries of my world? How can I rediscover my own voice and discover my own personal power?	**PERSONAL POWER** • Opening the space for learning, finding new meaning and perspectives; discovering contributions and one's voice • Transformation of deference to authority into accessing personal power strength; creating, mentoring, coaching
Taking it to heart Taking others' points of view to heart; loss of trust in instincts; negative self-talk *IMPACT: Loss of spirit and self-esteem; stop engaging*	*I wonder:* ➤ How do I reconnect to my own wisdom and instincts? How can I find where my own greatness lies?	**TRANSFORMATION** • Opening the space for connecting to larger purpose and meaning; accessing wisdom and vitality • Transformation of loss of trust into reconnection to the Vital Partnering Instincts

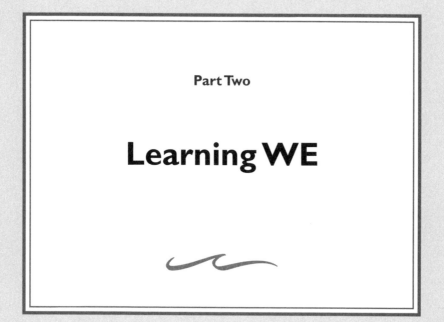

Part Two

Learning WE

4.

Hello, Can You Hear Me?

Understanding the Culture

*Never doubt that a small group of thoughtful,
committed citizens can change the world. Indeed,
it is the only thing that ever has.*

MARGARET MEAD, CULTURAL ANTHROPOLOGIST

IT IS NOT POSSIBLE TO CREATE a WE-centric organization without a deep belief that Being WE is both important and doable. Believing WE—understanding the true nature of authority, the roots of territoriality, and the constant challenge of self-interest—all are essential. But beliefs alone won't do it. You need to acquire and hone a set of essential skills that enable you to act upon your beliefs over and over again.

The first skill to be learned in Creating WE is the ability to see, appreciate, honor, and, if necessary, participate in transforming the prevailing culture of your organization. If you're not aware of the culture, if you cannot see how it works either to encourage or discourage I-centric behaviors, then you cannot begin to transform it and reshape it in the direction of WE. Awareness and understanding are essential before you can take any positive steps.

Gaining that awareness is not easy. Like fish swimming in a tank, completely oblivious to the water that surrounds them, we are often unconscious of the cultures in which we swim. After all, we're not aware of the instincts that operate below the surface of our own consciousness—instincts that drive our behavior in such a powerful way that they create an internal culture within each one of us. Do you truly feel as if you can see—much less change—all the existing cultures and behaviors in your workplace?

Transforming the prevailing culture is even more daunting when that culture is one that celebrates "consensus" and "alignment"—but isn't accomplishing either in an effective way. Too often, you will find management proud to say the culture is "a consensus culture," yet behind the scenes, employees are disagreeing with management and with one another and are unable to bring up the issues for fear of retribution.

Why? Most human beings hate conflict. Most people despise getting into arguments. In some companies, there is pride in being known as a consensus culture. On the surface, this means that we all agree. Under the surface, it often means we can't speak up. Leaders in such companies have learned to seek alignment. When we attain that "perfect state of alignment," unfortunately, we can lose the very voices that take us forward into new places—voices that express the new ideas, the new wisdom, and the new inventions for the future. Creating WE requires that we engage in active, robust conversations in which we speak up, and push back. And through these conversations we come to see challenges from many different perspectives and end up with a creation that represents our best collective input. In this chapter, we focus on learning how to create cultures in which people can speak up, push back, challenge the status quo, and open the space for healthy dialogue and debate.

Fear of Standing Out in a Crowd

In 1996, the day before my first visit to Donna Karan International to meet Donna and her senior leadership team, I spent a lot of time thinking about and planning what I would wear. At the time I did not own one piece of her line of clothing, although I would have loved to. At the time, I would buy designer clothes only when they were on sale, and I did not have a favorite designer. From time to time I shopped at designer outlets to find my "status apparel," which I proudly wore to the appropriate parties. While I almost became a designer out of high school, that was long ago. My design instincts for apparel had given way to my instincts for helping executives create the future of their businesses, and I was okay with that trade-off, until I met Donna Karan and her thirty-one senior executives.

The suit I chose for my first visit was quite beautiful: a taupe and white wool with an Italian designer's name on the label—someone I never bought from before, or after. It had a Chanel look, and in my mind, I was dressed appropriately for the occasion. I even treated myself to a new pair of shoes on my way over to her offices. Feeling I was taking all the right steps to "fit in," I proudly headed for her 1440 Broadway office in New York City.

One of my friends had told me a story about the day he left a client meeting, having just closed a big deal. He was walking with his head in the air, strutting around wanting to yell to the world about his success. As he strutted with his head in the air, oops! He fell right into loose cement in a newly paved sidewalk. Standing there with his leg covered in wet cement up to his knee, he realized that when we are too cocky, we fall. As I strutted to the offices of Donna Karan International, feeling cocky, with my head high in the air, oops! I fell down and tore my brand-new stockings and scraped my brand-new shoes. Okay, so I got my first wake-up call about what I was stepping into.

I arrived at their offices and sat in the lobby for almost twenty minutes. I was feeling like maybe they forgot me. I did the best I could to hide the torn stocking and scuffed shoe. I called a few people on the phone to pass the time, read every magazine in the lobby, and then was finally called in to talk with twenty-four of the top senior executives in the company, including the presidents of each division. I stood up, feeling like I was ready, in spite of the past two hours, to make a good impression. As the door opened, I got the shock of my life. It took a few seconds to fully sink in.

There I stood—all alone—in my beautiful taupe suite, sur-rounded by two dozen executives all wearing black—black suits, black pants, black tops. The room looked like a funeral parlor. As forty-eight eyes stared at me and I stared at them, I realized I was being checked out at all levels. Would I pass this test? What *was* the test? Those twenty-five seconds felt like two decades. The sweat formed under my arms. I realized something was going to happen that I was not prepared for. Before I opened my mouth, the die was cast! Whether I wanted this to happen or not, I certainly stood out in *that* crowd.

Unbeknownst to me, black was Donna Karan's company dress code. Everyone wore black, as it turned out, because Donna felt she could design better without lots of colors around her to interfere "mentally and physically" with her design mind.

We agreed that I would work on retainer, and spend four to five days a week with Donna and her senior team. Our first event was called a VisionQuest, and took place over a three-day period. I was coming to work in "toned-down" clothes, and caught on to the black theme quickly. However there were more lessons to learn.

The week before the VisionQuest, Donna told her assistant to "take me to the closet." This felt reminiscent of sitting on the dunce chair in elementary school for being bad. In the closet, however, were wonderful things from which I could choose to outfit myself for the VisionQuest. If the company was going to be led up the mountain to reach their new vision, I had to look the part, and wearing any-thing other than DK clothes was a no-no. Donna's assistant's job was to dress me, and Jose (my partner), for the VisionQuest. I was told never to wear my Ferragamo shoes again—even if they were black. You don't mix Ferragamo with Donna Karan apparel—*ever*. Better I should wear white sneakers than black Ferragamo. And then there is Ellen Tracy—not a designer worth buying ever again. And so my jacket was retired. Two hours—and three outfits—later, I was ready to face the senior team with a new sense of power and equality.

Once I was brought in as a full-time consultant, I purchased and wore Donna Karan black clothes, acquiring dozens of black items. Strangely enough, over time I became sensitive to the variations in black and, after a while, my black wardrobe started to feel inter-esting. There was blue-black and gray-black. There was red-black and brown-black. Dye lots are all different, and over time my perception of variations of black expanded, so that I could actually see when blacks didn't match.

What I discovered, as we all do, is that when we step outside the culture by acting, behaving, speaking, and dressing differently, people react to us as though we are outcasts, or we feel like outcasts. Learning how to fit in, and at the same time speaking our own voice, is the challenge of this chapter.

Over time I started to realize that I could "test the cultural waters" and include beige, tan, white, and blue in my wardrobe without feeling like I was "challenging the cultural norm." This took time for me, as I was feeling what it was like to enter a new culture and adapt to it. Pushing back on a significant norm, in the beginning, caused me anxiety. I did not have the boldness to test the waters without fear of losing my newly contracted business relationship.

In the beginning, all I saw was black surrounding me, so I dressed in black. Once I settled in, I found myself getting more comfortable, and as this occurred, I was able to see different things in my environment. This is an important principle for us all to recognize. Fear influences our attention by filtering out lots of things from our awareness. While I was orienting myself to the new culture, I saw only black. Black became a "rule"—it was an "all or nothing" rule that I created to fit in. As I lowered my protective shell and felt more comfortable, I began to see other colors. The rule changed to black, plus tan, or black, plus white.

I found my wardrobe diversifying as I became more comfortable in this new culture. From time to time Donna would remind me when I faltered on my design choices (like the time I wore another designer's stockings to a sales force design meeting). How she could tell they were not mine is part of Donna's talent. She could see the smallest of differences not visible to the naked eye. When I walked, the stockings didn't hug my legs the way her stockings did. In this very wonderful moment of embarrassment, she asked me to raise my leg and show everyone in the room—all sixty-five salespeople—what not to wear to work!

This is what we all face when we join a culture. When we are in line with the norms, we are rewarded. When we are not in line, we are punished and then it's up to us to determine how much we can comfortably push back.

The flip side of "wearing black" is that each culture has and creates its identity. Once you sense what it is, you decide if you want to join. You do what is expected and are rewarded: you are invited to the right meetings, you get to sit in the power seats, and you are asked for your opinion when it counts. The clues for fitting in become transparent over time, as we watch those who embrace the sometimes cultlike behaviors that win favor.

In some cultures, speaking up gets rewarded, while in many others, speaking up does not. In some cultures, it's okay to be late to meetings, because it means you are "important" and have been invited to many other meetings. In some cultures, it's a sign of being a hero when you can talk about having 100 e-mails in your box every morning; in other cultures, the hero story would be how many meetings you were invited to attend.

Some of us might feel that living the norms is a form of conformity, and therefore akin to a military academy dress code, and in reality, it is. And for those who choose to join the academy or sorority, it is a sign you have opted in. Sometimes outsiders do feel excluded or left out. In some cultures, dress code is not as important as it would be in a design firm.

Another of my clients, Paul Carlucci—the CEO of News America Marketing, a division of News Corp—didn't like "dress-down" Fridays. In fact, he didn't like dress-down any day. He felt his sales executives needed to be ready to meet a client on a moment's notice and so every day was a dress-up day. No one pushed back on this rule, or if they did they were called on the mat for it, and often it was from another colleague rather than Paul himself.

Dress-code conformity is one small part of the equation. Conversational conformity is another aspect of culture, and one that is the most powerful.

Some cultures are "consensus cultures." This means that the norm is for everyone to meet, talk, and discuss—and then, at the end, everyone magically agrees. If the team does not, somehow it becomes more important for the individual to give up an alternative point of view and get on the train. Sound like a good idea? On the surface it may sound like the right direction so that decisions can be made; however, in some cultures, what really happens is that the dissenters go underground and find others who agree with them; they collude with others of like mind and then initiate a front of internal resistance toward the previously agreed upon direction.

In consensus cultures, people sometimes realize that there will not be a consensus and therefore they give up early in the discussion. They say to themselves, "I know where this is going." They stop pushing back way too early and become silent, and then outside the meeting they complain. Culture is the invisible air we breathe, the wallpaper in the room, the glue that holds us all together.

Whether the norms are about physical dress, or about ethics, values, or conversational norms, they are a powerful impact on how people figure out how to act every day. People quickly sense norms. We know when a boss reacts negatively to our "speaking up" or "pushing back" that we have hit an unspoken norm. When we go out of our way for a disgruntled customer and get a great response, we know that we have acted to support a positive norm.

Most of the time, norms are invisible unless the organization makes a conscious effort to make them explicit, such as through rituals or public recognition of them.

Values are what we say is important to us. Some companies codify their values and create Value Statements that they post on their Web site or hang on the office walls. Norms are the behaviors that support those values. They may agree or not agree. When they do not agree, it sends very confusing mixed signals throughout the organization, and it weakens the health of the overall system. When they are in sync, values and norms can become part of the distinct identity of a company. As we discussed in the previous chapter, Fifth Dimension learned to value creativity and, to support that, they created norms around having employees bring new ideas for a business to the executives for consideration. The company created an identity in the marketplace for being a full-service, highly creative organization with incredibly talented employees. Together and when in sync, values and norms can generate a groundswell of positive support from customers.

What Is Culture, Really?

Every company has a culture. Every culture is different and is based on how people relate to power, with and through one another. Culture is the behavior that is valued and the behavior that is not valued. In some work cultures, speaking up is rewarded; in many it is not. Speaking up requires risk-taking, which is one of the hardest things to do. When we take risks we feel vulnerable. We may be wrong, fail, or look stupid, and most of us try to avoid any of these experiences. So instead of speaking up, we shut up. We pattern our communication and behavior after our leaders, who set the tone and influence the culture in ways that are often very subtle.

I spent a few years working with VeriSign, a very successful company in the Internet security business where the founding principles (the CEO and CFO) were very much key players and actively involved in growing the business. A few years ago, the company stock was selling for $250 a share. Even though the price had been knocked down by the fall of Internet stocks, the company was a survivor amidst the shake-out. In fact, the company is likely to continue to be a pillar stock in the Internet security world.

The CEO is charming and is an incredible visionary. He is smart and engaging, and employees love to have the opportunity to work with him and be in his presence. When he answers questions, he often starts sentences with the word *so*. During interviews with his senior team, I realized that everyone I interviewed also answered my questions starting with the word *so*.

Leaders have influence on a culture in a wide range of ways—from the words they use to the cultural norms they inspire that drive everyone's behavior. Founders of companies usually have the greatest influence in shaping culture. Over time, the organization moves from dependency on the owner's spoken or unspoken ground rules to development of more extensive, codified practices, procedures, and processes that drive the enterprise engine. When that happens, a unique culture emerges with its own unspoken rules, ethics, and standards of behavior.

Culture refers to *norms of behavior* and *shared values* among a group of colleagues, and speaking up (or shutting up) are powerful norms that either open up an environment for learning, growth, and creativity, or close it down. Norms of behavior are the common, accepted patterns of interacting and communicating within a group. Culture acts as a template, shaping behavior and consciousness within a company or within a society from generation to generation.

Cultural behaviors persist because they are taught to each new company member. Those who fit in are rewarded and those who do not are punished. Concerns and goals shared by most colleagues in a group tend to shape group behavior and often persist over time, even when group membership changes.

Culture can:

1. Determine the way you communicate.
   Example: Open-door policy or closed-door policy.

2. Determine how you show up at meetings.
   Example: You may speak up at them when you have things to say that are counter to the ongoing discussion, or you may speak up in the ladies' room to others who were also silent during the discussion.

3. Create learned prejudices and biases about expressing feelings, ones that go along with the beliefs of the tribe, often to the detriment of all.
   Example: Your culture may think it is bad for you to speak honestly about your own feelings.

4. Define your ability to take risks.
   Example: Your culture punishes risk-taking, so you feel restrained from acting on your business and leadership instincts.

Culture can trap you in a prison of false beliefs or liberate you and allow you to realize your greatest aspirations. Culture can make you "right" and others "wrong." It can be replete with villains and heroes who strive to leave their legacies, or it can be full of mysterious, dramatic possibilities that only a courageous few discover.

Culture consists of the agreements we make with each other about how we relate to each other, how we communicate, how we behave. Culture creates do's and taboos. To be accepted, you need to agree to these often unspoken principles. As a result, there are those who are in and those who are out.

Culture Is a Container

Culture is a container that holds a company's potential. Sometimes the organizational space becomes too small for the human spirit to thrive. Sometimes the rules we ask colleagues to live by are actually threatening to the health of the company as a whole. They ask us to give up too much in order to retain our membership.

When we can't speak up, when we can't ask questions, we can't surface issues that are important to discuss, and we can't tell the truth without being scorned.

To learn the culture, you come to work and observe others. You may be in a "feel-good culture," people-friendly and welcoming. Or, you may be in a ferocious culture, one that is highly competitive and weeds out those who can't keep up the pace. Yours might be a culture built on image, arrogance, and self-importance. Or, it might be a top-down culture in which decisions are made by the senior management team and everyone else merely implements those decisions.

By contrast, you can have a culture with minimal boundaries, in which colleagues have almost completely eliminated hierarchy and autocratic patterns. Some cultures encourage achievement and performance; there are others that even encourage pioneering.

Sometimes, shifts in the marketplace push against the culture, asking people to perform in ways that they cannot. And, to compound these challenges, when the competition is fierce and practices from the past no longer lead to success in the future, everyone's strength is tested. Fear and anxiety about the future and the challenges we face cause us to instinctually become territorial, protect ourselves from harm, and withdraw and hold on to what we have—the status quo.

When the competition is intense, our territorial instincts begin to dominate the organizational landscape, filling the space with toxic behaviors that negatively impact performance, distract people from getting work done, and snuff out the flame of passion for work. This is when Vital Leadership is most important, when you need to focus on shifting I-centric fear-based thinking to WE-centric engagement.

Why Focus on Understanding Culture?

Nothing is permanent. We can be successful one day and unsuccessful the next. Competition and shifts in the marketplace require leaders to live in a constant state of vigilance and concern. Culture is the glue that holds us all together, yet there are many unexpected outside and inside forces that threaten a business and its culture. Understanding what they are is the first step in learning strategies for Creating WE.

There are many forces that threaten a WE culture. Some come from outside, such as shifts in marketplace dynamics and competition. Others come from inside, such as complacency, egocentrism, or hubris. All come from the relationship of who we are, our current identity, to the world around us, be it internal or external. All require some form of action, to readjust and adapt to the shift. Many times, these unexpected forces cause fear and anxiety, leading to I-centric solo-responses. Instead, thinking like a WE-centric leader brings people together to tackle the challenges head-on with greater wisdom and insight.

Forces that threaten a WE culture are:

1. **Business erosion:** Due to changes in the marketplace, we see our future slipping away, our market share eroding, and our shareholder support going south.
   - **Challenge:** Our leaders need to determine the cause and re-strategize, yet they may not have all the answers. Becoming

exclusive and only turning to the top few people creates more of an I-centric environment.

- **Question:** How can we reposition ourselves to compensate for the radical changes in the marketplace?

2. **Declining markets:** We've spent years, if not decades, building the markets for our future success. We used to have the right products at the right time and the right talent to sustain growth. Now our leading products are seeing no growth; in fact, growth is declining. Our whole business sector is declining and new, disruptive technologies are entering the marketplace.

- **Challenge:** Our leaders need to rethink strategy and reinvent themselves.
- **Question:** How do we tackle this difficult challenge together?

3. **Growth of competitive challenges:** A tough competitor has come out of nowhere, and we've gone from being a success one day to falling off investors' radar screens the next.

- **Challenge:** Our leaders need to regroup, possibly reposition the company. It's a big job.
- **Question:** How can we come out on top again?

4. **New acquisition or merger:** To remain number one, our company buys its biggest competitor or potential competitor. The top team of the acquired company is let go. There is great shuffling around at the top and new blood is brought in.

- **Challenge:** How can our leaders leverage the new acquisition and integrate the cultures without great distress?
- **Question:** How can we leverage the talent and knowledge of both organizations?

5. **Merging existing units:** Our leaders have combined two divisions in an attempt to create a new entity with more robust capabilities, which will help us sustain market leadership. This is not an easy task, since both sets of leaders believe they have the right answers and the best talent.

- **Challenge:** How can we use these changes to boost performance and seize new market opportunities—without the leaders on both sides vying for control?

- **Question:** How can we create a significant leadership role for each person?

6. **Conflicts among key players:** We've just been acquired by another company and the new, combined leadership just isn't on the same page. There are too many heads, too many divergent ideas, and too many people feeling they have the ultimate power. Decisions are being made covertly, and those with the loudest voices are dominating the executive suite.
   - **Challenge:** How can the leaders create an environment in which multiple perspectives on the business can be heard?
   - **Question:** How can our leaders learn to communicate and interact in a healthy way?

7. **Emotionally loaded, buried issues:** During the course of events, we are caught in a deadlock in making key decisions. Unable to work through the issues, our leadership team splits up and creates a WE/THEY atmosphere that everyone in the company experiences.
   - **Challenge:** Our leaders are unable to bring the issues to the surface and handle highly charged, deep-rooted problems.
   - **Question:** How can they get past this impasse?

8. **Loss of "edge":** Our leaders have lost their edge. They are giving up and giving in and have stopped working with passion to get the answers. They throw their hands up and just say, "That's the way it is around here."
   - **Challenge:** Transformation takes a lot of energy and sometimes even the leaders give in to the status quo and think it's "reality."
   - **Question:** How can the leaders open their blinders to a new, more powerful view of reality?

9. **Need to rejuvenate and revitalize:** Our team has been working at 150 percent, and everyone is exhausted. The colleagues are all on the verge of breakdowns, yet no one is able to acknowledge it because this is how we all work here!
   - **Challenge:** Anyone giving less than 150 percent is considered a weakness.
   - **Question:** What can the leaders do to rejuvenate and revitalize everyone, so we can can work 100 percent and get more done in better ways?

We Feel Culture

Everyone feels their company's culture. When that culture is exclusive rather than inclusive, it closes down and territorial instincts become prominent, blurring the company's common focus. There is nothing more important than opening the space for heart-to-heart dialogue to ensure negative beliefs can be examined and corrected, eroding relationships can be repaired, and the space for outrageous futures can emerge. (Thanks to Linda Buggy for the term "outrageous futures"—a name she is now using for a workshop she offers executives.)

Sometimes, it seems easier to leave a company than to go through another painful experience of change and receive even more permanent scars. Sometimes, bad experiences foster the belief that change cannot happen without serious trauma, or that the cost of change is not worth the effort. Cynicism, skepticism, and resistance are the unintended consequences of a change process gone sour.

Some people take change personally when they should not. For them, just the word *change* has negative connotations that lead them to hear that who they are isn't good enough. The first important mind shift we need to make to prepare ourselves for change is to realize that the process of change is not so much about change as it is about growth—that it is not about going from point A to point B; it's about expanding A, expanding B, or combining A and B into something completely new. We may choose to eliminate something in the process, but that happens because we are focused on what we want to become, not on what we lack. How can we create environments for growth? How can we create environments where speaking up is the cultural norm?

Transforming a Company, a Category, an Industry

Clairol, the high-profile consumer products company specializing in women's hair care products, was struggling in the early 1990s to stay in business and reinvent itself. Clairol started in the 1960s with the incredibly effective advertising campaign "Do Blondes Have More

Fun!" Clairol shaped the industry and made coloring your hair something all women wanted to do to stay young-looking and attractive.

By the 1990s, however, the hair-coloring industry—actually, the hair-*dying* industry—was a dying industry that lacked new product innovation. For Clairol the business was flat, so to speak, so much so that they were considering getting out of the business. Women did not want to dye their hair, and the trend for natural products was on the rise.

Steve Sadove was brought in as the CEO of Clairol to either revitalize the business or sell it off. The culture was very territorial, full of executives and employees going their own way, based on personal agendas and self-interest. There were many "unhealthy cells" breeding conflict and competition internally, taking the focus off the customer and business. Steve faced frustration every day as he worked his way through the challenging decisions about what needed to be done. Steve saw performance falling and the company losing market share. There was no clear strategy and people were finger-pointing. The culture was toxic and dysfunctional. At first Steve was not sure where the toxicity was, yet he knew that there was an unhealthy mindset influencing how people behaved, and he was going to get at the bottom of it. Some people felt that the company was in a losing battle, yet Steve saw this as a challenging opportunity for growth.

As he did his due diligence on the company, he recognized that the culture was hierarchical and every decision was being made at the top. Everything was dependent on those at the top and when the "top" wasn't communicating, nothing happened. The culture had a very high *fear of change*, driven by the fast growth of the 1970s and 1980s. People were afraid to change the factors that had led to previous success. They were frozen in past history, repeating past success practices and strategies. The people in the company lacked sensitivity toward one another, and territorial and autocratic leadership reigned supreme.

As a leader, Steve felt he needed to shift the culture from one of control to one of innovation, change, empowerment, speed of action, and decision-making.

He thought about it at great length and decided he needed to really shake up the old culture by introducing practices that were countercultural to what existed. That is often the hardest challenge of a leader—to change the norms of an existing culture. If the culture is strong enough, it can reject the new leader, so how a leader goes about creating change in norms will determine its success.

I started to work as a communications consultant and executive coach with Steve and his senior team when they were inside the middle of this large transformational challenge. We provided him with guidance and a team of resources to help build a communications framework for enabling the organization to be part of creating and implementing the new strategy. Steve decided he wanted to create a radical shift from a status quo culture to one of innovation and team-building. As he learned more about the organization, he realized it was full of silos. Sales didn't work with marketing. Finance was not involved in shaping the customer relationship. When he thought about the culture, it felt like an eight-headed monster moving its legs, yet stuck in the sand.

Steve first decided to create a team-based culture, to educate everyone on category management and the role each person played in creating it with customers. I worked closely with Carl Freund, the key executive driving category leadership across the organization. By establishing cross-cultural teams, Steve could break down the silo thinking that was preventing cross-company communication. He made it the job of the team leaders to develop and nurture these teams to have P and L (profit and loss) responsibilities, grow their brands, and drive the business.

Over the course of the first years, Steve focused on creating a culture in which teams could survive and thrive. To enable the organization to really see what was needed, Steve created a vision of leadership for all to embrace: Leadership drives culture, which drives innovation, which drives results. His goal was to help people focus on establishing the type of culture that would drive innovation. The team became the catalyst. He spent all his time on nurturing the teams and building the culture.

In one of our conversations that took place in 2003, long after the Clairol transformation, Steve confided in me about what it was like back then:

"The hardest thing is moving the culture and getting people to move on. There were resistors and fence sitters waiting to see what would happen with a 'this too will fail' mindset. The active resistors wanted to sit on the side and watch it fail. We had to find the early adopters and build a coalition—people at all levels who would embrace where we were going. At least a third of my time was spent working on the culture."

By "working on the culture," Steve was referring to time he spent talking about where the company was going, shaping the type of environment the team wanted, and celebrating people's contributions and ideas.

In the beginning, it was lonely for Steve and he felt like a one-man band. But soon people got caught up in the excitement and joined in the commitment. One interesting shift involved one of his classic fence sitters, who was a visible leader in the organization but didn't believe in "this sort of thing" and "didn't have time for culture." Steve didn't give up on him. He kept talking about what "we want to do" and celebrating the early successes. Soon the naysayer became the biggest convert. He went from being the most vocal skeptic to being the best leader for change. Early on, he was very autocratic, thus disempowering. He soon saw that there was much more leverage in shifting to a more inclusive leadership.

The New Rules of Engagement

One of the observations Steve made was about how he used his staff: "Seventy percent of the time was spent talking about culture—things like alignment, decision-making, how to shape the culture, and rules of engagement. While Clairol *was* interested in results, we focused on what kind of company we wanted to become, so the team could get those results."

If the role of leaders is only to approve or disapprove of ideas people present to them, then they are just bureaucrats rather than developers of other leaders or shapers of culture. Steve and his senior team created a culture of early involvement; talking about ideas and nurturing them with others was the norm. Creating an environment in which all the members of the leadership *team* could roll up their sleeves and join in brought others into engagement with the top executives.

Steve believed leadership was an art: "You have to create an environment where people can open up and share their ideas, not an atmosphere where people feel graded. It's always two steps forward and one backward. People will be watching and you have to know what you're doing. You have to hit this head-on. Rather than appearing arbitrary or too controlling, you have to explain why, so people know what your intentions are. People need to know that it's okay for the leader to disagree with the direction in which a team is going. But this has to be established. Leaders *can* override decisions, but they must recognize that this frays the fabric of the culture whenever they do so arbitrarily—but if they handle it right, they can minimize the implications. This requires clear communication."

Steve had a lot of *touching-base* meetings with all his staff. They were collaborative. He had to spend that much more time to make sure discussions were going on across the organization. He would call people on it whenever they tried to bring in a third party to represent their interests. Steve wanted direct, honest communication, and when he didn't get it, he would stop meetings.

Monitoring the culture was as important as monitoring the results. He believed that most leaders look at sales numbers all the time, but that they need to put the same focus on what the culture is doing. You need to find ways to track culture to take the pulse—through surveys, focus groups, and breakfasts with employees. You have to learn to handle things right away, not let them fester.

Steve and his team called the transformation at Clairol the Clairol Makeover. Today it would be referred to as an "extreme makeover"! These are the seven lessons Steve Sadove learned in making over the company culture at Clairol:

1. **Communicate:** "We need to overcommunicate. Communicate all the time. Through meetings, forums, newsletters, and videos

so that people know what is going on. This also helps people understand the brand positioning."

2. **President's Club:** "We found people across the company who embodied the culture and we awarded them with membership in the President's Club. They were selected and given public recognition. They modeled the behaviors of the culture that we wanted to sustain. We talked with them regularly about the culture and how to sustain its health. Everyone could understand why these people were chosen. It's a great way to reinforce the culture. People wanted to be selected to be in the President's Club."

3. **Recognition:** "We gave out 'clucks' or 'Clairol Bucks,' to people who did a great job of shaping the culture. Clucks became part of the cultural evolution." It was an economic reward to spend on products, and it was another way for those who lived the culture to be rewarded for it.

4. **Patience:** "Changing a culture really takes time. It's a lot of work and staying the course. We had to find ways to catalyze the marketplace. One of our great reinventions was Herbal Essence. By taking an old product and reinventing it, we made the statement that Clairol can change with the changing times, and can meet the customer's new tastes and needs. We used that to help us reinforce the Clairol culture and the Clairol brand."

5. **Cultural Stories:** "Once we were able to turn the company culture and our product lines around, we would take those success stories and use them to build more success. There were stories of risk-taking, rule-breaking that supported the process. Every day we were looking for stories to make our points."

6. **Experimentation:** "Early on, we did lots of experimentation. Some things worked, others didn't. We had to experiment, try new things, and build on what worked. We raised the bar for innovation. We showed the customer that we could have continuous innovation. Not everything was a major breakthrough. It was a positioning breakthrough."

7. **Think Differently:** "We made changes to our products, but the most important change was to help people think differently. This transforms a company."

The New Culture Brings Results

Clairol wanted to become a "category leader" in the industry, bringing their new natural hair color and hair care products to market. By creating a culture of innovation, of self-expression, of influence and positive pushback, Clairol changed their culture, their industry, and the marketplace.

How did they do this? The culture changed from the inside out. Executives became WE-centric in the way they ran their company internally and externally. They met with retailers and made them partners in developing their business. The Clairol team introduced the Color Choice System, a new 24-foot-long shelf-display system that transformed how consumers bought hair color products—and, in the process, changed the industry. The shelving system displayed hair color products from lightest, on the left, to darkest, on the right. It also positioned the least permanent at the top of the shelf and the most permanent at the bottom. The invention offered the customer, for the first time, an easy way to make hair color decisions—and the sale of Clairol products soared.

The most important aspect to the innovative shelving system was that it not only housed Clairol's products, it housed the competitor's products as well. It was like a store inside a store. The Color Choice System became the place where all hair color products from all companies were displayed. This broke the mold for retail display units. Until then, products had never been organized according to how customers buy. Never before was there a unit that housed competitors together. The CCS was an industry first. In other words, *competitors were sharing the shelf space for the benefit of the customer and retailer.*

This was a revolutionary concept. No one in their industry had ever offered to give up shelf space to competitors, but Clairol did. Clairol's principle was that what needed to be on the shelf were the products that the customers wanted to buy. This generous act created a deeper trust and loyalty to Clairol products and to the Clairol sales organization. In essence, they understood that, by creating and sharing a whole new story about how to do business in their category in a WE-centric way, they could assert their company's leadership in the industry—and it worked!

Inside the company, Steve Sadove, Tim Meeker (the vice president of sales), and Carl Freund (the director of category management) contracted with us to design, develop, and produce a powerful communications program that shared the "success stories" throughout the organization. We built three communication vehicles, and through these vehicles called "The Manager, the Challenge, and Visions" (a video newsletter), the new story of Clairol's success was disseminated—and discussed—throughout the organization. Inside the stories were the success principles that each person was learning to help create the Clairol Makeover. Through this communication strategy and the unyielding commitment of the CEO and the senior team, the organization shifted and the perception of Clairol subsequently shifted in the marketplace. The new principles for success were being created and shared at lightning speed, and the organization experienced a *lift* to a new level of success. By the mid-1990s, Clairol owned the hair color marketplace. In 2001, the Clairol Division of Bristol-Myers Squibb was sold to Procter & Gamble for a whopping $4.5 billion. What a return on investment that makeover was!

Three Organizational Challenges to Culture Change

It is one thing to change individuals, another to change entire teams and companies: The resistance that builds up in teams and organizations is much stronger and more difficult to shift. We face our biggest challenges when we try to change behavior in a larger arena. Yet it certainly can be done and has been done!

Challenge 1: How to Develop New Belief Systems

Create a positive environment in which people can talk about their beliefs in order to root out territoriality. Our minds are maps of the future. How we think determines the journey we will take. Surfacing and exploring these patterns of thought in a safe environment enables us to make serious choices about how we will participate in creating shared "maps" for the benefit of the whole.

Challenge 2: How to Focus on Shared Challenges

A culture becomes strong when people focus on significant business issues and challenges. As marketplace dynamics and competitive issues become clearer to you and your team, what you need to do to win also becomes clearer. At that point a sense of common ownership of the future emerges.

Something special happens to people when they struggle through a crisis together. They must depend on and trust each other in new ways. They must communicate with a different level of passion and self-expression. They become more intimate and more compassionate. Crisis and challenge connect people in ways not typically found in "business as usual" situations. Also, people feel more alive when they are challenged to do their best and "rise to the occasion." They grow more confident and are more daring. Vital Journeys and team challenges create a shared bond and will ultimately have a positive effect not only on staff, but on customers and clients as well.

Challenge 3: How to Become a Co-creating Culture

As a leader, you can help employees face challenges together in completely new ways. Irrespective of hierarchy and position, everyone can be a contributor and, through a highly targeted process, can help shape the future of the business.

Focusing on skills for working together—no matter how monumental or daunting the challenge—brings people together with a common purpose. It helps them work through the necessary trade-offs. As the game plan unfolds, employees at all levels can become part of the powerful team experience that creates the organization's strategic intent.

A co-creating culture is not a change-management program, nor is it a one-time event. It is a life-changing turnaround that recalibrates and reconnects employees in conscious and unconscious ways. It is as though an invisible garment were woven around those involved, shifting the way people work and interact, and enlarging organizational capacity to achieve extraordinary business results. The process powerfully changes human dynamics even as it changes business dynamics.

The process works for teams, divisions, and organizations. It works for virtual as well as co-communal teams. Within this new model there are visionary practices that can be woven into meetings, retreats, and day-to-day encounters. This will raise the team's capacity for Letting Go of the past and creating the future. These practices create a tough-mindedness about dealing with business reality and, at the same time, a compassionate way of dealing with people They are practices that, when put into place in enough companies, lay the foundation for changing the fabric of the business and ultimately the world.

Break the Code of Silence

In addition to the three organizational challenges, there is another problem both leaders and employees must face: They need to break the Code of Silence. When anyone is afraid to speak up or is unsure of how to express frustrations, a number of behavior patterns emerge that feed the flame of fear. These include:

- Finger-pointing
- Making someone else the cause of your distress
- Telling a third person of your anger, rather than the actual person with whom you are angry

In many cultures, a Code of Silence evolves from territorial trauma, and as a consequence, few people have the courage or the tools to address this openly. The Code of Silence is a dynamic that blocks growth and change in those organizations overrun by politics or by positional power practices. The Code of Silence is an unwritten doctrine that prevents colleagues from talking about the things that can create fundamental change—for example, the arrogance of a boss, the insensitivity of a coworker, broken promises, backstabbing, hidden agendas, power struggles, and turf wars.

Organizations that are serious about taking on the challenge of shifting from a command-and-control culture to one in which power is more evenly distributed and individual contributions are rewarded must find a way to break the Code of Silence. If they do not, all efforts at creating a culture of reinvention will fall short. Educating employees on how to have open conversations gives them the tools to break the Code of Silence.

The Code of Silence represents a tacit agreement among colleagues not to communicate publicly about certain topics that are considered undiscussable. In most cases, talking about these undiscussables creates backstage dramas. We need to help people shift their conversations to center stage and feel good about it. It is the most critical factor in an organization's success.

Breaking the Code of Silence allows colleagues to identify the fears and the obstacles that prevent them from taking a more active role in growing the organization. The Code of Silence creates victims, people who feel they have no power. Breaking the Code encourages colleagues to act accountably and responsibly, enabling them to enter into critical conversations that can change the course of a company's future.

Reinventing a Challenging Culture

Creating WE-centric environments enables executives and colleagues to face the challenges of change with courage and capability. There are four requirements for reversing (reinventing) challenging cultures and creating WE-centric environments:

1. Create a neutral space for change.
2. Realize the power of speaking up.
3. Discover the courage to ask and the courage to listen.
4 Build skills to handle conflict and complexity.

Create a Neutral Space for Change

For you and your organization to create WE, you need to create "neutral spaces" in which colleagues can have open, honest communication about what is really going on. Most environments punish honesty. You need to educate employees on the conversational skills for neutralizing the feel of the environment. Grasping these skills helps employees balance the emotional tone and reduce the assumption-building that causes environments to become toxic.

We all need to learn how to listen to others without judgment, so we can discover what does and does not work. In organizations where the drive for discovery and innovation replaces territorialism and subgroup divisions, the change process has a greater chance of proceeding rapidly.

When you put yourself in the heart of the action with others, and everyone involved can talk freely about what might work, you enable change rather than disable it. When you participate in a culture-changing transformational process, you hold up the torch for change. Rather than imposing the "final answers" as an autocrat might, you allow colleagues to nourish each other as equals in the context of change. Transformational and fundamental change at this level cultivates the soil in which the seeds of success can take root and grow.

Realize the Power of Speaking Up

Why is speaking up so difficult? Why is it so hard for leaders to help employees break the Code of Silence? Because being different and holding different ideas than the majority requires a boldness that we often can't summon up when surrounded by dozens of eyes looking at us with skepticism. Being able to take risks by expressing a contrary point of view when others are challenging you triggers either a desire to fight or a desire to give in—neither are constructive—and both take you down a similar rabbit hole. You lose your voice, then go underground to find others who will listen.

Learning how to create a cultural norm that encourages risk-taking, speaking up, pushing back, and holding different points of view is critical to creating a culture in which employees feel they have a hand in shaping a desired, collective future. When this takes place, we enable each person to step into his or her own unique leadership role. Employees learn how to "own" what happens every day through dialogue and conversation about the present and future, and they build commitment to action.

This work involves the investment of "sweat equity" by employees at all levels. They must challenge what they know, challenge each other to think in new ways, learn to create a new context for thinking about the culture, and expand their ability to arrive at a new perspective on the organization's future.

The Courage to Ask—and Listen

For you and your organization to achieve a breakthrough, you need to encourage conversations in which people can ask tough questions and listen to the answers without becoming defensive.

When you are afraid to speak up about problems and conflicts, or when there are no formal practices in your culture that allow for honest conversations or for giving and receiving feedback, the organization becomes toxic to both management and employees. Tensions inside a company mount, and management may become convinced it is an employee problem, just as employees may become convinced it is a management problem. Pointing fingers is easier than looking at the patterns in which the whole company is trapped.

In companies where there is tension between employees and management or between employees, there is a lot going on below the surface that the leaders need to face. Learning to have Vital Conversations provides a safe framework.

There are many reasons things go wrong in companies, but few solutions on how to turn those situations around. If management asks questions and listens without judgment, they will uncover any frustration and pent-up anger or resentment that may exist in the organization. This discovery phase—when the leader is asking tough questions and really listening—sets the stage for the interactive dynamics necessary for breakthrough.

Build Skills to Handle Conflict and Complexity

Again, for you and your organization to reach a breakthrough, you need to build the competencies for handling conflict and complexity. You need to enable colleagues to learn how to think together to work through difficult problems and handle complex power struggles. This is vital to the success of the change process and to the health of the organization.

To do this, you need to learn how to build teams, handle difficult discussions, resolve conflicts, and turn challenges into opportunities. These are the skills that help employees learn how to build partnerships.

Partnerships are coalitions—alliances of people who have come together to form a whole. To coalesce means to grow together, to fuse, to unite, and to nourish. Partnership, another term for teamwork, is the primary dynamic that enables organizations to break from the past and create a bigger and better future for their company. Partnership is the joining together of like-minded people on common ground. Partnerships are a powerful community of colleagues working together to produce change.

For transformation to occur, the organization must also go through the process of bringing talented new colleagues onboard, and of providing old and new colleagues with the skills and insights to handle difficult situations and conflicts.

Try This

Whenever you are having a meeting, you can start it by doing an exercise on Creating Your Rules of Engagement. This is a way to establish the group dynamics the way you believe will most benefit your meeting, your team, and your business objective. Here are the instructions:

- Use a flip chart and some colored markers.
- At the top, put the words "Rules of Engagement."
- Go around the room and ask people to suggest ideas for how they would like the meeting to go—what would they want to create during the course of the meeting. Here are some examples:

  It's okay to . . .
  1. Nurture and support other people's ideas.
  2. Ask questions to learn more if you don't agree.
  3. Cultivate new thinking.
  4. Challenge assumptions.
  5. Let go of old ways of doing and thinking.
  6. Be confused.
  7. Have more than one good idea.
  8. Make mistakes.
  9. Free associate.
  10. Take excursions for insight and bring them back to the main discussion.

- Run your meeting with these on the wall.
- At the end of the meeting, go back and see if you were living the norms you set up.
- Go around the room and ask people, one at a time, how they felt living in these norms.
- Celebrate your success!

WE-aving It All Together

Every organization has a culture, and every culture is made up of norms, rules, and practices that influence how we behave. Most often these norms, rules, and practices are not visible to the eye. We may, in fact, behave within that culture in ways that we would not when we are outside of it; yet, while we are inside, we adapt to the way things are, or we push back and speak up.

Some cultures allow us to speak up and others do not. Some cultures focus on intimidation and fear to motivate people to action, and others focus on inspiration and empowerment. In some cultures, you are safer if you criticize and judge others rather than being open, honest, and direct. In some cultures, there is such pride in how things have always been that the individuals within that culture no longer connect with customers as they are in the present. Every culture is different. When you care about the well-being of others and the success of the whole enterprise and not just your piece, the *I* becomes *WE* and you are interlinked at a profound level—you trigger the instinct of mutual learning, growth, and nourishment. You have a true partnership. In a business partnership, you stand a better chance of success if you practice the following guidelines:

- When in a partnership, communicate regularly, playing back your understanding of what you are doing.
- Watch for areas of agreement and disagreement, and issues that reside under the surface—the undiscussables.
- When you are unsure, ask.
- Don't make too many assumptions—test everything.
- Get agreement on what you need in order to move forward.
- Listen to your partner to work out the details of how you will—together—execute and implement plans.
- Clarify the next steps in a game plan.
- Identify others who need to be involved and their roles.
- Identify resources needed to support the process.
- Set up a timetable—meetings, phone calls, memos, e-mails—to communicate with key players, especially to ensure there are accountabilities and responsibilities for taking action.
- Establish a timetable to track progress.
- Establish benchmarks for measuring success.
- Look back and talk about lessons learned. Ask each other, "What did we learn?" and "What would we do differently next time?"

How WE-Centric Is Your Culture?

Instructions: As you reflect on the dynamics of your culture and your organization, you will see that you have choices. Understanding the dynamic tension between protecting what we have and creating what we aspire to is the primary dynamic in shaping a culture. Understanding the pushes and pulls of these dynamic tensions gives you a better handle on driving energy in positive ways and reducing the negative pull of downward spirals.

C COMPETITIVE/EXCLUSION   **Co-creating**   COMMUNITY/INCLUSION

1 2 3 4 5 6 7 8 9 10

H DISTRUST/JUDGING   **Humanizing**   TRUST/RESPECT/APPRECIATION

1 2 3 4 5 6 7 8 9 10

O STAGNANT/LIMITING   **Optimizing**   GROWTH/POSSIBILITIES/EXPANDING

1 2 3 4 5 6 7 8 9 10

I WITHHOLDING/SILOS   **Interacting**   SHARING/EXPLORING

1 2 3 4 5 6 7 8 9 10

C COMPETING/PERSUADING   **Catalyzing**   WONDERING/INNOVATING

1 2 3 4 5 6 7 8 9 10

E DICTATE/CONTROL   **Expressing**   ENCOURAGING/DEVELOPING

1 2 3 4 5 6 7 8 9 10

S COMPLIANT/RESISTANCE   **Synchronizing**   SPIRIT/COMMITMENT/CREATING

1 2 3 4 5 6 7 8 9 10

Are You Up for the Challenge?

Learning WE calls for sharpening your skills at observing and understanding the culture of your organization and, if necessary, challenging that culture in those areas where it is failing to move toward WE. This chapter contains a Culture Assessment tool for you to use to define the "invisible" nature of your culture.

- Review the chart and think about your culture.
- What are the characteristics that define your culture. Those on the left tend to close down a culture and make it more

prone to unhealthy toxic syndromes. Those on the right tend to create a healthy culture, one that has a strong "immune system" for fighting off disease.

■ Make your assessment of your culture's current dynamics with one color ink. Then mark what you would like it to be with another color.

We began this chapter with nine business challenges that cause companies and individuals to turn to protective, territorial I-centric behaviors. Without realizing it, an organization can find itself in a fatal spiral, where people are reactive, defensive, and fearful and focus more on saving face than building the business

This chapter reminds you that you have a choice—by choosing to learn and practice partnering behaviors, you will be adding new skills and competencies into your culture that will transform negativity into positive energy, fear into hope, silo building into silo breaking, and distrust into trust. In the next chapter we'll talk about taking those first steps out of the Comfort Zone, from where you are now to where you want to be.

5.

But That's How It's Always Been Done!

Embracing the Possibilities

*You will either step forward into growth or
you will step back into safety.*

ABRAHAM MASLOW, PSYCHOLOGIST AND AUTHOR

ONCE WE GET INTO ROUTINES, we feel comfortable. From comfort comes confidence. Yet, in the world of moving targets (ourselves included), we need to learn to be open to change. Sometimes we don't change because change means taking risks. We don't like to fail, and we protect ourselves from looking bad. Not changing feels like a familiar haven that protects us. It makes us feel smart because we repeat what we know and we think we know it all. We perpetuate the illusion of knowingness. What we don't realize—precisely because it all feels so safe and reassuring—is that we are trapped by our comfortable assumption as to what constitutes safety and success.

Inevitably, you will encounter many changes in your work life—changes that will require energy, focus, and commitment. Some changes will throw you into I-centric response as you will feel you need to protect what you have and prevent loss. Some changes will inevitably lead to defensiveness as you try to hold on to what you have created. In this chapter, you will learn about how to reframe, or shift your focus, from fear-based thinking to embracing the future.

This change in thinking will shift pessimism into optimism and transform habit patterns that be may holding you back into new patterns that will catapult you into creating a culture of WE in your organization.

Even the Smartest People Fear Change

John is a highly successful publishing executive. He created magazines for companies in the airline industry and others, then filled them with editorial content and sold the advertising.

John makes more money than almost anyone I know. He is creative and entrepreneurial, and comes up with off-the-wall ideas that he turns into revenue streams in niches that no one else sees. He grows his business by coming up with distribution channels for publishing content, which means he sells the same product over and over again. On top of all that, he is really nice and generous, always offering to help others.

My husband and I invited John and his wife to join us for a concert in New York City. We got the tickets and told him we'd meet them in front of the big music hall. We said we'd find them and give them their tickets. He must have called me five times that day, checking on where we'd meet, what time exactly, what we'd be wearing, and who we'd be with. I started to wonder if I had given him clear directions.

What I discovered later is that John is not used to New York City and hates crowds. He created a scenario in his head that went something like: "I'll drive all the way in from Connecticut, park in a parking lot, then not find them, and have to turn around and go home." His anxiety propelled him into worst-case scenario thinking. Having become accustomed to limos and drivers, he had no routine for "handling the New York scene." For this event he was on his own without a limo and driver, and he was afraid he'd screw up.

John was anxious about this trip. I could hear his inner thoughts: "What if I go and she's not there? What if I go and they run out of tickets? Am I a fool to trust her?" So he called again and again, just to make sure.

The bottom line is that adults don't like to be vulnerable, to make mistakes, or to lose. Once we are at the top of our game, as John is, we don't like to look foolish or be embarrassed in front of peers. We really like looking good. Looking bad causes us great anxiety. That's why many of us love buying the latest Mercedes, living in the biggest house, and being seen with the most "important" people. Having status and thus looking good is part of our identity, and when situations threaten to erode this image of success, we find them uncomfortable or even intolerable.

When John was young, he was smaller than his friends. He was picked on. He was not in the popular crowd. In fact, he was rarely invited over to people's houses. Those experiences continue to live inside John and are triggered in situations that raise similar fears of shame and exclusion.

John's life has been about breaking through barriers, pushing against unnecessary rules, living outside of his Comfort Zone, and creating things that never existed before. He is wildly successful in inventing new publishing products for hotels and airlines, a niche he invented and developed when there was none before. John is a true pioneer.

However, when in new territory, even the greatest pioneers sometimes have moments of fear and anxiety that they need to deal with. The day of the concert, John was not only concerned he was going to get lost and miss an enjoyable evening; he was also deeply concerned that he might afterward have to admit to having gotten lost and then he would lose face in front of his friends. People don't like to do that. Yet, for companies to move forward, employees and leaders have to experiment, navigate the unknown, become vulnerable, and learn to try new things—even at the risk of occasionally going down the wrong road.

If such anxiety arises on a small scale with a smart, sophisticated businessman merely navigating in New York City, imagine what happens when you are the CEO of a billion-dollar company and you are the executive decision-maker who must deliver results-driven change when the stock is plummeting.

Or think of what happens when you are a new leader taking on a group of direct reports for the first time and you need to delegate and give up decision-making power to your team, but you are uncertain if they can do it the way you would. Or maybe you are afraid they will do it better than you, and you will lose your job. The fear that "my people will learn too much and outshine me" is as big a fear as "people will underperform and make me look bad." In either case, our knee-jerk reaction is to overcontrol those who report to us. This one leadership behavior can lead to a fatal downfall.

Change Disrupts Our Old Patterns of Success

Why do we often see change as threatening? Change often means that we give up something rather than gain something. Change often means that we lose rather than win. Change often means that we are not in control and others are doing something to us—often harming us or preventing us from achieving our greatest aspirations.

Human beings are creatures of habit. We are much more comfortable when we know what we will do every day. We like to get out of the same bed, eat in the same kitchen, see the same people at work, and drive down familiar streets.

Change is not always predictable. We feel more centered, confident, and good about ourselves when we know our life is predictable. We work hard to establish successful routines and we repeat them so we can perform well at work. "If I do X, I will get Y." It's the pattern we follow over and over again, from the way we launch projects to the way we launch relationships.

Assess Your Mindset

Let's start with an audit of your mindset. The column on the left is a Probability Mindset, which is based on the past and what was. The column on the right is a Possibility Mindset and is based on the future and what you can discover and create. Which mindset reflects how you think?

Mindsets

Probability ... Comfort	Possibility ... Stretch
Past	Future
Cause and effect	Pattern interrupt
Fear	Courage
Scarcity	Abundance
Knowing	Wondering
Controlling	Expanding
Use energy	Create energy

Business is not predictable, and in fact, outside forces are always creating disruptions that require major shifts in how people work together. People join a company that is headed in one direction, and the next minute it's turning 180 degrees in another direction. You can't control all the market shifts; you can only respond to them or try to influence them and ensure that everyone moves with agility in the right direction. How do you get everyone to successfully shift, learn new skills, and embrace change for the good of the company?

In the process of change we, as leaders, are bombarded with an incredible amount of detail. Do we have to educate and train employees on a new business direction? Do we leave it to the human resources department, or do we educate a few who teach the rest? Who announces the shift and how? What happens if people are afraid of change or don't want to take on the new challenges, for fear that they will not be able to learn as fast as others or, worse still, that they may fail?

But what if *you* are the one having difficulty? You want to stay with your organization but don't like the direction it's headed. What do you do? Do you try overtly to influence other executives to change their minds? Or do you play politics behind the scenes, trying to keep everyone from changing? Answer the following self-assessment questions and try to get a realistic picture of how you fare when faced with changes and pressures in the workplace.

ᔑ Stepping Out Self-Assessment

1. When challenged by others:
    - ❑ Do you doubt your own abilities to lead and allow fear to drive you into defensive behaviors?
      Or
    - ❑ Do you focus on engaging with others to build partnerships for success?

2. When competition is fierce:
    - ❑ Do you hold on to your old avoidance behaviors or rely on old strategies that have helped in the past?
      Or
    - ❑ Do you focus on engaging with others to discover new strategies for success?

3. When expectations for performance are high:
    - ❑ Do you get upset with employees because they are not delivering results?
      Or
    - ❑ Do you focus on having developmental coaching discussions to help them reconnect to their aspirations and skills for success?

4. When your bonus is on the line:
    - ❑ Do you step in and get involved in your employees' work for fear they may make mistakes?
      Or
    - ❑ Do you focus on developing and coaching them to achieve their performance goals?

5. When you manage a team:
   ❑ Do you give people the freedom to make decisions and then take back their power when they do things differently than you would?
   Or
   ❑ Do you focus on Letting Go and allow them to discover their own answers?

6. When you are leading:
   ❑ Do you find employees retreating, avoiding confrontation, or losing faith in your management?
   Or
   ❑ Do you focus on encouraging employees to discover their leadership instincts?

7. When an employee's performance is low:
   ❑ Do you confront these problems by deciding it is easier to fire him?
   Or
   ❑ Do you focus on having courageous conversations and help her grow?

Should the Comfort Zone Be Comforting?

You can feel it in yourself. When you get to the edge of your Comfort Zone, do you ever experience fear and anxiety? If so, do you, like most people, withdraw and retreat back to the safety of the familiar? Our Comfort Zone is our world of knowing what we know, what is familiar. It's the place where we go inside our heads to feel confident and competent. By the time we are adults, we build a large repertoire of things we can do and things we know, and living inside this space gives us a sense of accomplishment and self-esteem. Sometimes, when we wander outside into the unknown, we feel less competent and unsure of ourselves. We, as humans, respond to discomfort by protecting ourselves and retreating back to comfort.

When we step out and take risks, speak up, and push back on conventional wisdom and in return, get a strange response that feels like our ego has been threatened, we often retreat into our Comfort Zone. Unfortunately, when we do retreat, we may stop speaking up, we may stop asking questions, and we may stop learning!

Our instincts to protect ourselves are constantly monitoring our environment. When our senses equate danger with change and safety with the status quo, we activate the fear response and all the controlling behaviors that go with it at the first signs of change.

There are perceived advantages to living in our Comfort Zone:

1. We are always right.
2. We won't get hurt.
3. We have a safe place to hide.
4. We will be successful at what we are doing.
5. We are safe from harm.

There are, however, real disadvantages to living in our Comfort Zone:

1. We may be wrong.
2. We can get hurt.
3. We cannot hide.
4. We will not always be successful at what we are doing.
5. We are not safe from harm.

Expanding Your Comfort Zone

Comfort Zones are illusions. We are only safe and out of harm's way—comfortable and successful—as long as the world around us stops changing. And, if we learn nothing else in life it is this—the only constant is change.

If you live in your Comfort Zone, chances are you are stuck in patterns that are no longer working or right for the situations that you are facing. Chances are you are no longer learning or growing. Chances are you are using a lot of energy to build walls around an unchanging set of assumptions about the world that may no longer be true, if they ever were—building walls around yourself so that others cannot see or threaten what's going on inside.

Pushing through your Comfort Zone takes courage and the willingness to take risks. I call this *stepping out*, and it is vital to your growth. It takes a certain willingness to be able to open up to new principles and situations and to challenge yourself to view the world in new ways. Right now, you need to think of your Comfort Zone as *discomforting* and see living without risk as a signal that you have stepped back from something you really need to learn to do.

Finding the edges of your Comfort Zone is a skill you can cultivate. You'll know it when it happens, because when you get to that edge, your mind will signal you to pull back. Your body will cause you to turn around and flee. Your emotions let you know because you will want to withdraw, attack the offending person or situation, or freeze up and stand still.

When we live in our Comfort Zone, we fail to challenge ourselves to learn and grow. We create a status quo that reinforces our old patterns and routines. Feeling the edge of transformation is good. Stepping out is good. Without it we lose our drive and motivation to reach our potential. Remember, from *breakdown* comes *breakthrough*.

Embrace What You Love

In the late 1970s my parents returned from Indonesia with a gift for me: a set of jaunting tools that batik artists and craftsmen use to design and create batiks on fabrics. I had a friend who was making silk batik dresses, and they were extraordinarily beautiful. She invited me to visit and watch her working at her craft. I fell in love with what I saw her doing. She looked enchanting working in silk, wax, and dyes, and I wanted to become what she was. From this experience I uncovered a desire to experiment and learn this new art form.

I explored fabric stores for waxes and dyes. I played and experimented with the materials and soon discovered I was teaching myself to batik. In the beginning, for every three I made, I tossed out two. As I practiced, I discovered I was learning to draw with my new tools, and soon found I could do simple things like flowers and birds. Later I found I could do landscapes and people. Over the weeks and months my confidence grew. A friend saw my work and found it quite unique. She told someone running an art show, and I was asked to submit my work. In two months I had to have forty paintings. I did them and half of them sold at the show.

Someone else saw them and suggested I enter a larger show. I did and then had to create twenty more batiks. They were bigger and more complex. I was asked to be a featured artist, and I sold half of my larger batiks. Someone else suggested another show, and I took first place!

Lee Keet, the person who bought my winning batik which I named "Jeremy's Dream," became my first corporate client. He loved my work so much he hired me to design his corporate marketing materials. He was the first CEO I worked with, and from that one opportunity my lifelong career in transformational consulting unfolded. One small step—inspired by the vision of a friend and the encouragement of a business colleague—helped me step out of my Comfort Zone and shifted a fear into a desire. I released old assumptions about who I am and what I am capable of doing. I embraced what I loved to do. And this love embraced me and took me on a whole new journey.

The Challenge of Change

Sometimes we get into grooves that just feel right and comfortable. We like feeling smart, knowledgeable, and proud of being an expert—called upon by others for what we know and do well. Sometimes, we just like feeling powerful, and so we bask in the light of our knowingness. In this state we are not learning, growing, and nourishing; we are feeling confident and proud of our past successes and success strategies, and may even defend them in the face of a world of change around us.

In most cases there are harsh business realities at work, demanding we approach challenges with a fresh point of view. Most often, our short moments of confidence are disrupted by the realities of business dynamics and the competitive marketplace. Sometimes we are on top of the mountain for only a short time; then someone comes along and knocks us off our mountaintop.

Power and control define big business. For example, the need to own bigger companies and acquire as many as we can is symptomatic of the need to be big and powerful, sometimes at all costs. Acquiring a company without integrating the new entity is a common pattern in companies today. Acquire one, then another one, and move on to the next—eat or be eaten; those are our natural hierarchical, territorial instincts, driving us to be on top, since on top means bigger and more powerful.

Our instincts to be the alpha, to dominate a marketplace, and to acquire other companies at all costs are born out of our territorial instincts. Ironically, even if it means charging into a situation that requires a radical change—such as integrating a newly acquired company—our instinct to protect ourselves by being the biggest and most powerful becomes just another way to expand our Comfort Zone. We expand our territory, but we don't deal with the real-world changes that come in the wake of that expansion.

This sad fact can be observed all too frequently when we follow acquisitions to see how they turn out. Less than a third turn out to produce the value and benefits imagined on paper. The reason is that when it comes down to doing the hard work of integrating companies, it's all about dealing with change—the very work we most fear doing. So we go after companies, we gobble them up, and then look good on paper. Now we are faced with the reality of the change we have initiated and we either retreat and avoid doing the integration work or we take a hard stand and dominate, applying our own norms and values to the newly combined enterprise—thereby demolishing the heart and soul of the acquisition.

In the 1990s, Chase Manhattan Bank merged with Chemical Bank. If you spoke with the Chemical executives, they would say they acquired Chase. If you spoke with the Chase executives, they would say they acquired Chemical. There was a lot of mixing around of executives at the top as they tried to figure out the power structure so that the final entity would be a combination of the best of both.

Today, many acquisitions later, Chase-Chemical became JPMorgan Chase & Company and now the merger of JPMorgan Chase and Bank One will make them one of the largest banks in the world. Are they merging differently as a result of past learnings? You bet they are, and with a mindfulness about the customer and why they are merging in the first place.

Some companies rush into acquisitions and become so big they lose sight of their customer. They get caught up in their own complex internal processes and lose sight of whom they are in business to serve. Others, in the throes of getting big, stop listening to those they believe they have left behind—such as smaller competitors or smaller customers. They become blind to feedback that would inform them that their business model is not working anymore. They are not listening; they are not learning.

They have grown by acquisition only. Until there is truly organic integration of cultures, there is no growth in the truest sense.

Rather than looking in the mirror, too often we start by pointing fingers at targets closest to the problem—our employees. Change is rarely just about buying a company, updating a process, or installing a new system. It's always about the realities we face when our jobs change, our reporting relationships shrink, our territory is reduced, and our feelings of security are eroded. Change impacts egos and how we feel about our size and stature in our team, community, or organization. Change affects our relationships with customers and what we will do to get and keep business.

Stuck in an Old Pattern

Major change—or transformation—usually involves a huge shift in power that takes place across a company. In the 1990s, a weight-loss company was experiencing customer defection at a high rate. They interviewed a number of consulting companies and chose us to work on what they called a "damage-control" project. The head of human resources wanted help in figuring out how to stop the alarming loss of customers and how to help the sales organization sell more effectively.

Customers were defecting from their programs and, worse than that, they were telling other potential customers that the company was awful. Customers were telling others, "They pressure you into buying big programs." The company was getting a bad reputation for high cost/low value. Their brand was becoming tarnished. Meanwhile, the smaller, lesser-known weight-control companies were finding a way into the hearts and minds of women seeking to improve their physical appearance, without being pressured into buying something expensive.

The company leaders didn't believe how serious the situation was. They felt that Weight Watchers and Jenny Craig were no match for their billion-dollar powerhouse. But they were wrong, and the feedback proved it.

To launch the project, we did extensive customer research, as well as franchise research among their 4,500 sales consultants, and discovered that the hard-sell style did indeed cause customers to rebel at some point and to spread the word that the company was insensitive, pushy, and only out for money.

With the help of the entire organization, in a very WE-centric design approach, we engaged hundreds of internal consultants and totally revamped the sales approach and, most of all, its relationship to its customer. The company changed its value proposition from weight control to weight management, and based on this repositioning, we created a sales-training process to teach everyone how to be sensitive to customers, to talk and partner with them. In fact, the program was called "Partnership Selling," and we rolled it out to the entire company. Using the top salespeople as the "modelers" of the new approach, we videotaped them so everyone could see what partnership selling was all about.

Customers loved the new approach, and sales consultants did, too. Interestingly, however, the new approach created great problems for the leadership team.

The previous hard-sell approach, while distasteful to the customer, enabled the company to track each sales consultant's every move. Each was trained to memorize a sales script and not divert from it—even by one word. From the moment a customer first called to the final close of the sale, the best consultants knew what to say—word for word. Ironically, their strength was their weakness. This highly structured, predictable, customer-insensitive approach enabled them as a company to track what everyone did and said down to the last word, giving the company control of every customer interaction. They rewarded sales consultants for getting the pitch perfect. At the same time, the customers rebelled and defected.

The new customer-focused process reduced the control of the corporate headquarters and increased control for the sales consultants to manage the "customer experience." Corporate went along with the new approach for a short while, maybe six months, then retracted the whole value proposition, for fear they were losing control. Corporate was unable to ensure that everyone followed the same process. They therefore were unable to reward the best sales consultants for following the script. They never thought to reward sales consultants based on customer satisfaction or referring other customers. Their focus was totally internal and control-based.

Also, during this time, the former president returned to run the company. He favored the canned and controlled interaction with customers and reinstated the old approach to selling. The hard sell returned and the customers left. The company downsized and reorganized. Jenny Craig and Weight Watchers took their place in the minds of millions of men and women who were, basically, just looking for someone who cared.

The company executives were fearful of losing control. As smart as they were about creating an incredible weight-loss program, they were not as smart about being sensitive to the customer. The founders—who were savvy businesspeople, pedigreed M.D.s and Ph.D.s—feared loss of control so much it caused them to retract the new selling system that customers loved. They were incapable of stepping out of their Comfort Zone of control.

And, of course, the company lost out to more sensitive, customer-centric competitors. I remember that when we were going through this ill-fated project, I tried to help the senior executives focus on the up-and-coming small competitors moving into their space. I was told by one of the officers, "These are not competitors. We are the biggest, we have the best resources, and we are a formidable force in the industry. We own the sector. These other fads will disappear."

During the process, they were hell-bent on reinforcing their own way of doing business, dominating the customer and the sales organization, and being in total control. After they went out of business, a few of the executives realized they had authored their own demise.

This was a challenging time for me as a young consultant. The executives were at the edge of new insights. They were taking the coaching and doing well. Then their insecurities kicked in, the fear of losing control returned, and they went back to square one. They could not leave their Comfort Zones of doing things the way they'd always been done. The only WE they could see was the familiar WE of their fellow senior executives, not the inclusive WE of the enterprise as a whole, and certainly not the WE of the customers.

When organizations are faced with change, fear often causes them to freeze and hold on to a current way of doing things, even if it's not working. In the beginning, executives were willing to learn more about their customers' feedback and do something about it. We engaged the organization in providing feedback to gain insight and clarity about what was not working. The company's executives listened to the customer and discovered why they were unhappy. It was inspiring to be part of the openness and dialogue that developed among the executives. We were on our way to inventing a new company identity and a new relationship to the customer.

When the previous president returned to run the company, he had not been part of the engagement and learning process—he was still coming from I-centric thinking. He had not evolved to the new way of thinking, inspired by the incredible collaborative work and input of so many people. Rather than continue the process of healthy dialogue and discovery, his hierarchical approach halted the change. His leadership approach restored the organization to "his Comfort Zone."

Unhealthy cells stop taking nourishment from outside, stop taking feedback, and defend their position; and the president responded in the same way. He stopped listening to the marketplace, to the customer, and defended his point of view; he was not open to feedback or to new ways of thinking. People had to please the boss, and they did. The weight-loss company lost its "immune system" response and was unable to survive the competitive challenges ahead. The weight-loss company returned to its old ways, and soon faced Chapter 11.

In contrast to this weight-loss company, in 1999, Web-based NutriSystem was created, based on a highly innovative WE-centric approach. In this unique model, NutriSystem offers women direct-to-customer weight-loss services. People go online, interact with a weight-loss counselor online or on the phone, select a food plan, and receive home delivery as easily as striking a key on the computer. No one needs to sit in a center feeling embarrassed about their weight. The 1,200-calorie NutriSystem plan comes directly to the client's home, prepacked and ready to go for the busy man or woman on the go—a customer-centric and WE-centric approach that follows a winning formula. One of NutriSystem's slogans—"never pay extra for support"—is all about a low-cost, high-value approach to weight loss.

Conversations for Embracing Change

The reality is that change doesn't have to be negative. Too often we think of change as something to fear. Instead, let's define change as a positive challenge that helps us grow. Let's go a step further and define change as an opportunity to discover new possibilities for the future—opportunities that open up and expand our lives and minds in new and exciting ways. There are a variety of skills that can help you shift your mindset about change:

1. Find excitement inside ambiguity and change.
2. Expand your Comfort Zone.
3. Embrace what you love.

Find Excitement Inside
Ambiguity and Change

This is what we as leaders face every day. We have many choices to make and the bottom line is that we must learn how to adapt to change in the competitive marketplace and successfully manage the impact of change on our business. For many of us, this requires moving out of our Comfort Zone, where we are certain about what to do, and entering our disComfort Zone, where we face situations and challenges for which we don't have all the answers.

Success patterns are difficult to change. When something has made us successful in the past, we like to re-create it over and over. Human beings will, in fact, stick with a pattern even after it has lost its ability to produce results. We become pattern fixated and come to love the pattern more than the end results—it becomes a part of our very identity.

In the 1980s, IBM sold big mainframe equipment. They missed the small-computer market when other companies were responding to the customers' cries for small, personal productivity tools. Levi Strauss, one of the largest jeans manufacturers in the world, missed out on getting into the designer jeans marketplace. They were fix-ated on work jeans and missed the move to designer jeans, leaving room for Calvin Klein and others to take the lead.

By contrast, Coach Inc. was known for making very traditional handbags and accessories. In 1995, their consumer research began to show that the buying trends of consumers were changing. The trend toward "business casual" along with women's and even younger women's desire for accessories for fun, fashion, and femininity created a wake-up call at Coach. The rate of growth slowed in a way that caused the executive team at Coach to do what they do best: turn toward the customer, embracing the feedback even if it meant a complete extreme makeover. Through one of the most successful companywide efforts, the makeover has been breathtaking. Since 2000, the company's compound annual sales growth has been 25 percent. Coach has become one of the most desired lifestyle brands, continuing to wow the marketplace going forward. Lew Frankfurt, the CEO of Coach, first decided to bring in Reed Krakoff from Tommy Hilfiger as his new creative director, with a mandate to rethink the product line. He then hired Keith Manda as COO, bringing extensive industry expertise. Soon the Coach organization was bringing to market a whole new line of lighter-weight bags, with the Coach logo to fill out the traditional leather bags. The line expanded into other accessories—and from a twice-a-year design schedule, they began offering bags every four weeks. Coach broke through their proverbial Comfort Zone by using extensive outreach to customers and inclusion with employees. From the late '80s, Coach had been interviewing customers and running focus groups. In fact, today they interview 10,000 customers individually every year to better understand how the brand is being perceived in the customer's mind. Through this, they are able to *gauge* how to readjust their production.

Coach does an extraordinary job in both its commitment to its customers and the inclusion of its employees. From the CEO out to the customer-centric teams, everyone takes part in creating the brand. Employees throughout the company participate in training and education regularly. While our company has worked with the retail, wholesale, and operations teams for years, we are still impressed with the incredibly high level of commitment to learning, growing, and educating employees that takes place in this very people-centric organization. Coach executives not only listen to the customer—they fully engage the employees in creating the transformation. Today, the company is headed into another year of explosive success; their stock has split twice since their IPO, and their revenues now exceed $1 billion, and growing, annually.

Expand Your Comfort Zone

In the face of continuous market changes, the people in companies that are most successful turn to each other and study change; they study the unknown, and make the unfamiliar familiar. They turn to each other to create a new capability for transforming fear into flexibility and resilience. Since companies are people, it is within people that the real shifts need to take place. There is no organizational change without personal change. The most common reaction to change is fear; yet, when people turn to each other, they reduce the level of fear and increase the level of support—triggering their Vital Instincts.

Environments That Create Success

What kind of environment are you creating for transformation to take place in your organization? Fear triggers Fatal Instincts of territoriality, self-interest, and autocratic behaviors. When you live in a state of fear, you may be carrying that toxic, unhealthy state into your workplace, and unknowingly trigger more fear in others.

How you approach change and transformation determines the environment you create. Are you retreating into your reptilian brain, where fear dominates your mental state—and thus triggering that response in others? Are you driving yourself and others into self-protective behaviors and, in doing so, cutting off your nourishment from the outside world?

How comfortable are you with change? How do you approach change? Do you withdraw? Do you get upset and angry with others and yourself? Do you blame those who are apparently creating the change? Change is filled with ambiguity; sometimes, when we are in the middle of it, we just don't know how to interpret where we are. Are you willing to step up and challenge the direction a team is headed if you are the only voice—the only boat heading upstream? How comfortable are you with learning new skills?

How comfortable are you with taking feedback from a superior who feels you are not turning your boat around fast enough? How willing are you to change your behavior if you have been getting results by "ordering people around" and now you need to learn the softer side of influence? Do you feel that any form of influence other than giving direct orders is weak willed and makes you a pushover? On the other hand, when you are told to toughen up and be more assertive, are you willing to try it out even if you have never influenced people that way before?

To expand your Comfort Zone, you need to reframe how you think about "comfort" and what it means to you. You may like your life the way it is and not want to change, particularly if your identity is intricately woven into the way you are now. You may like your habits and routines because they bring you the peace and comfort that comes with knowing what will happen next. Change of routine is often disconcerting to us, even on a small scale. For some people, navigating the unknown creates anxiety and fear, and even the brightest leaders may be resistant to change.

Instead, think about change in terms of the wonderful discoveries that you will make along your journey. Think about how wonderful it will be to live in a world full of learning, growth, and nourishment of your mind, body, and soul.

You are navigating and pioneering new facets of your life. If you don't start, you may never discover all the incredible things about yourself!

When we live in our Comfort Zone and fail to challenge ourselves to grow, we create a status quo that reinforces our old patterns and routines. Right now, think of your Comfort Zone as *discomfort*ing, and think of living without risk as a signal that you have stepped back from something you really need to learn to do.

Ask yourself where you feel stuck or are living in a holding pattern:

- What can I learn that will help me expand my leadership portfolio and my ability to influence others in positive ways?
- How can I expand my people resources?
- How can I expand my strategies and new ways of thinking?
- How can I expand my moves and my opportunities?
- How can I acquire and leverage new skills?

Find a Coach

Working on your deepest character flaws may make you angry with yourself or may even make you unhappy. In these instances, a coach can be helpful to you during times of change. There is a new form of coaching called "organizational coaching." It starts with coaching for the leaders, yet the content of the coaching is to help leaders expand their point of view from I-centric to WE-centric, which opens the space for mutual growth.

Coaches can be external coaches—like I am—or they can be internal coaches or consultants who are hired on a full-time basis to help the organization with its growth initiatives.

Whether internal or external, coaches can help the organization raise its consciousness and facilitate a growth process for discovering potential—at the individual, team, and organizational levels. Coaches can reinvigorate organizations for the journey ahead and show organizations how to grow into their aspirational potential. Desire drives development and, working together with a skilled coach, an organization can change its growth trajectory, its business, and in some cases, the industry. Whether the coach is an internal coach, a peer coach, or an external coach—he or she can help create a powerful road map for success. Most of all, coaches can provide executives and organizations with deep insights on Creating WE.

Every day you have choices to make, and important choices will either send you into a fatal spiral (an unconscious, self-sabotaging behavioral pattern that you unknowingly create) or they will equip you for being a WE-centric leader.

As you continue through this book, you are priming yourself to see the crossroad choices you will face as you reach each potentially dangerous intersection. Think about how you interact with people at work now. Do you get caught in the fatal spirals driven by fear that cause you to retreat into your Comfort Zone, or are you focusing on achieving your aspirations and building support for Vital Spirals to emerge?

Vital Spirals emerge when individuals work together to achieve audacious goals. It's when individuals feel like they have bonded together and the energy of each one energizes the whole. It's like being in a WE-zone that seems to have an unending source of power to propel the team forward. The result is what I call an *arc of innovation*. The team leaps forward, exceeding expectations. It's a powerful, energetic feeling that activates our best performances.

It's easy to get caught in fatal spirals. They suck you in. Fearing what we don't know is a powerful motivator to freeze, hide, or give up—to retreat, go into your Comfort Zone, and stay there. Instead, help yourself and others become WE-centric leaders and focus on what you want to create in the world, rather than what you don't want to risk losing.

Adopt a new way of looking at your role at work, at your ability to lead, and at how you can create conditions for mutual success with others. Aspirations are our North Star. They help us discover what we love to do, what we hope to become, and what we are put on this planet to bring to the world. As we make space for our own growth aspirations to flourish, we expand the life force for everyone.

Try This!

When we call something a fear, we trigger our own "fear habit patterns." We avoid, we withdraw, and we tell ourselves we can't do it. The following situations call for courageous conversations. Identify your fears and release them. How might you transform each of these situations into a positive experience?

▶ **Letting an employee who has not met your expectations know how she needs to improve.**

Comfort Zone: Wait until the end of the year and don't give her a raise.

Stepping Out: Let her know how to achieve the high standards you hold for her.

▶ **Handling criticism and confrontation where you may have to be vulnerable in front of others.**

Comfort Zone: Fear of failure and of looking foolish in front of others.

Stepping Out: Take risks; experiment and learn important lessons that will help you and others be successful in the future.

▶ **Pushing back on others when they don't see your point of view.**

Comfort Zone (your answer): _____

Stepping Out (your answer): _____

▶ **Handling difficult issues with interpersonal relationships in your workplace.**

Comfort Zone (your answer): _____

Stepping Out (your answer): _____

▶ **Pushing yourself to take risks by speaking up about what you believe in.**

Comfort Zone (your answer): _____

Stepping Out (your answer): _____

▶ **Expressing your anger and disappointment with others.**

Comfort Zone (your answer): _____

Stepping Out (your answer): _____

▶ **Breaking out of the pack.**

Comfort Zone (your answer): _____

Stepping Out (your answer): _____

▶ **Sharing what you know when it's different from others' points of view.**

Comfort Zone (your answer): _____

Stepping Out (your answer): _____

▶ **Speaking up and saying what's on your mind, anticipating potential conflicts that doing so might create.**

Comfort Zone (your answer): _____

Stepping Out (your answer): _____

▶ **Challenging the status quo.**

Comfort Zone (your answer): _____

Stepping Out (your answer): _____

Break Through Belief Obstacles

Sometimes, we can step out of our Comfort Zones and create breakthoughs in our lives by reframing "belief obstacles." Here are seven belief obstacles to Creating WE. See which ones apply to you and then apply the reframing wisdom for your transformation.

Co-creating

Belief Obstacle: As I've grown up, I've learned there are places I can't go. I've learned that telling the truth, being honest, and trusting others can get me in trouble. I've learned that politicking is the only way to survive. I exclude people to protect myself from getting hurt.

Reframe: Co-creating is about believing that you are uniquely equipped to learn how to navigate "difficult" organizational spaces by interacting with others in a positive way and building a sense of community. Learning how to establish trust, honor, and respect of others and to include others in your future is an artful skill that expands the capacity of the organization and yourself. Honor your ability for being inclusive.

Humanizing

Belief Obstacle: When people discover who I really am, they will see all of my shortcomings. I therefore must only reveal myself when I am powerful or at my best; otherwise they won't appreciate me.

Reframe: Humanizing is about believing that you and others are unique human beings, with special gifts to contribute to your family, your work environment, and your community. Unfolding your humanity is a Journey of Discovery of appreciation. Honor it and the wisdom it brings.

Optimizing

Belief Obstacle: When difficulties stand in the way of what I want or dream about, I often step back from wanting and give up trying.

Reframe: Optimizing, by its very nature, envisions more than simply settling for what is adequate. Having outrageous aspirations is about believing in the potential that resides within and holding that passion in front of you as you are climbing the mountain. Recognize the power that aspiring to an optimal future brings.

Integrating

Belief Obstacle: Sometimes I believe that when I share what I know, I become less powerful and lose my uniqueness. When I give away what makes me the best, I lose my edge. I give up my identity.

Reframe: Integrating is about believing that you can become part of a community and expand power and influence by sharing what you know. When you offer to integrate and share with others, you become part of a process of expanding power and influence, which in return enables you to gain even more from the process. Sharing success builds more success and hope.

Catalyzing

Belief Obstacle: The world is changing at such a rapid rate that sometimes I become fearful and hold on to my own perspective because it is the one thing that I know and feel I can be certain of.

Reframe: Catalyzing is about believing that the world is in constant evolution and transformation. For you to sing with the potential of the universe you need to move from trying to persuade others of your point of view to challenging what you know—and thus becoming a catalyst for transformation at every level. See and feel the transformational power of catalyzing.

Expressing

Belief Obstacle: Sometimes when I join a community, I feel that it's safer to accept reality as others see it. Deferring to authority has its rewards.

Reframe: Expression is about intentionally finding and listening to your own inner voice of wisdom and learning how to share it and express it, and not being frightened when your point of view differs from others. Intentionally learning how to express yourself in a larger context of expansion, rather than from conflict, empowers everyone. Honor the insights that come from the synergy of your heart and your mind.

Synchronizing

Belief Obstacle: My power comes from what I know and see. The physical world is reality. That is what I see and trust.

Reframe: Synchronizing enables us to value not only that which we know and see but also that which is outside of our control and purview. Embracing the belief that colleagues have something valuable to contribute allows us to synchronize with one another and achieve a higher purpose—we create something of bigger value; we tap into a more powerful energy and wisdom and open up wonderful possibilities that don't yet exist.

Do Alone or with Others Exercise

You can do this exercise on your own or with partners. It's valuable to share aspirations with others because it helps you affirm your commitment to action. The following exercise will give you an opportunity to draw out how you think about your Comfort Zone. Follow these six steps. The goal is for you to see where your edges are in life, what you are holding on to, and what lies on the other side. These are the places where breakthroughs will occur for you.

Step 1: Explore the following areas. Draw a large circle with a smaller circle inside. Identify situations in each, and place specific issues in either your Comfort Zone (the center) or your Desire (the outer ring). Remember: Desires are aspirations waiting to be born. Consider categories such as these:

- Big Audacious Goals
- Business Challenges
- Aspirations
- Leadership
- Business Growth
- Opportunities

Step 2: Identify the challenge you (or your team) are facing in each area.

Step 3: Identify three key steps you can take to move forward in each area.

Step 4: Identify three key resources you can rely on to move forward in each area.

Step 5: Identify three metrics for success: What result will give you the greatest satisfaction? How will you know when you are successful? How you will celebrate the milestones?

Step 6: Remember to repeat the steps and stretch your aspirations.

WE-aving It All Together

Too often when we face challenges that seem too big to handle from where we stand now, we become frightened, we retreat, and we step back from taking on the challenge with gusto and passion. In learning to create a WE-centric world, the best time to reach out is when we are at the edge. More often than not, this is when we find that others are more than willing to help. You just need to bring them in to help you with the challenge.

Are You Up for the Challenge?

On the next page is a self-assessment. How willing are you to step out of the crowd and challenge the cultural norms that are not working for you? How willing are you to be the one to catalyze change? How willing are you to push back? How willing are you to be the voice that stands alone? How willing are you to take the risk to make a difference? See where you stand, and where you are willing to step out.

The assessment is designed for you to see that sometimes change does not need to be as hard and challenging as we make it seem in our heads. We do everything to avoid change, for fear that we will lose more than we will gain. Yet, more often than not, small changes in beliefs can set the stage for large transformations. Identify your assumptions and release them.

Shift from Stepping Back to Stepping Up

Release Courage to Create Transformations in Yourself and Others

Dimension	Challenge	Personal Power and Influence
How to Develop COURAGE	**Lack of Clear Direction** *You, and/or colleagues, seem unsure of the direction of the company yet are not speaking up.*	**COURAGE** "Let's set up a meeting to do some strategic dialogue about the direction of our strategy. Let's all push back on what we feel is unclear, and let's see what we can come up with to create clarity and direction."
How to Develop RESILIENCE	**We've Failed** *You, and/or colleagues, experimented with some new tactics and strategies and they did not produce the desired results.*	**RESILIENCE** "There's so much we can learn from experimenting. Let's run a debrief on lessons learned and see how to navigate the next project."
How to Develop HONESTY	**One Strike and We're Out** *You, and/or colleagues, put your best effort into launching a new product and it did not have the desired impact.*	**HONESTY** "I was really pleased at what we accomplished in helping us move forward. Let's sit down and talk about our strategies and tactics and see what worked and didn't work so we can put together a different approach next time."
How to Develop OPTIMISM	**There's No Hope** *You, and/or colleagues, appear to be fearful of the unknown future.*	**OPTIMISM** "Every business has challenges, and now the business landscape is changing. Let's focus on our key challenges and how we can strategize new opportunities together."

(continued)

Shift from Stepping Back to Stepping Up (continued)

Release Courage to Create Transformations in Yourself and Others

Dimension	Challenge	Personal Power and Influence
How to Develop EXPANSIVENESS	**We Know Best** *You, and/or colleagues, are acting like you know it all and you are not open to input on how to launch the new system.*	**EXPANSIVENESS** "Let's talk out our approach. There may be some things none of us have thought of that could catch us at the end."
How to Develop PERSONAL POWER	**Known Is Better than the Unknown** *You, and/or colleagues appear to be too accepting of the status quo.*	**PERSONAL POWER** "We don't need to wait until things are broken. What are some things we need to challenge, to improve, and to enhance in our workplace?"
How to Develop RISK-TAKING	**Safety from Not Speaking Up** *You, and/or colleagues, are withdrawing and not speaking up.*	**RISK-TAKING** "Sometimes we all need to experiment with ideas to find out what doesn't work first. What were some of the worst ideas you explored? How did they inspire new thinking?"

Years of coaching executives have taught my clients and me a very powerful lesson: Staying in our Comfort Zones and holding on to old patterns of success may seem to protect us from the potential of failure; however, in reality, this causes us to stop growing. Failure is a place to go for new lessons and new learnings. Failure teaches us how to grow and do things better.

In the chapters that follow, you will read about one of the biggest challenges plaguing work environments: how to face difficult people and have difficult conversations. These chapters are about sharing and breaking down barriers; they will help you focus in a way that creates a more collaborative environment and growth for all parties involved—without alienating or attacking anyone.

When it comes to your relationships with others, are you living in your Comfort Zone? Are you avoiding the most important conversations out of fear of rejection? Do you anticipate that the person on the other end will cut you off, get angry, or become an adversary?

Step out anyway, release those outmoded beliefs, and learn new ways of thinking about risk and change. Living without risk, fear, and uncertainty may mean you have stepped back from learning something you really need to learn to get to your next level of success. Stretch yourself to try new things. Encourage yourself to experiment. Take small steps one at a time and enjoy the journey.

6.

Are We Really
on the Same Team?

Opening the Space

~~~~~

*Creativity is a central source of meaning in our lives . . .
{and} when we are involved in it, we feel that we are
living more fully than during the rest of life.*
MIHALY CSIKSZENTMIHALYI, AUTHOR OF *FLOW THEORY*

AS LONG AS WE FEEL THE TEAM IS GAINING, not losing, it's easy for
everyone to play as a WE. The fear is that you will get more than
I will, or if I open up and share, you will run with the goods and I'll
be left alone and powerless. The underlying fear is that I'll trust you
and you'll stick a knife in my back.

One of the negative meanings of the word *collaboration* is working
with the "enemy." And, of course, it is dangerous to be in bed with
an enemy—as long as we think of them as an enemy. At any moment,
a friend can become a foe, a supporter can become a slammer, and a
colleague can become a competitor. This is true in our lives—we see
it and feel it every day. Yet living on the side of fear only increases the
chances that we will produce the exact state we don't want. The challenge is how to expand and create the space for colleagues to open up
with one another and, in the process, get back more than anyone ever
expected.

As a global community, we have been working at collaborating for a long time. It's human nature to work with others, to form communities, to get along. Yet the instinct to protect what is ours—*ours alone*—is stronger than the instinct to collaborate.

When we throw the net of inclusion wider than our immediate circle to include partners outside of our conventional thinking about what WE comprises, we begin to include new potential relationships for enhancing our sphere of influence, and our range of impact. Our net encompasses stakeholders, allies, and partners beyond the traditional boundaries of the enterprise—including vendors, customers, and donors. When we throw our net wider, we expand the way we work, how we generate value, and how we can partner. After all these years we are starting to see how shifting boundaries—throwing the net wider—is a way to create alliances in a new way. This chapter speaks to how to Learn WE by opening up, expanding, and creating the space for a *bigger* WE.

The Golden Thread of Trust

The ability to work together interdependently is one of our least-developed skills. This is so vital that, in its absence, good leaders turn bad, good executives become ineffective, and good colleagues turn into adversaries. The skill of opening up to others—and of creating the emotional space for others to open up—requires deep trust. Trust is the most precious of the golden threads. Without it, there can be no WE. With the golden thread of trust, we can weave our lives together like a beautiful tapestry.

WE-centric relationships are built on trust. I trust *you will not harm me* and you trust *I will not harm you*. When we have that level of trust, we don't feel the need to duck into protective behaviors. We automatically assume a mutual support and we move forward from there.

When we experience doubt about the good intentions of others, for whatever reason, we need to recognize the importance of having the kind of conversations that bring us back to trust. Creating the space for open dialogues enables us to reclaim trust with others.

Building Trust Takes Commitment

When we get married, we establish a relationship based on mutual love and appreciation, and we hope for unconditional love every day. While we may aspire to unconditional acceptance and respect at work, we find that these relationships are often temporal. And there are many more of them to manage. Because of the nature of work and business, relationships take effort to sustain, and establishing positive, growing relationships takes a lot of back-and-forth checking, updating, and clarifying. All of these are necessary to create a sense of community and collaboration. Such an environment is feedback-rich.

Our ability to communicate indicates the quality of the connectivity between us as individuals, teams, or larger organizational units. While we don't always talk about it, we feel it. Knowing where we stand is vital to our success, and when we feel we are on the outs, it negatively impacts our performance. We start acting strangely—we protect, we hide, we defend—all because we feel we are being judged or rejected.

Too often, we see management and employees as separate. In reality, both are part of a larger system of colleagues working together to create positive business results. The challenge for you as a leader and as a colleague is to understand how to create "mutual trust" through the way you communicate with colleagues every day.

New Beginnings

Cisco, one of the world's largest Internet companies, grew over a ten-year period through thirty-nine acquisitions and 100 alliances. Large pharmaceutical companies such as Pfizer, Roche, and Novartis have grown through acquiring smaller companies with innovative product lines in existing or new therapeutic areas. Financially, the purpose of these acquisitions is to increase market share. Yet, along with the bottom-line growth comes the important culture integration that is necessary to leverage the value of the larger entity.

Companies like Pfizer and Cisco are examples of companies that have leveraged the proposed integration by managing the cultural integration effectively. When employees join a new company—through an acquisition, merger, or even just as a new employee—there is a foundation of trust at the start of the relationship. Both entities believe that the joining will turn out well, and all parties will benefit. Why else do it?

A year ago, I worked as a coach in a manufacturing company. My assignment was to coach a VP who had been with the company for a year. When she was brought onboard, she was instantly her boss's favorite executive. She was bright, charming, and very extroverted.

In the beginning, the boss trusted her so much that he gave over many of his tasks and decision-making activities to her. He did what a good leader does: he trusted in her and delegated responsibilities to her. This fit in with his leadership style, which was to create an open environment of engagement and sharing in the company.

However, while her peers watched her status grow in the eyes of the boss, their feelings of exclusion grew, causing them to talk behind her back, find fault, and exclude her from critical meetings. Trust among peers became an issue, and distrust was becoming the team norm.

The boss soon discovered that his special attention to his golden-haired VP had caused a breakdown in communication across his senior team. Soon, this perception rippled out into other parts of the organization and caused communication issues among the VP and other team leaders. I-centric behaviors began attacking the team left and right, and what had been a collaborative organization soon fell into a dysfunctional team—lots of individuals touting their strengths to win the boss's approval, protection of turf, and disharmony all around. The VP was enjoying her coveted status, unaware of the negative impact on others or how this eroded trust among peers. Trust building is an essential activity for a healthy organization, without which we cannot aspire to become a WE-centric leader. Understanding what breaks trust is as important as understanding what builds it.

How Does One Become a WE-centric Leader?

A decade ago, power, control, and authority were considered acceptable behaviors. Today, we measure ourselves against a new yardstick of leadership success. It is interconnectivity that counts—and how we as leaders create a WE-centric workplace.

As a leader who wants to make a difference in your organization, you hold the key. It all starts with you. You influence the power dynamics in your organization. When you create a sense of community and inclusion, colleagues feel they are trusted, accepted, and valued and they will strive to live up to that higher level of performance. When you broadcast, even unconsciously, that you are unhappy with or, worse, unaware of the value colleagues bring, they feel the lack of appreciation and trust and they will underperform.

Once you become mindful of the difference and can consciously shift your orientation as a leader, your organization will explode with productivity. This deep level of awareness provides you the power to engage your organization positively and proactively in the process of becoming extraordinary.

You can do this by becoming conscious of how masterfully you use WE-centric language to pull people toward you rather than push them away, inspire others to greater heights, and fuel everyone's Leadership Journey. You have the ability—by being mindful of how your communication impacts others—to transform relationships, teams, and organizations. With this awareness you can use conversation to turn positional power into mutual power, fear into opportunity, and territorial energy into positive, trusting vital energy. When this happens, you also change the mindset of the company from powerless to powerful—and incredibly, progress begins.

Creating Our WE-centric Story at the Edge

Creating the space for open, trusted, and nonjudgmental conversions is a WE-centric skill. As we have conversations and listen, we are able to sort out what affects our personal future and what does not. The amygdala in our brain senses threats and tries to prevent them from harming us. It senses where we are in the pecking order and who is friend or foe. This kind of subconscious listening is fundamentally I-centric by nature.

Listening I-centrically causes us to be apprehensive in our conversations with others and cautious about their intentions and motivations. Because most of us fear confrontation, and because one of our least-developed skills is the ability to confront another person and have a difficult conversation, we reactively take on the posture of being an enemy ourselves when we sense that we are facing an enemy.

Even thinking of the word *confrontation* causes our blood to boil, or our fears to rise. The word is fraught with meanings that keep us at a distance from others. The dictionary defines it as "to stand over or against in a role of adversary or enemy." While the word also means "to meet or to face someone; to encounter another person," we often project onto the word all of the bad experiences we have had when we face others. Over time the word itself has become tinged with fear and apprehension.

When we think of "confrontation" or of having a "difficult conversation" it takes most of us to the edge of our Comfort Zone, and we will do everything imaginable to avoid it. Having difficult conversations scares most people into thinking they will lose a friendship, and so we avoid confronting the truth. When we feel frustrated or angry with someone who has stood in the way of our success or undermined us and caused us to lose face—at least from our point of view—we get so upset that we just can't find the words to express ourselves. We end up angry and express our most reptilian behaviors. Worse than that, we hold it all inside until we boil up and over with frustration and then we blast that person.

Confronting others honestly requires we share mutually in building our relationship, with both parties feeling the power of the exchange; these are *power-with* relationships. When we feel others want to own us or our power—a *power-over* relationship—we fear harm and cannot open up with honesty. If we think of our conversations as a *power-over* experience, it's impossible to be comfortable confronting others honestly; it's impossible to trust.

Additionally, when confronting another person brings up potentially volatile emotions, we move with caution and keep our real feelings close to our chest. In the most extreme cases, when we are faced
with situations that stir up highly charged emotional content, most
of the tension and drama is actually taking place in our own minds.
This is our "story" and how we have put words to the drama of our
experience. Much of our frustration is coming from the words we use
to tell this story to ourselves and to others.

Yet behind the scenes is the reality of the challenge: How do
we communicate with each other when we feel we are pushed to the
edge? How do we deal with others in a way that builds trusting
relationships rather than erodes them? How do we masterfully keep
ourselves in a state of openness, with our assumptions and inferences
in check? Stephen Balkam faced the challenge and discovered how
to open the space for Creating WE—even though he faced some
extremely powerful obstacles.

A Creative Meeting and Merging of Minds

In 1998, the German government honored Stephen Balkam,
then executive director of the Recreational Software Advisory Council
(RSAC), for creating the conceptual framework for the Internet software that would rate and filter objectionable material not appropriate
for minors.

RSAC's innovative software gives content providers a conve-
nient way to label Internet content and for parents to filter potentially
harmful sites. When the self-regulating labeling and filtering compo-
nents work together, young children can freely access acceptable programming and Web providers can target their material to appropriate
audiences. Browsers, contained in software from Microsoft, AOL, or
others, provide the interlink between the two audiences. They handle
the go/no-go messaging that needs to take place inside computers to
help people navigate through acceptable and inappropriate sites.

Stephen and I (as his external consultant) were given the important job of facilitating an RSAC board meeting in Washington,

convened to shape RSAC's future global strategy. The organization was transforming into a global nonprofit organization, from RSAC to ICRA (Internet Content Rating Association). This meeting would launch the new global strategy to invent the first global self-regulatory system for protecting minors while supporting free speech on the Internet. Representatives from major Internet companies and software vendors such as AOL, Telecom, Microsoft, and IBM attended the Washington board meeting. Each company wanted to champion free speech, but they also wanted to ensure that those who care for minors would be able to censor inappropriate material. Stephen hoped their input would help the board reshape the mission, redefine the market, and transform how they perceived their product—the RSAC rating and filtering system.

We've all attended meetings in which the participants bring vested interests to the process. We all feel it when our colleagues speak with preconceived outcomes in mind. In these meetings we often see people making suggestions, but not listening to others. We see people selling their ideas, but not considering the ideas of others. The atmosphere often becomes adversarial and competitive.

Of course, such groups may make important decisions, but the results usually reflect what people brought to the meeting in the first place. Rather than developing new ideas, they simply play out variations on old ideas.

Everyone concurred that in bad meetings certain individuals try to dominate with their own agendas, while in good meetings everyone harvests new ideas that spring up from collaborative give-and-take discussions.

At the outset of the ICRA meeting, the group was asked if anyone wished to offer an opinion on the desired outcome of the session. A few people raised their hands and said they were about 70 percent sure about what should happen, signaling the fact that before they could create something new, they had to "undo" some old thinking.

Participants then paired up and shared experiences of both great and awful meetings. At the end of this opening exercise, they concluded that they would shun speechmaking and selling in favor of drawing out and experimenting with new ideas.

It's one thing to agree to set aside pre-existing agendas and instead play with new scenarios; it's another thing to make it happen. For some people, even just *talking* about new possibilities and scenarios causes visceral reactions. Words trigger fear and hope responses that can actually be measured on a machine called a Galvanic Skin Response (GSR) meter. The machine is designed to measure the electrical impulses discharged by the body. Most typically it's used for lie-detection. Not surprisingly, certain words send the GSR wild, especially words with emotional overtones or that trigger strong personal memories. But you don't need a GSR to sense people's reactions to words. It just takes sensitivity. We can all learn simply by paying close attention.

If *talking* about something unnerves someone, that probably signals that the person links *talking about it* with actually *doing it*. For example, let's say we want to *talk about* making major changes in a system, process, or department because we want to imagine what would happen if we were to introduce a new technology or merge two divisions or radically shift how we work across organizational boundaries. It is a very human response for simply talking about it to ignite fear of loss, fear of conflict, or fear of change. And fear is the archenemy of even modest preparations for change, such as scenario-building and testing.

With that in mind, we started the ICRA meeting by asking participants to literally draw their ideas. On paper, individuals sketched both what the old RSAC system looked like and what the new system could look like. Once the ideas had been captured on flip charts, people drew, resized, combined, and reinvented new and even more radical scenarios.

Participants used colored markers so that they could create overlays to existing diagrams, which they would never have created using words alone. Ideas started to link to other ideas. When the group seemed most stuck, we introduced metaphors and images to inspire them to think of things in new ways. The ICRA team had been struggling with how to create a new system architecture that content providers could use in evaluating appropriate material for the Web. By the time the session ended, the ICRA board had literally invented just such an architecture. They were able to do this because a space had been opened up and expanded within which they could create and thrive as WE.

Intentionally Removing Barriers

The biggest challenge facing the executives at the ICRA meeting was that each came from another company, like AOL, IBM, and Microsoft—each with its own vested interests. AOL was creating Internet controls for its customers; Microsoft was creating its own controls. Yet, as members of ICRA, the executives were now being asked to temper their primary company's vested interests for the sake of ICRA's interests.

Faced with these challenges, at times during the meeting each executive wondered "whose team was I on anyway?" If the ICRA team developed a global system, would it interfere and compete with what IBM or Microsoft would do with its own content-screening products? How could each executive be open and participate without jeopardizing his or her own company's proprietary product information?

Translated to our own experience, when we join a team, we each own critical knowledge that makes us unique and valuable to our organization. If we share this knowledge or give it away, do we lose our competitive edge? Do we weaken our power, or is there a way to give away power to gain more power? These are the questions that we all face as we learn to figure out how to create more space rather than shrink it down, so new ideas can flourish.

Sometimes we have a bold person inside us and yet, when we speak, what comes out is less powerful than we hope. We choose words that are not as edgy or ideas that are a bit less profound, because we think others will not accept our beliefs and thoughts, or because we want to hold them inside so we don't give away what we believe are our critical secrets. So we close up, or shrink down our communications to avoid the larger challenge of trusting and sharing. When what we have to say seems to be in conflict with others, we may step back from speaking up or reduce our thoughts to a miniature version of what we intended. Perhaps being bold once cost us some points when we got pushback from an authority figure who was in control of our year-end bonus.

In Learning WE, we need to be able to create the space for our full selves to come to work every day and, when we do this, we create a stronger, more powerful WE. So what stops us from bringing our full, robust selves into conversations? What courageous conversations can we introduce to create a stronger WE-centric workplace?

What causes us to communicate in gray instead of full color? In most cases, it's the perception that there are forces in the culture that are holding us back from being as open, as bold, and as honest as we would like. Explore these potential mental obstacles:

1. Power
2. Attachment to being right
3. Old grooves
4. Fear
5. Groupthink

Power

There are few parts of our life that are neutral. Organizations are based on relationships, and most relationships involve positional power. Most decision-making involves power and what we often fear most is that someone will use power in abusive ways. We don't open up when we feel that we will encounter and engage with other powerful people who have their own self-interest in mind. In environments where acquisitions and mergers are commonplace, or restructuring and re-engineering are day-to-day activities, we often revert to our self-protective behaviors to ensure that in the end we will hold a position of value. Any shift in relationships offers the possibility that someone might be demoted or even fired. It makes sense. Too often changes and reorganizations begin with a "housecleaning." It's no wonder when change is afoot that colleagues are concerned about losing rank and power.

Question: What courageous conversations can you encourage colleagues to have with you to reduce the threat of positional power and create an openness in your communication and opportunities for learning, growing, and nourishing?

Attachment to Being Right

Under stress, and in the face of dramatic business challenges, we want to have answers. We want a feeling of safety and security. We want to live in our Comfort Zones. Yet, this is rarely possible. When we are attached to being right, we defend our point of view. We are not open to learning. We are persuading. We are influencing with a push of energy, and most often colleagues will push back. Sometimes our desire to be right accelerates to such a level that we want to be right at all cost, even if it means losing a relationship. Being right provides false confidence in the face of complexity and ambiguity. When we are "all-knowing," we feel superior over others. Sometimes, in the spirit of being right, we explicitly prove others wrong.

Question: What courageous conversations can you encourage colleagues to have with you to reduce the negative impact of "righteousness" and the need to be right? How will this positively impact your relationships with others, build trust and openness, and create opportunities for learning, growth, and nourishment?

Old Grooves

When we undergo major changes in our strategies, our direction, and our ability to address marketplace competition, our brain often reverts to a default setting. That means that we fall back into old familiar habits and behavior patterns. We are not open to change; we are not open to thinking about new strategies. We close down and fall into the old, worn grooves that feel good—where comfort in the known feels more desirable than facing the challenges of the unknown. When we face rapid change and marketplace shifts, our fear of not having the answers causes unsettling feelings. Human beings have trouble staying open to learning new things. We want quick answers, and we want closure. Staying open pushes us out of our Comfort Zones. Old grooves are comforting. However, these well-worn, habitual practices, while consistent with the past, are often not right for the future. Old ways of approaching new challenges can undermine success in new ventures.

Question: What courageous conversations can you encourage colleagues to have with you to reduce the negative impact of old grooves. How will you positively impact your relationships with others to build trust and openness and create opportunities for learning, growing, and nourishing?

Fear

Fear causes us to default to our self-protective behaviors. It is not reality that triggers this response, but the "feared implications" of an imagined future reality. Feared implications are the often hidden concerns that we all have about how any change in the organization might negatively impact us. They are hidden because they are implications we are generally afraid to discuss. Example: "If they sell our division, I'll lose my job." Or, "If I don't make the cut, I'll be demoted."

Sometimes, these are issues we are not comfortable sharing with others, such as feared implications about the motivations and behavior of our boss: "My boss is a jerk. He's so insensitive. He's arrogant and doesn't care about anyone but himself." In reality, once we learn how to create safe environments in which we can openly share these fears and concerns, we can do something about them. Discussing them openly is the key to change!

There are other types of protective behaviors that hold us back:

- Fear of giving up control
- Fear of success
- Fear of failure
- Fear of the future
- Fear that nothing will really change

Question: What courageous conversations can you encourage colleagues to have with you to turn fears into possibilities and create opportunities for learning, growing, and nourishing?

Groupthink

While research suggests that team decisions are formulated on better judgments than those made by individuals, this is not always the case. When Groupthink is at work, the group may limit its wisdom and make misguided, wrong decisions. It is a process for gaining consensus at all cost. While Groupthink may sound like it's a positive process for getting everyone onboard, it really is not. It's actually a covert process for, in some cases, strongly intimidating those with different opinions to cave in and agree with the majority. On the surface, Groupthink appeals to our notions of WE-centricity; however, it is a different animal altogether—it is I-centricity disguised as WE!

Groupthink has a metalanguage, or a hidden line of communication among the team, that suggests "you better go along with what the top dog, the boss, or the company wants" or you will be rejected from the group. Groupthink sets the norm of compliance in place and limits innovative thinking, pushback, and challenging conversations.

Groupthink also forces convergent thinking, which limits exploration, closes down options, and hides inconsistent data from the group's review. Since groups often seek consensus, those individuals with differing points of view often feel like they need to abandon their divergent ideas for fear they will be rejected by their peers. And because such rejection can go beyond the ideas themselves to personal rejection, we often don't risk opening up. Sometimes good ideas are squelched well before the important gems surface. Groupthink screens out some of the most important data that could prompt a new course of action. When pressured by time, judgmental postures, and a few powerful talkers, the group literally stops thinking together and adopts a singular course. By eliminating the potential conflict, the group might also eliminate the higher truth—the bigger ideas and the best insights.

Groupthink forces out novel contributions, conflicting ideas, and unique participation, often at great expense of a forced decision. It causes premature closure and convergent thinking, and it can have a negative impact on the quality of decisions. Handled properly, however, a divergent group process can help a team keep minds open long enough to spark breakthroughs in thinking. This is the challenge—and the opportunity—in group decision-making.

Question: What courageous conversations can you encourage colleagues to have with you to reduce the negative impact of Groupthink and create opportunities for opening up to learning, growing, and nourishing?

How Fear Closes Down Organizational Space

In the face of group pressure, telling the truth, speaking up, and holding a different point of view takes courage. Encouraging positive pushback and courageous conversations enables colleagues to break the Code of Silence.

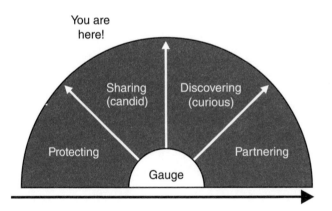

There is a natural tendency for individuals to believe truth-telling is dangerous, as in the following: "If I say what's on my mind, I'll get fired!" and "How can I be candid, and why would I confront someone? They might fight back, and then what?" Notice how the language we use to describe this phenomenon—undiscussables—sets us up for failure even before we try. If we expect confrontation, we get it. If we find things undiscussable, they will become undiscussable.

Here are some examples:

I-centric Example: Anger at You
"Let me tell you the truth. You are really upsetting me. You never follow up on our agreed-upon action steps. You are sloppy in your work and you are not a team player."

WE-centric Example: Being Candid
"I am really upset. I count on you to be my partner and follow up on our agreed-upon action steps. I need you to be a team player and make sure your work is organized and has no typos. What can I do to help you achieve that goal?"

Too often "their" truth and yours don't agree. While they are being "candid" and telling you what's on their mind, they are setting up a challenging dynamic. If you agree, it's okay. If you disagree, their candor could provoke a conflict that sends you both into protective and defensive behavior, creating an unending cycle of fear—one that reinforces territoriality and fear of speaking up.

Three Tips for Creating WE with Candor
1. **Make I statements only.** When you start from YOU, you are in attack mode.
2. **Watch your style of language:** Be clear, be concise, and make sure you lead from assertiveness and not from anger. Do not attack another person or belittle his or her complaints. Simply state how that person's behavior affects you.
3. **Make amends for your behavior.** Relationships are a two-way street. Maybe you need to own some of your own behavior. When you are resisting, backstabbing, or refusing to return phone calls, you are operating out of passive-aggressive behavior. To resolve a problem, the only behavior you need to take responsibility for is your own. When confronting someone, make sure you have inventoried your part in things.

Candor, collaboration, and cooperation are almost impossible to establish in environments where turf wars and one-upsmanship exist.

No one wants to lose. Competition is ingrained in our corporate culture. Trust does not come easily when we feel someone—maybe even our friend—might be out for our job.

In addition to consulting in companies, I also consult with boards. Recently, at the time of the election of a new president, I got a call to consult about some backstabbing going on among potential presidents-elect. As it turned out, the new incoming president was being challenged by an opponent. The opponent, whom I'll call Marsha, wanted to become the next president of this organization so much that she put on a full-court campaign like no other I'd seen before.

She uncovered that the new incoming president, whom I'll call Carol, had recently fallen into Chapter 11. It was around the September 11 time frame, and Carol's client contracts dried up. Carol was left with a huge overhead and a large staff, and the best way to handle her business challenge was Chapter 11.

Marsha discovered this information by digging around in the D&B (Dun & Bradstreet, a business credit and information service), looking for a case to build against her opponent. She not only uncovered this information, she disseminated it to the top ten board members, stating that she felt with this record, Carol should not become the next president. She then began to set up meetings with association members to promote her own interests.

I was called in to help the current president and board members decide what to do. Was Marsha right in presenting the Chapter 11 story to the board? Was she right in framing it as a failure story and demeaning the president-elect? Was she right in claiming the role as opponent?

No, no, no. She was out for the presidency at all costs and was enflaming alliances, friendships, and stirring up ethical issues in her wake.

Some of the board asked me to call her to the mat. Others asked if the current president should send out an e-mail blast claiming her support of the incumbent, Carol. Marsha was out for her own interests and used an underhanded technique to open the door for her "heroic performance."

My coaching to the team was to take the high road. I suggested that each board member should call friends and colleagues and make sure they knew what a great board member Carol had been, that she had a solid record of leadership as past VP, and that as committee leader for over ten years, she had the right stuff to prepare her for her new role as president. I suggested a positive campaign to create clarity and recognition for her commitment to the organization. And I suggested the attention be placed on elevating awareness rather than getting caught up in character assassinations.

The board took my advice and moved forward with a positive strategy. The night of the elections, Carol won 90 percent of the vote. Had they publicly gone after Marsha using an e-mail blast, the whole organization would have learned about Marsha, and she would not have had a strong platform to cajole others to her side. Instead the board took the high road and created a WE-centric rather than a WE/THEY campaign.

In this situation, there was time to do some thinking about a strategy, and there were people who sensed an injustice. In every workplace, there are Marsha-like people who are really nasty and self-interested—people who scramble to accomplish their objectives at all costs. There's no guarding against every person who won't get with the program, and you can be harmed even if you do everything right; but, if you keep working on changing the cultural norms, eventually these people reveal themselves and do get their comeuppance.

In addition, today many companies are implementing ways employees can get help if they feel they are encountering a "kill at all costs" boss or colleague. These are EAPs (Employee Assistance Programs) and internal legal councils. There are now many companies that offer coaching from either internal coaches or from external coaches like myself, for just these types of people. Most importantly, as we develop our ability to have courageous conversations with one another, we will hit the challenges sooner, and stop the disruptive, unhealthy behaviors well before they fester and erode the culture.

Additionally, most clients are putting a lot of time, money, and energy into teaching courses on emotional intelligence and appreciative inquiry as a way to prevent toxic behaviors from invading their environment and workplace. Coaching is growing at an incredible rate as a workplace solution. Soon, and I hope sooner rather than later, every employee will learn and use the skills of coaching as a way of sustaining health. The value to the organization far exceeds the cost or time to learn.

Most importantly, were companies to create a coaching culture in which each person is able to honor the Vital Partnering Instincts, they would be creating environments for health by ensuring that everyone understands how to:

- Be sensitive to others and provide rich feedback.
- Be open and transparent in sharing and building a commonly shared approach to manage health and ward off toxicity— "a natural immune system."
- Focus on creating the future together rather than defending the past.

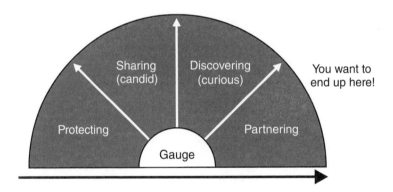

WE/THEY mentality is another challenge to building strong partnerships, and it has become so commonplace in many organizations that it is fundamentally destructive to working through change. We accept the WE/THEY paradigm too easily. We accept that it's okay to live with WE/THEY norms. We accept that it's okay to talk behind people's backs rather than face-to-face, where we have the best chance of fixing underlying problems.

Everything embodies its opposite. Coalitions and partnerships can be nurturing and positive, or they can evolve into groups of people seeking out supporters for their position in the battle against an enemy. The key to change is to shift the language we use, the meanings we create, and the beliefs we hold. The key is to understand how to move from breakdown to breakthrough.

Influence Through Courageous Conversations

The root cause of why relationships turn sour, teams fall apart, or divisions fail to achieve their goals is often that people don't know how to open up to each other in a positive way about the challenges they face. Issues become insurmountable, challenges too big to tackle, and conflicts too emotional to resolve. Encouraging courageous conversations fuels movement out of Comfort Zones on the way to breakthrough. It's how we can develop power and influence across the organization.

When we are caught up in being "candid," we are actually pushing (and sometimes dumping) as we tell people what's on our mind from an I-centric point of view. We are pushing on others. To transform the push into an open, honest conversation, you need to shift from trying to "sell someone" on your ideas—*push*—to asking questions to open up discussion—*pull*.

It takes courage to open up. It takes courage to challenge the status quo, to push back on conventional wisdom and against fears, and to move forward toward better solutions and new possibilities. Positive pushing back sends the message that we don't have to accept *what is*, but instead can create *what could be*.

Having courageous conversations, being open to share what's on your mind in a positive WE-centric way, facilitates Creating WE. Being bold and courageous may mean pushing back on others' points of view—challenging them or giving alternative perspectives. We often feel that if we push back, we will break rapport, lose a friendship, or alienate others. We fear that if we push back we will be seen as too aggressive or assertive, and so we avoid or disengage from taking a stand on what we believe.

To be able to push back with others, you need to realize that it's more about opening up and sharing than arguing and being in conflict. Modeling this behavior is critical not only for ourselves, but for the next generation of leaders as well. The leadership DNA of a culture can only evolve if we, in this generation, make the pivotal shift to courageous conversations.

Every day in your conversations with others, notice when you lose the courage to stay open. Notice when you are feeling that you have labeled a conversation a confrontation, so you can—in the moment—do a *reframing*. Reframing means to change the context (or connotation) from negative to a positive. It means to change the point of view so you can see the conversation in light of the value you are bringing each other, rather than the conflict and resistance you might be imagining.

Staying open in challenging discussions is the essence of a healthy, feedback-rich culture. Without it, we stagnate, accept mediocrity, and ultimately become underperformers. What kind of courage does it take for you to confront your own fears, to be real with yourself, and to encourage that level of openness and honesty with others?

The Magic Triangle

To gain the courage we need, it helps to understand an under-lying dynamic process that takes place between and among people—a process that was previously invisible. I call this process the "Magic Triangle." It is magic to watch what happens when we teach executives what it is and how it works. Learning to use the Magic Triangle turns hesitant communicators into bold communicators, and turns breakdowns into breakthroughs.

I discovered the Magic Triangle almost two decades ago while working with a colleague, Rich Rearon, a senior organizational development executive at Union Carbide. We were brought in to help convert mired and entrenched teams into productive teams. As we observed the teams, we measured the ratio of how often they asked questions to how often they made statements. Over and over again, we discovered they made statements about 85 to 95 percent of the time and asked questions 5 to 15 percent of the time—more often at the lower end of that range.

We observed that colleagues were *selling* their ideas to each other and were not open to *being influenced*. We discovered that most people operated out of "persuasion" and were in a win/lose mode of discussion. We observed that, after their meetings, many people were unhappy and felt left out or overridden by their more vocal and powerful colleagues. The frustrations didn't stop after the meetings. Colleagues harbored bad feelings about others, which they carried around and shared. Consequently, the performance of the teams went down, politics went up, and the customers felt unsatisfied.

Rich and I invented the Magic Triangle through brainstorming, experimenting, and sharing our insights and perceptions. We wanted to help the Union Carbide teams see what we were seeing by making their dialogue process transparent. Then we wanted to give them a process for working through their conversations in a more productive way, one that tapped the wisdom and insight of everyone in the room. The teams went through rigorous workshops in how to ask questions and how to listen from an open point of view. They studied team dynamics and human behavior, and they applied their learnings to real-life situations and challenges. The result of this work was outstanding.

Every team not only turned into a high-performing, productive team, but they also discovered they were coming up with exciting, new ideas to help the business. They shifted from an I-centric focus to a WE-centric focus—from their own self-interest to the enterprise's interest. They started saving the company lots of money, they invented new technology, and many of the executives who went through the process were promoted to help build teams with this competence in other parts of the organization.

How Does It Work?

The Magic Triangle process is simple. Observe yourself and others at meetings. Are you sitting on the top of the triangle persuading others of your ideas? Are you entrenched in your own position? Are the conversations going nowhere? Are you at the top of the

Ladder of Conclusions with strong beliefs that are unchangeable? If so, you need to come down the ladder, open up to listening, and ask "Discovery Questions" to learn where others stand—to shift from Persuasion to Discovery. Discovery Questions can be:

- What is at stake?
- What can we gain, rather than lose?
- What do I need to do to help the process move forward?
- What are our interdependencies?
- What are the feared implications we need to explore and eliminate?
- How can I support my colleagues?
- How can I support my enterprise?
- How can I move the internal dialogue of fear and concern out onto the table?
- How can we manage the fear in a positive way?
- Can we work through the challenges and gain agreement about what to do in a more transparent way?
- What can we create together?

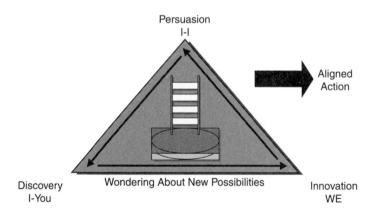

Discovery: Making New Connections

As you move around the Magic Triangle from Persuasion to Discovery, you will notice that something begins to shift inside of you. You are less focused on holding on to your own beliefs and you become interested in what you are discovering from others. You are open to being influenced; your curiosity and wonder help you navigate into the world of feelings, insights, and wisdom. Some people describe it as a Letting Go.

Remember to ask open-ended questions. Open-ended questions are those for which you do not have the answers and for which there is no easy one-word answer—like "yes" or "no." As you ask and listen, you will also discover that your mind opens up. Rather than living in "defense" or "protect," you will be opening yourself up to think in new ways. Gauge yourself, and you will see that you feel different, and you will begin to resource new ways of thinking.

Innovation: Wondering about New Possibilities

As you move around the Magic Triangle from Discovery to Innovation, you will notice that something else begins to shift inside of you. You and your colleague will begin to think as one brain. You will start to see the same challenge from all different sides, and each member of the team will begin to use phrases such as "What if we did this?" or "What would this do?" You will begin to shape and craft new ways of thinking inside of one another that will occur simultaneously. At the moment this occurs, people say they feel like a WE is emerging. The shift from I to WE is happening and you feel like you are now in partnership. You are simultaneously uplifting one another to access a new level of imagination, releasing fear, and focusing on invention.

Following are the type of Innovation questions to ask one another as you make this journey together:

- If we could wish for the impossible, what would we do?
- If we had unlimited resources, what would we do?
- What if the opposite were true?
- If money were no problem, what would we do?
- If we had everyone supporting us, what would we do?
- If we could implement any solution, what would we go for?
- If we could picture the best solution, what would it be?
- If we were to have no limitations, what would we do?
- What would a significant breakthrough look like?

- If we were someone else, what would we do?
- If we started backward, what would we do?

Continuing around the Magic Triangle to the top again, you and your colleagues stand together in mutual commitment and support. This is WE-centric persuasion, both of you holding new ideas and beliefs you together can take out on the road for action. The difference is that you are engaged in a new way, in support of something you have created together. You shift from *power-over* others into *power-with* others.

The Leadership Trilogy

It is one thing to change individuals, another to change entire teams and companies. The resistance that builds up in teams and organizations is much stronger and more difficult to shift. We face our biggest challenges when we try to change behavior in a larger arena. Yet it can be done by mastering the Magic Triangle and applying this process to how you and other colleagues discuss and work on leadership challenges.

The Magic Triangle, applied to business challenges and practiced every day during conversations, lifts you out of old grooves, interrupts the patterns of positional power, and prevents Groupthink from taking a team into premature consensus. Remember, as the leader, you set the tone!

There are three keys to utilizing and applying the Magic Triangle to everyday work life:

- Open Space for New Wisdom
- Sharing Key Business Challenges and Uplifting Experiences (Discovery)
- Crafting Breakthrough Conversations about the Future (Innovation)

Challenge 1: Open Space for New Wisdom

You must commit to creating a positive, open environment in which colleagues can speak up and talk about their beliefs. They need to intentionally root out territorialism and prevent silo building. This will provide energy so colleagues can focus on creating the future together, rather than reinforcing the past. Our minds are maps of the future. How we think determines the journey we will take. Surfacing and exploring these patterns of thought in a safe environment enables us to make serious choices about how we will participate in creating new belief systems for the benefit of the whole organization. Focusing on opening the space for conversation enables others to speak up without fear.

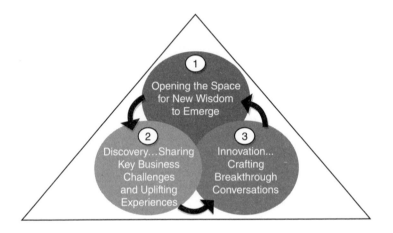

Challenge 2: Sharing Key Business Challenges and Uplifting Experiences

A culture becomes strong when people focus together on surfacing and working on significant business issues and challenges. By sharing rich feedback about marketplace dynamics and competitive issues, they become clearer to you and your team, and what you need to do to win also becomes clearer. At that point you are sharing an uplifting experience together and a sense of common ownership of the future emerges.

Something special happens to colleagues when they struggle through a crisis together. They must depend upon and trust each other in new ways. They turn to each other and open up. They communicate with a higher level of passion and self-expression. They become more intimate and more compassionate. Crisis and challenge connect colleagues in ways that are not found in "business as usual." Also, people feel more alive when they are challenged to do their best and "rise to the occasion." They grow more confident and are more daring. Initiating Vital Leadership Journeys and team challenges creates a shared bond and will ultimately have a positive effect not only on staff, but on customers and clients as well.

Challenge 3: Crafting Breakthrough Conversations about the Future

As the leader, you can help employees face challenges together in completely new ways. Irrespective of hierarchy and position, everyone is a contributor, and by creating open spaces for dialogue, you create a way for colleagues to work together to shape the future of the business.

Focusing on skills for opening up and holding the space for dialogue, no matter how monumental or daunting the challenges you are facing, brings colleagues together with a common purpose and helps them work through the necessary tradeoffs for coming to the best decisions. As the game plan unfolds, employees at all levels can become part of the powerful team experience that creates the organization's strategic intent.

You set the tone. By becoming a co-creating leader, you show the organization how to do this. Creating conversational space is not a change-management program, nor is it a one-time event. These are powerful conversations that create life-changing turnarounds with the power to reconnect employees in conscious and unconscious ways to work together in harmony and achieve audacious goals.

The spirit of cooperation that emerges from these conversations helps shift the way colleagues work and the way people interact, creating an ongoing organizational capacity for achieving extraordinary business results. These conversations powerfully change human dynamics as they change business dynamics.

Your role as a co-creating leader unleashes energy in others. You catalyze teams, divisions, and the whole organization. You can create the same energy in virtual as well as face-to-face teams. Within this powerful conversational strategy are the vital practices that you can weave into meetings, day-to-day encounters, and retreats. These will raise your team's capacity for Letting Go of the past and creating the future.

These practices create a tough-mindedness for dealing with business reality and, at the same time, a compassionate way of dealing with people. They are practices that, when put into place in enough companies, can lay the foundation for changing the way we conduct business in general.

Try This!

10-Step Process Guide for Innovation

Step 1: Choose a leader.

Step 2: Define the situation/challenge.

Step 3: Define the desired outcomes.

Step 4: Define any new terms/ideas/issues that the team needs to share in common.

Step 5: Acknowledge and confirm the team norms. Decide how you will handle disagreement, conflict, and excursions: free-for-all or one at a time, etc.

Step 6: Share points of view on the challenge, one at a time with team members.

Step 7: Use Discovery skills to build understanding.
- Explore its issues: convictions, assumptions, and feared implications (fears that people need to put on the table).
- Explore current thinking (conventional wisdom).

Step 8: Use Innovation skills to expand understanding.
- Explore/create/innovate new ways to look at the situation (unconventional wisdom). Ask what-if questions . . .
- Foster breakthroughs: combine ideas, turn them upside down and inside out. Post them on flip charts for all to see.
- Combine ideas into a bigger idea.

Step 9: Validate ideas, suggestions, and new ways of thinking.
- Capture the best ideas around the room on big flip charts.

- Ask people to go around the room and add sticky notes to the flip charts with suggestions for how to turn these ideas into reality.

Step 10: From Ideas to Reality—create accountability charts for who will be responsible for what, when, and how.

- Determine the roles of those who need to be involved, responsible, or part of the next steps. Make roles and accountabilities clear.
- Define roles for those who need to communicate to others not present, and outside the group.
- Go around the room and ask people to say one word that describes how they feel.

WE-aving It All Together

When given a choice, most of us would prefer to create positive change rather than inhibit it. At the same time, our instincts to protect our territory and be fearful of the enemy are triggered when potential changes are contemplated. The natural fear of the negative impact of change (i.e., "I may lose my job") often triggers fear and the perception that "something is being done to me that I won't like." The unintended consequences of these fears are a cycle of behavioral posturing that turns into resistance to change. Why? Because these dynamics create power-over rather than power-with relationships.

It's easier to say that it's someone else's fault than it is to work through the dynamics and have the kind of discussions to get to the heart of a problem. In many companies that are experiencing growth and cultural challenges, the essence of the problem stems from fear of speaking up in the face of authority—the fear of opening up and getting pushback.

In many cases, people are afraid to push back in the face of five powerful dynamics in the culture. When you make these dynamics visible, you help remove the stigma of pushback and enable people to open up and take risks with one another that release positive energy into the environment.

We began this chapter with a discussion about trust and openness, and the skills and processes for having open conversations with others. Most of all, we learned how to express what is on our mind in a way that creates, rather than erodes, WE.

This chapter reminds you that you have a choice. By choosing to learn and practice vital behaviors that keep the space open for healthy dialogue, you will be infusing new skills and competencies into your culture that will transform negativity into positive energy, fear into hope, silo building into silo breaking, and distrust into trust.

Over the years, we have researched behaviors that help create WE, and the following chart is a one-page summary of those behaviors in action. Imagine yourself in meetings at work. Picture the kinds of behaviors that show up as people communicate, and work on challenges together. Some people seem to have a facilitative influence on conversations. They are able to draw out a topic and draw out people. They encourage speaking up and demonstrate how to speak up without dominating. They are candid and honest, without being caustic and critical.

Are You Up for the Challenge?

Each of us has the ability to lead in a WE-centric way. The skills entitled "Expanding Spaces" on the right side of the chart create energy for engagement and make speaking up a desired norm. The skills on the left side—"Closing Spaces"—create an atmosphere of protectiveness and defensiveness and make shutting up a norm. As you interact with your colleagues every day, become an observer and participant in Creating WE. Learn and practice the skills that catalyze imagination, sustain positive energy, build powerful relationships, and lift organizational spirit.

Think of the best times you've had at work. They are the times when you and your colleagues get so excited about what you are creating together that it doesn't matter who is the originator—"because we all are." Think about these wonderful times when you start a

Vital Communications

Closing Spaces	Expanding Spaces
Communication that triggers defensiveness and fear and limits imagination and wonder	Communication that catalyzes imagination, sustains positive energy, builds powerful relationships, and lifts organizational spirit

	Relationship-Focused	Task-Focused

Blocking
Arguing several positions; returning to "dead issues"; "nit-picking"; vested interests

Participating and Including
Helping communication remain open; getting other people to participate

Initiating Rules of Engagement
Establishing rules of engagement for effective conversations to achieve mutual success

Withdrawing/Disengaging
Removing oneself from participation mentally and/or physically; repeated side conversations; avoiding

Supporting and Encouraging
Using positive, nonjudgmental words and nonverbals to let others know you have heard them

Information Gathering
Requesting "feelings" as well as facts/information; asking for information necessary for achieving success

Digressing/Gossiping
Taking colleagues down a path of unrelated issues/information; telling war stories; complaining about other colleagues

Openness
Willingness to share what's on your mind; willingness to be influenced by other's opinions; admitting mistakes

Information Generating
Giving facts and suggestions in service of the team's task; stating or providing beliefs about the situation

Seeking Recognition
Loud or excessive joking or cheap shots aimed at diverting attention from business and drawing attention to oneself

Testing Agreement/Reality
Using periodic checks to test others' satisfaction with the process; pointing out norms that may need to be tested/changed

Decision Testing
Offering to test whether colleagues are close to a decision; proposing a possible direction

Interrupting
Using irrelevant input to abruptly stop dialogue/discussion; repeatedly cutting off others in midsentence

Harmonizing
Encouraging colleagues to explore difficulties and perspectives; not judging; asking more questions than telling

Problem/Challenge Clarifying
Helping clear up confusion by interpreting input; suggesting alternatives

Hidden Agenda
Using the "yes, but" routine; manipulating colleagues to focus on your own personal agenda — never explicitly stated

Listening
Listening for feelings as well as content; reflecting back understanding; clarifying

Summarizing for Direction
Restating where colleagues are in discussions; pulling together related ideas

meeting. Get your head into the spirit of Creating WE, and guess what? You will be leading the way!

Now that you understand how to create the space for inspired discussions and innovative thinking, the next practices to learn more about are how you can shape conversations for positive influence, how you can master your intention, and how you can transform culture every day.

7.

Get Over It!

Shaping the Conversations

The fishermen know that the sea is dangerous and the storm terrible, but they have never found those dangers sufficient reason for remaining ashore.

VINCENT VAN GOGH, PAINTER

EVERYTHING HAPPENS THROUGH CONVERSATIONS. A seemingly simple act such as talking with a colleague—a small momentary exchange of words in a hallway—has the ability to alter someone's life permanently. Phrases like "I can't do that!" and "If I only knew how!" may take only seconds to utter, but they can be life changing. There is little connection between the time it takes to say the words and the impact they may have on a person, a relationship, or an organization.

Conversations have the ability to trigger emotional reactions. Words carry baggage. They are rarely neutral. Words carry a history of years of use. Each time another experience overlays another meaning and it all gets collected somewhere in our brain—the vault—it's there, ready to be activated during conversations. Conversations carry meaning that becomes more embedded in the listener than the speaker. We communicate with each other through conversations; we connect to others through conversations. Once the umbilical cord is cut, conversations are the connectivity that keeps us all together.

However, words are not external, objective reality. They are projections of our own inner reality.

Language is instinctual. It is also utilitarian. All animals use language to communicate, and most of all to signal each other about how to explore, navigate, and survive the environments in which they live.

Understanding the communication process enables us to use language to create WE. In this chapter we will focus on how to shape and craft conversations through a variety of processes—the most important of which is the ability to change history, change memories, release, and Let Go.

Meeting Voices from the Past

Imagine for a moment that you have just been recruited onto a project team that's been assigned by the executive vice president of your division to do special work around customer relations.

You've wanted to be on a special project team since the beginning of your career. It's a dream come true. You show up for the first meeting and discover that the senior executive has recruited about a dozen people from across the company, and one of them is someone you worked with in the past and did not get along with at all. Together you were like oil and water. You said black; she said white. She was one of those people who was always talking about people behind their backs and couldn't hold confidences.

Without much effort, you start to remember what it was like working with her and your blood starts to boil. You wonder how she could have been chosen for this project. You know it's not healthy to carry around baggage from the past, and you're pretty good at letting things go, but you just don't trust this person. She's one of those people who, you believe, is out to win for herself at all cost. Your dreams about being on an exciting project team and working with people who you know will challenge you and work creatively with you are now crumbling in front of your eyes.

In an ideal world, we get to choose the colleagues we want to work with. It starts with choosing a company, then a boss, and then teammates. Yet, in today's world of constant change where teams are formed and unformed so often, we are more frequently dropped into an ongoing drama where there is some past history to deal with. Inevitably, you will know some of the people from previous situations.

You may have heard about them from colleagues and friends. They may remind you of your father, whom you never got along with, or at the opposite end of the spectrum, they may remind you of your old roommate from college who turned out to be your best thought-partner. By the time we become adults, we have so many memories to connect with and so much knowledge and wisdom from our journey, it's rare, very rare, that we enter a team environment with a clean slate.

Searching for Comparables in Our Mental Dictionary

When traveling from one situation to the next, we bring our past along to guide our way. We are resourceful. We tap into points of view, know-how, rules of conduct, rules of behavior, likes and dis-likes—all giving us the conceptual tools to make decisions and judgment calls regarding what to do and why.

Instead of entering a situation with an unbiased and open mind, just the opposite occurs. In new situations, or new teams, or new anything, you begin what I call "searching for comparables." You go into your memory bank of similar examples and bring them up to consciousness to uncover the rules, interpretations, and understandings you need to bring forward to help you in this situation. You begin to have a dialogue with yourself, and perhaps others, about what this new situation is going to be like, drawing on your past knowledge, insight, and wisdom to help you out.

Your self-dialogue will take you down a path of familiar streets and signs, telling you what you might expect will happen. Your mind can process the situation faster than you can put words to it. Patterns from the past invisibly surface, so that you can feel grounded in the newness of the unfamiliar. You may call upon comparables from your actual experience or comparables from things you've read or heard to help you navigate the new terrain. Sometimes data from the past are valuable to hold on to and other times they get in the way. Let's see how.

Trapped in the Past

Since less than 30 percent of acquisitions, mergers, or transformations prove successful, there are many who believe that bringing in new leadership can help make the change successful. Replacing the leader poses its own new set of challenges. It is a course that doesn't always result in success.

Design International was a $150 million business that appeared to be very successful, offering great-looking apparel for the "upscale" customer. At a time when design manufacturers were having trouble, this company appeared to be doing fairly well—that is, until the real numbers were uncovered. The growth strategy was to push for a heavy sell-in to the retailer. This made Design International's bottom line look great, with sales increasing in every market. Yet when the numbers were all put on the table—with returns and markdowns factored in—the bottom line no longer looked so good.

Within six months, the old CEO and president were let go—a common way companies begin the process of Letting Go of the past, to release old meanings, old beliefs, and old interpretations from a "system." As the senior management of the parent company worked through the actual numbers and discovered the manner in which the profits had been reported, they realized how far from secure the business actually was. Dozens of people were asked to leave, and a new CEO was brought in to retrench and reshape the business. In the meantime, those employees who stayed felt deceived. As they looked back over the past few years, they were able to make sense of things that, at the time, were not clear. They were upset at themselves for believing illusions of success and upset at the previous leadership for not telling them the truth.

As the next few months unfolded, the emotions moved from disillusionment to anger. Colleagues consoled each other and talked about the past. They tried to put it away, but every time they discovered more details, they became angrier. The level of anger became so distracting that no one could do his or her best work to turn the business around. I was brought in to work with the new CEO as an executive and organizational coach.

Holding On and Letting Go

Every day of your life, the consequences of your interactions are stored in your memory bank, compartmentalized in your mind's own filing system. In the broadest sense, you are filing memories as "feel good" or "feel bad" experiences. In more finite ways, you are filing memories in mental buckets from which you can later retrieve points of view, opinions, and interpretations that help you navigate the corporate terrain.

Memories with strong emotions linger. It's as though the brain more easily files and calls up memories attached to strong sensory data. Smells, tastes, emotions of any sort attached to a memory give it a compelling distinctiveness that enable you to call it up more easily, to pull it out of the mental database from among the other less-intense experiences. But this mechanism, while often helpful, has a downside: The experiences are hard to control and can burst out all on their own. With little provocation, we can call up a bad experience at a moment's notice. Haven't you ever had a bad experience with a boss, one in which he or she drove you nuts and wouldn't leave you alone about something you did? If you're really upset, you'll talk about it forever, complaining to your friends, your colleagues, and anyone who will listen.

Emotional trauma or experiences that threaten our ego, well-being, and self-esteem—or push our hot button—don't just happen and then go away. They linger in our minds and in our workplaces, creating toxic effects that, over time, become the stories everyone wants to tell over and over again.

Inside conversations are stories that embody emotions. They are prisms that bend and refract relationships. They are reality exchanges

Finding New Meaning from Letting Go

As we release ourselves from the past, we open the space for our lives to transform. We allow the brain's neural connections to become free to accept and attract energy and new meaning, and in doing so, bring vitality into our lives. Our relationships with others become richer and fuller, our sensitivity expands, and we set higher standards and aspirations for the future. Life takes on new meaning and we enjoy taking risks while exploring and experiencing others and ourselves in new ways.

Letting Go has a facilitative effect on opening up new pathways to co-creation and to the new outrageous futures that lie ahead. Letting Go opens up and cleanses our inner spaces, in some cases providing us with the energy to break from the past and interrupt old patterns that are no longer serving us well.

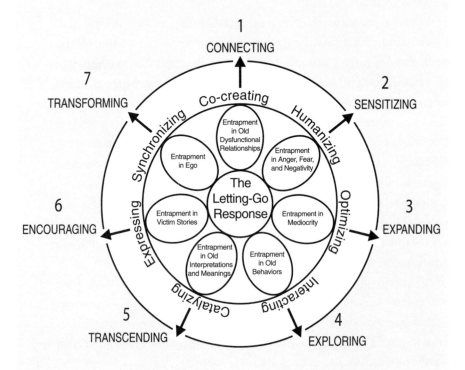

from one person to another—but the reality is never real. It is merely a *story*. The Design International executives were so mired in the past, they were uncoachable. They were each so convinced of their "truth" that they were not open to any other point of view. In this case, the fatal spiral had created so much downward energy that the best coach in the world could not have righted the system.

The executives, even with intense coaching, were unable to Let Go of the past. They cycled and recycled the stories from one person to another—and, like snowballs rolling downhill, the stories became bigger and bigger to a point that they took on their own toxic presence. Name-calling and blaming became the conversational norm. They were all so bent on ditching one another, that instead they ditched the company. With their market share eroding from the internal focus and cut-throat conflicts, they had no energy left to focus on creating the future and turning things around. Customers went elsewhere, other design firms went after their shelf space, and soon the company faced Chapter 11.

For individuals and teams to live in a trusting, future-oriented space, they need to learn and practice "releasing" when stuff gets in the way, as well as when they want to launch a new perspective on the future. Releasing means Letting Go of the past (old relationships, fears, behaviors, and interpretations; negativity; mediocrity and acceptance of the status quo; victim stories; and entrapment in ego).

Environmental Triggers

While we can't see what's going on inside our heads, the brain is active during our conversations, providing us with our own set of internal instruments for sensing whether our environment is filled with friends or foes.

The amygdala activates in survival situations—or situations in which a threat may be impending. The amygdala triggers the fight-flight response to impending danger. Without it, our enemies and predators might overcome us. In business, if we believe we're losing market share, we react. In relationships, when we believe we're being taken advantage of, we react. The responsive amygdala goes into overdrive when our environment triggers our survival instincts.

There are times when we should be grateful these systems are fully charged and effectively operating. Our overactive reptilian brain gets us into trouble, however, when we fall into internal battles and turf wars, when we perceive the enemy as another division within our organization or another person on our team. At the moment of attack, it's virtually impossible to sort out what we are making up and what is real. Attacks are attacks and threats are threats. When someone is after us, we don't lie down and offer ourselves up as dinner; we have

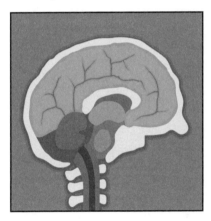

to do something. Where we get into trouble is when we overreact and assume that the only response is to take out our club and kill the attacker, before we find out if what is in his or her hand is a loaded gun or a peace pipe.

Our quick response to threats often leads us to believe someone is after our job or is intentionally trying to make us look bad to advance his or her own career. When under apparent threat, we usually start with an I-centric protective response. Stepping back to seek an alternative requires learning to think WE.

When we sense danger, what is going on inside the brain? At the moment of an attack, why don't we simply ignore the attacker? Few of us can just dismiss an assault on our ego without counterattacking in some way. Our reptilian brains—where the fight-flight instincts reside—are hard-wired to ensure that we don't just offer ourselves up as prey without a fight. When you are attacked in public, depending on your nature, you can do any or all of the following:

- Withdraw (Flee) and simmer inside, keeping the emotion alive by telling stories to yourself and building up a strong case about the offending person, then sharing your wounds with others whom you trust will respond with compassion. This is known as case-building.

■ Attack (Fight), verbally accelerating the emotion to a higher level, intimidating the attacker. You become the aggressor and victimize your prey. This is known as aggression.

■ Acquiesce (Fright) and get them back later, which gives you time to build your attack strategy. You may not fully go after the person, but instead plan strategically to make sure they feel it later. You can give in now, suggesting you're in a weaker position, and then collect your team to go after your attacker with a vengeance. This is known as passive-aggressive.

■ Confront (Connect) and constructively and courageously deal with the situation. This means facing your challenge, being direct and assertive, and openly communicating and setting boundaries around the behavior that you are not willing to tolerate. You are also potentially coaching others in the direction of the desired results. Some executives are able to rise to the occasion.

Warding off the Negative Energies

Ward Mooney's division of Gordon Brothers, called the Retail Finance Division—was newly acquired by BankBoston to help them penetrate the growing world of retail with their unique boutique-lending offerings. The new division was uniquely positioned to provide loans to retailers in growth cycles. The new division was a small company acquired by a larger company. Since then, BankBoston has been acquired by Fleet, and, most recently, Fleet has been acquired by Bank of America.

I worked as an executive coach to Ward, the CEO, and his team when they were still with Gordon Brothers prior to the acquisition, and moved forward to work with him as an executive and organizational coach for the BankBoston venture. As CEO of this new venture, Ward Mooney had a lot of decisions to make early on. He wanted to launch his team with the best resources, wisdom, and possibilities.

Regardless of what happened with other acquisitions in the past, Ward was determined that his team would be an example of what success looked like. He wanted the bank to say, "We made a great acquisition; this business is better than what we expected." Yet, as good as his team was, it was hard to predict how individuals would handle something as dramatic as what they were about to enter into.

Acquisitions and mergers represent huge challenges to Creating WE. They can trigger every territorial instinct we have, making us question everything—from who will get the best and biggest office to who will be promoted, demoted, or let go. Depending on our individual sense of security, we can quickly encumber the new situation with baggage from the past in an effort to navigate our way into the future.

Perhaps the biggest challenge for BankBoston Retail Finance was that while the new entity had an official name, there was no official history to the name. There was no legacy to bring forward except the individual experiences of those who came forward—no real identity except for the titles of each person in the hierarchy. Identity is something we build over time. It's more than a title, and it is something we "share" when we are part of a company, a brand, or an organization. Ward's new venture had no clear identity, mission, strategies, or vision. They were purchased for their economic value, and that was still to be fully realized.

In spite of how good his team was in the past, Ward Mooney realized he had to create a new team and to do this he had to create a new, shared experience around which to build a new identity. Ward decided to run a Leadership Journey to ensure that the team members brought forward the wisdom they needed and Let Go of the past that was standing in the way of their future success. He wanted to be in the fortunate minority—the 30 percent who succeed. He wanted to give his team a way to start fresh and create a pathway for success. Within seven months after their Leadership Journey experience, Ward's team produced results that exceeded their year-end expectations. What happened during this experience that made such a powerful difference?

Much to his surprise, Ward's team embraced the Leadership Journey with great enthusiasm. Prior to the meeting, there were undercurrents of skepticism about the roles people would play when they became part of BankBoston. Many of the team members came in to the process with the "stories" they had heard from others about how companies get acquired, and the first thing they do is fire the existing team. Ward felt that if the team came in with a positive mindset—without old baggage from the past and with an openness to embrace the change—then they would be more prepared to show dramatic results immediately.

Creating New Meaning in the First 100 Days

Ward also talked with his team about the "First 100 Days." He believed that this period was critical for a newly acquired team. During the First 100 Days, senior executives and team members need to understand the new culture they are entering and, at the same time, bring their competencies and talents to the new venture. Together they need to "meld meaning" and "create meaning," so that everyone is speaking the same language. Most of all, everyone needs to understand what success looks like—and create common views of the endgame they are shooting for.

Like Ward, you need to approach a merger or acquisition from the point of view of a WE-centric leader. In doing so, you will enable the positive transformation of yourself, your team, and your organization. If you are starting out in a new company, a new leadership position, or a new venture, there are a few key prescriptive steps to follow to create WE:

1. Build your team around a shared meaning for success.

Getting your team in place precedes anything. You are not alone on the Leadership Journey, and each of your key people will make a difference in the organization's overall success. Talk about what success looks like—define it with others—take it out and look at it from all angles, rather than assuming that everyone knows what it is. Typically, we have different pictures in our heads. Bring these pictures to the table as resources to create the larger view that will become the shared view you create. The view needs to contain aspirational energy to express what the team as a whole aspires to create.

2. Adopt a strategy for creating the shared vision.

Decide how you want to engage with others to create the vision, how much interaction, how much pushback, how much empowerment, and when. Become mindful of how you want decisions and implementation of strategy to unfold—ensure people are looped in. Create it together, rather than handing it over on a silver platter. The words people choose to describe the vision become beacons drawing them toward a goal—even in the murkiest situations.

3. Set thirty-, sixty-, and ninety-day priorities, and build your plan with others.

Don't fly solo. Your team is waiting for you to ask them for their suggestions. They have instinctual insights, wisdom, and knowledge to share. To give everyone an opportunity to learn to work together and make decisions together, create a month-by-month plan so that everyone can practice moving from ideas to realities together—step by step. This creates a new pattern of engagement and team decision-making. Draw upon the team for the larger plan so they can be part of setting and achieving milestones. Don't rely on one perspective—your own—because it's easier. Remember to be inclusive. The road ahead will be navigated by the insights of your collective team. Allow them to build the map with you—their input creates their commitment.

4. Build momentum and energy at the top, bottom, and throughout.

Create energy by engaging with your team on the vision and how to expand your value in the marketplace. Introduce words like value creation, which will elevate the team's thinking to a new level usually reserved for the CEO or office of the chairman. Exchange ideas; draw people into conversation. Enable people to participate. Remember: Everything happens through conversations. Make it a transforming vision. Engage in conversations with customers, employees, colleagues, and alliance partners to ensure you capture everyone's input in shaping and crafting the future.

5. Communicate intimately and globally.

Create constant touch points with people; engage with your organization and with the outside world. Dialogue is the cornerstone of your success. If you err, do so by communicating more, rather than less. Realize that as you take in new input you will be revising the picture of success. Visions are not set in stone; they emerge more clearly as people touch and hold them. Capture the words people use to sharpen the picture. Language is a new lens to see into the future.

6. Appreciate the value each employee brings.

Even though you may have new ideas to introduce and implement, value those who have built the organization before you as well as those who are entering for the first time. Rather than dictate the vision, engage others in creating it. You will move forward and create change only if others are willing to listen to you. Validate their experience—then nurture their awareness of new possibilities.

7. Adopt symbols of change.

Make change visible to your organization through symbolic and tangible things people can see. Create a "Journey of Discovery" so people know you are moving from where you are to something new. Engage people as pioneers with you along the new journey. Capture and share the Best Practices along the way.

8. Achieve small wins.

Mark the team's success so people learn what winning means. Define winning and share success stories throughout your team and organization. Positive energy creates more positive energy, and the momentum of success has a power to propel the largest entity forward. Create a sense of shared reality and a sense of excitement.

9. Celebrate success.

Recognize your wins publicly; allow people to see that contribution and commitment pay off. It doesn't need to be in the form of financial rewards. It's more about taking the time to appreciate good work toward a common goal. When people know what success looks like and how to define it, they are more apt to create it. Too often we fail to define success and winning and instead we punish people who don't deliver. If they knew what success looked like, they would have been better prepared to create it the first time.

10. Deliver on promises and commitments.

Building your credibility will be the key to your ongoing success as a leader. Learn the distinctions between trying to do something and delivering on the promise. These fine distinctions are huge distinctions. As people go through transformations and take on greater challenges, it's easy to say, "I'll try to do it." Trying is not the same as doing. Even just using the language of "trying" allows for us to ease up when the journey gets rough. Engage others at the level of commitment not compliance; contract with others for accountability, communication, and results. Work with each other to support rather than criticize.

Coaching Conversations: Reshape Reality

One of the most important ways for executives to help both organizations and employees expand their capacity for growth in the face of an ever-changing marketplace and to stay in sync with each other is to become a peer coach. Coaching enables you, and other colleagues, to shift relationships from WE/THEY to WE.

Peer coaching enables you to Let Go of and eliminate negative beliefs, and strengthen relationships across the organization. Peer coaching can be colleague to colleague; it can be colleagues on the same team or colleagues from different divisions in the company. The common thread is that both parties agree to become open to feedback, to suggestions, to seeking new perspectives, and to helping each other succeed.

On an individual level, coaching helps you preserve the core of what is good, unique, and special about a person. It enables you and your colleague to learn to have healthy conversations, to articulate and communicate with each other, and to align with each other around what is real and what is not and what is success and what is not.

What type of peer coach are you? What type of peer coach do you want to become? How do you set the tone for healthy conversations—ones that are open, honest, and candid? How can you have conversations that speak your truth and at the same time strengthen relationships with others? How can you help others grow and how can you nourish them and address issues that may be getting in the way?

Do Alone Exercise

Sometimes we can be our own coach. When you find you are thinking of others judgmentally, triggering your amygdala, you can transform your mental space and, through this shift, transform your environment.

Here are some questions to ask yourself that will challenge you to shift the energy in your mind from "judge" to "grow," from fear to possibility, from caution to courage. Remember: You set the tone.

1. **Building a strong culture:** To what extent and in what ways are your conversations setting a tone for collaboration and ongoing change, helping people see that they can contribute and participate in creating a great culture and great community?

2. **Communicating with honesty and trust:** To what extent and in what ways are your conversations setting the tone for open, honest communication, helping people learn how to express what they are feeling and helping the organization move from

being politically driven to respectful, supportive, direct, and open in all communications?

3. **Stretching to achieve new heights:** To what extent and in what ways are your conversations helping people move from giving up their dreams, setting small sights, and accepting the status quo to embracing exciting and challenging possibilities for creating outrageous futures?

4. **Mining for Best Practices:** To what extent and in what ways are your conversations setting a tone for cross-company sharing of information and exchanging of Best Practices; reducing the need to protect turf and supporting the need to break down silos; and testing the waters and pioneering uncharted territories?

5. **Generating new ways of thinking:** To what extent and in what ways are your conversations setting the tone to help people move from being stuck in the past—their old ways and old grooves—to being innovative and creative, leading to new ways to satisfy current customers and create new loyal customers?

Coach Yourself

Give yourself permission to be your own coach, or to find someone to coach you when you revert to your "default" setting. When you find yourself backsliding, use the following conversation:

I have been doing a great job of creating a new future.

I am making great progress and am changing the following things:_____, _____, and _____.

I am proud of myself for putting effort into these things: _____, _____, and _____.

In the future, I will do _____ instead of _____.

Then picture yourself doing _____ and celebrating your success.

6. **Taking a leadership stand:** To what extent and in what way are your conversations setting the tone for the next generation of leaders to be able to emerge and drive the enterprise forward? How are you teaching people ways to challenge authority, Groupthink, and consensus?

7. **Building enterprise spirit:** To what extent and in what ways are your conversations setting the tone for enterprise spirit and celebration, helping people move from a singular focus on "making the numbers" to seeking a higher purpose in contributing to the ongoing evolution of the enterprise and, most importantly, their own growth and ability to achieve higher and higher goals?

Coaching conversations help people achieve their highest aspirations, stretch themselves, and realize they can do more than they expected. Your role is critical. You set the tone by leaving behind judgment and believing in your colleagues' ability to grow and learn. As you review the next few pages, look for ways to coach yourself and others to higher levels of openness, creativity, and performance.

Try This!

When people peer coach, they learn from one another and are more apt to develop the higher-level skills and wisdom needed to meet the organization's performance goals. When we coach, we learn how to turn breakdowns (conflicts) into breakthroughs (new opportunities for mutual success)—we become high performing. When acting as a peer coach, there are a set of questions to guide you forward successfully. Keep in mind that the best coaches ask questions rather than give answers. As a peer coach, you can use coaching conversations to:

1. Discover Your Colleague's View of the World
Ask open-ended questions and then sit back and observe your colleague to see what she or he says and how. By listening carefully, you will learn more about how she views herself, her team, and the

organization. Listen to the words she uses to gain an insight into her world before you give advice.

2. Discover Your Colleague's View of Dynamic Relationships

During the coaching conversation, ask questions that draw specific situations out of your colleague, so that you can learn more about which relationships challenge her most and how she deals with them. She may describe some relationships as healthy with a lot of give-and-take, respect, and openness. In other cases, she may speak about an individual's flaws, lack of character, and skill, expressing her disappointment as she talks. Notice how she labels her frustration by labeling people who cause it for her.

3. Discover Your Colleague's Real Blind Spots

As your colleague's story unfolds and she enters a place in the story where she is most disappointed about a person or how a situation has transpired, she will become very emotional, her posture will shift, and she will take on a composure that may upset even you as the coach. Then you know you have found the "golden center"—a spot to enter with your colleague where she needs your insight as a coach because she is blind to a piece of reality.

4. Discover How to Reframe

At this moment, go inside the situation with your colleague as her coach and follow these four steps.

Step 1: Reflect the emotions.
You Say: You are incredibly angry at David. Your anger feels ____
_____ (scary, hurtful, aggressive . . .) to me. If I were David, I'd want to retreat from you.

Step 2: Call on the intention.
You Say: What where you hoping to accomplish with David? How did you want David to feel? What was the outcome you wanted to achieve?

Step 3: Reflect your experience of your colleague's impact.

You Say: At this moment, I am experiencing what David must have felt like. I can feel your emotion. It is powerful. It feels aggressive. I actually feel I need to be cautious with you right now. Are you aware that you project a very powerful and often aggressive energy when you are communicating about something that is important to you?

Step 4: Close the loop between intention and impact.

You Say: How could you communicate what's on your mind candidly without creating the reaction in David that you did? David is afraid to talk with you openly and honestly for fear you will jump down his throat. How else can you communicate with him to encourage him to see you as a collaborative leader who has his best interests in mind?

As an expert executive coach, you have learned how to be in the *real action* with your colleague—giving him a mirror to his words and actions in a way that will benefit him greatly. Rather than just talk about situations from a third-person perspective, you need to be in a coaching dialogue with your colleague that gets to the heart of the matter.

The heart of the matter is this: In almost all cases, a leader with blind spots is someone who has ego issues, gets caught in politics, uses inappropriate and inflammatory language that triggers defensive behaviors, and expresses herself in a "candid" yet inappropriate style.

One way you can change this dynamic is to use another person to help you vent and then prepare for straight talk with the person with whom you are having difficulty. I call this straight talk "Vital Conversations"—ways of using language to build, rather than weaken, relationships.

In Vital Conversations, we seek to partner with others, rather than protect ourselves. Moving intentionally from protect to partner means moving from I to WE in the most fundamental way, by using our most fundamental tool: language.

Practice Living in New Realities

Choose a situation in which you would like to have acted differently—where you may not have been at your best. Then respond to the following:

1. Imagine what "best" would look like. Remember yourself being at your best. Call up that memory in your mind as robustly as you can. Remember how you talked, how you felt, and how you spoke. Hold that vision and enjoy it.
2. Remember another person being at her best in a similar situation. How did she act. How did she speak? How did she impact others? Remember that image.
3. Envision yourself in that situation behaving in ways that create the outcomes you desire and that capture the way you need to look, feel, act, and speak.
4. Envision yourself in a movie being the way described in numbers 1 through 3.
5. Envision how others will respond to you.
6. Play the movie over and over, taking in the experience of being in that space in that way.
7. Find situations similar to the one you want to change.
8. Enter those situations in real life, bringing with you the memories of yourself being the way you want to be.
9. Enjoy the experience!
10. Share your positive experience with your teammates—people who care.
11. Think about it later and re-enjoy it. Talk about it and live it!

A Team Journey for Releasing and Letting Go

It can be healthy to create a break from the past—to launch a team of people into a new space of clean, fresh possibilities for the future. Here is a simple, yet effective, way to do it:

1. Create a vision of the future you would like to have together. Make the vision as real and as photographic as you can. Have people discuss the future with rich, vivid descriptions. You can even have people paint pictures, cut out pictures from magazines—whatever it takes to encourage a common view to emerge.

2. Create two walls: one marked "Releasing," and another that reads "Embracing." Have people write down what they would like to "Let Go of or Release" on Post-it notes and stick them on one wall. Then have them do the same for things they would like to "Embrace." Make half of the group responsible for interpreting and summarizing the "Let Go of" wall and the other half the group responsible for the "Embrace" wall. Share and discuss.

3. Option 2: A particularly powerful version of this exercise is to have people individually write on pieces of paper specific things they want to "Let Go of or Release." Create a circle ceremony in which all the team members get the opportunity to speak, into the team space, what it is they want to Let Go of (speaking into the space is helpful for releasing). Then they crumble up their written piece of paper and throw it into the center circle. This publicly releases the negativity.

4. Discuss what else needs to change to support the Embrace wall. This could set the stage for lots of expansive discussions on how to revitalize and reinvent your team, your organization, etc.

5. At the end of the exercise, each person will write up his or her own personal commitments for what they need to Let Go of and what they need to Embrace for the team to be successful.

6. Each person will find a partner and share his or her commitments with that person.

7. Agree to check on your partner every week to see how he or she is doing.

8. Support each other in the process. Be coaches.

How to Know When You are Creating WE!

How we use language causes us to either feel we need to protect ourselves or to partner with others. When we feel we need to protect ourselves, we become defensive, withdraw, retreat, cover up, or attack. When we are in an I-centric "protect" mode, we no longer think about protecting our brand or team, we think about protecting our self, turning to reactive behaviors aimed at avoiding being hurt. With this attitude, we abdicate our leadership, separate ourselves from our employees, and create a true leadership vacuum. WE-centric leadership brings us closer to others, enabling us to see the truth, to tackle real issues head-on, to build a mutually shared view of reality, and to create the future.

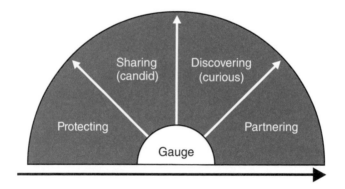

As you read through the next few pages, envision this Gauge in your mind. Observing interactions through this framework will enable you to make the invisible visible and will help you become more conscious of how you transform relationships through conversation. At any time, you can choose to communicate from either an I-centric or WE-centric point of view. Each has a dramatically different impact on outcomes. How well do you know where you are coming from? How well do you know the impact your words are having on others? How often are you coming from I when you really want to be coming from WE?

Protecting Conversations
PROTECT . . . What does protecting look like?

I-centric	WE-centric
Not speaking up; delivering a difficult message through someone else.	Delivering a difficult message directly, and asking questions to uncover important concerns.
Competing unhealthily with colleagues for growth opportunities.	Collaborating to establish growth opportunities for everyone.
Fear of making mistakes and taking risks.	Addressing the fears openly.
Avoiding a potential conflict by not speaking up or expressing your point of view.	Suggesting ways to positively disengage rather than avoid, so you can come back and discuss it later.
Fighting over resources.	Pushing back to create mutual clarity and understanding of what we can do together.
Acquiescing to someone with strong opinions and later getting angry about it.	Challenging yourself and others to think of alternatives rather than giving in.
Withholding important information that is critical to a division or team's success.	Giving and exchanging information for mutual benefit.

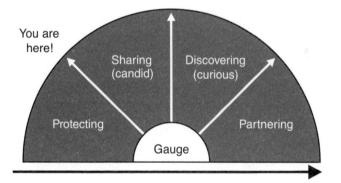

Interpretation: This Gauge suggests you are demonstrating protective behaviors with other colleagues and divisions, such as fighting over resources, withholding information, and avoiding having difficult conversations. You believe you are playing it safe; however, the impact is that you are coming across as negative and territorial.

Leadership Impact: You are creating territorialism, fear, and competition; are not perceived as collaborative; and are not a valued partner.

What positive impact will you experience by uplifting conversations to WE?
1. Less fear; 2. Less resistance; 3. More positive engagement

Candid Conversations
CANDID . . . What does candid look like?

I-centric	WE-centric
Criticizing others for failing to meet expectations.	Providing feedback; letting the person know your expectations and what you want and need.
Delivering a difficult message by being upset, angry, and in-your-face.	Being straightforward in delivering a difficult message.
Pushing your judgmental opinions on others; always being right.	Shifting from being right to sharing your perspective openly.
Being aggressively outspoken.	Sharing your honest feelings; sharing how you are feeling about the situation, challenges, or a person.
Being hurtfully frank.	Sensitively having difficult conversations.
Being insensitive and judgmental about the person.	Speaking about your feeling and how the situation has impacted you.
Thinking only you speak the truth; thinking that your feelings are facts.	Distinguishing fact from feelings and from opinion.

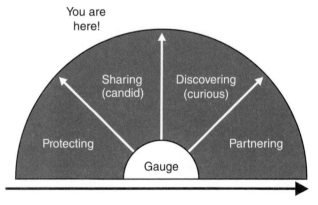

Interpretation: This Gauge suggests you are moving from protect to candid. You are experimenting with what candid is and is not, and have not yet figured it out. You believe you are being candid; however, you are, in reality, more often projecting judgment on others in the name of being honest with your feelings. You come across as very critical of others, often too frank, and sometimes aggressive.

Leadership Impact: You are creating fear, and while people respect your authority on the surface, they are talking behind your back. You are not giving clear directions, yet are expecting others to read your mind. You are not leveraging your talent.

What positive impact will you experience by uplifting conversations to WE?
1. Open two-way conversation; 2. People feeling "tough love" rather than just "tough"; 3. More positive engagement and influence

Curious Conversations
CURIOUS... What does curious look like?

I-centric	WE-centric
Only experimenting in your Comfort Zone.	Breaking out of your Comfort Zone.
Thinking about only what's important to you.	Asking what's important to others and not judging them for having different values than you.
Probing aggressively for what's on people's minds.	Spending more time listening and asking open-ended questions.
Investigating the situation with the goal of finding blame.	Discovering the difference between facts and opinions.
Scrutinizing, questioning, and doubting what you hear.	Questioning from a state of wonder and appreciation.
Caring about and exploring only your own perspective.	Open to influence and to other's perspectives.
Curious tenacity about your position.	Being more open to changing your mind.

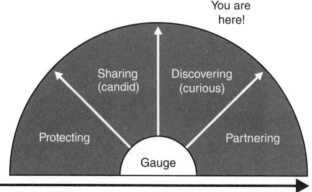

Interpretation: This Gauge suggests you are stepping into WE-centric behaviors. Others see you as curious, open, honest, and candid. You are focusing on creating energy and excitement around the brand. Sometimes, however, you mistake curiosity and probing; sometimes people feel interrogated, and sometimes you send others back into a protect mode. You really want to build high levels of trust and openness to create mutual success.

Leadership Impact: You are moving toward creating a healthy, thriving workplace with a high level of trust and mutual support.

What positive impact will you experience by uplifting conversations to WE?
1. We learn, grow, and nourish each other; 2. We harvest wisdom in ourselves and others; 3. We become open to testing, experimenting, learning, and risk-taking

Partnering Conversations
Partner . . . What does partnering look like?

I-centric	WE-centric
Forcing compliance to a vision.	Inspiring inclusion, engagement, and commitment.
Forcing consensus and agreement without accepting pushback.	Building support for new ideas to emerge, and allowing lots of pushback to get there.
Assuming and forcing alignment when little exists.	Engaging in lots of "open space" discussions to discover agreement and catalyze new thinking.
Coercing others to your point of view, or sending signals of great disappointment when others show disagreement with you.	Seeking ways we can join forces and include many points of view, many options, many alternatives.
Pretending to agree to avoid conflict; then talking up your ideas behind the scenes, gaining support for what you want to do.	Creating a space for sharing disagreements, exploring the ideas behind them, opening up new ways of thinking.
Giving in to someone so he will stop arguing or disagreeing; supporting the Groupthink mentality.	Pushing back, because you decide it's important to disagree. Opening the space to experimenting with options.
Hiding issues under the table to avoid being challenged, speaking up, and telling the truth.	Putting issues on the table to harvest insights and wisdom, and to gain support and help from others.

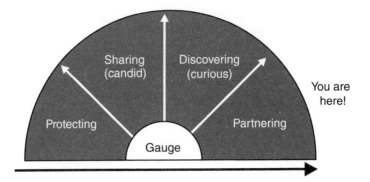

Interpretation: This Gauge suggests that you are demonstrating a high level of partnering behaviors, including seeking ways to include lots of employees in decisions, and encouraging pushback. However, at times you are getting frustrated with the amount of engagement and you turn to giving orders or pushing for alignment when you want immediate action. You want to practice being less coercive.

Leadership Impact: You are working on creating an inspired workplace where employees can anticipate and work on critical challenges. Work with your coach to get clarity on what partnering looks like.

What positive impact will you experience by uplifting conversations to WE?
1. New opportunities and ideas flood in for everyone;   2. We discover the world of resources is bigger than we ever imagined;   3. We create win/wins

The Map Is Not the Territory

Often, we fall back into territorial I-centric thinking because we dislike confrontation. Confrontation comes from a variety of places:

- Confronting the fact that your expectations will not be met.
- Confronting a challenging situation that you thought you could tackle, only to find out you are not equipped.
- Confronting a colleague who has failed to deliver when you needed him most.
- Confronting your own mistakes made in front of others (confronting embarrassment).
- Confronting your own lackluster performance as a leader.

Confronting the truth takes courage. Yet, it doesn't have to be confrontational. Instead, it can become a process based on learning, growing, and nourishing yourself and others. Confrontation can become something to look forward to. It requires putting into place a new platform for dialogue about what is—our current reality—and what could be—our future possibilities. In this process, we address with others what works and what doesn't work so that we can shape and craft the future we want together—we define what good looks like and we step into that new vision.

When fear of confrontation generalizes into fear of communication, it stops us from communicating many things that may be important for us to be discussing. When we avoid communicating because we don't want to hear what someone has to say or we imagine potential conflicts with our position on an issue, we lose out on shaping and crafting the future. We bury the issues rather than discuss them openly, or we complain to others not directly involved in solving the challenge. When we do this, we become the enemy. In so doing, we fail to engage in the essence of WE-centric leadership.

WE-centric leaders can see the endgame before it happens, and courageously set the context for difficult discussions to take place. Especially when there is a potential for conflict, they create a healthy environment where colleagues can work through difficult challenges.

As a result, they help develop their colleagues' skills for navigating challenges, for turning breakdowns into breakthroughs, and for growing the business in exciting and previously unimaginable ways.

By reframing (or relanguaging) the context of a conflict into a "shared and mutual" experience, the WE-centric leader fosters honest communication, sets high and clear expectations, and encourages colleagues to openly face tough issues. Using these skills turns territorial conflicts into business breakthroughs.

Monitor yourself and see how you're doing as a leader. Audit your conversations every day. What context are you creating? Opportunities abound in the workplace every day to create WE, and you don't have to wait until a team-building off-site meeting to ensure that happens. The key to your success will be to identify these critical moments, make a choice, and create a powerful shift. In doing so, you create WE and shift your culture from living in a world of probabilities to living in a robust world of possibility!

Two Different Worlds:
Are You an I-centric or a WE-centric Leader?

As a leader, you will discover new wisdom in this process. Keep in mind that the key to transforming culture is to develop a keen sensitivity to how conversations influence outcomes. Do your conversations push you away from others or bring you closer?

As you interact, reflect on your intention behind your communication and how that is reflected in your choice of words, your positioning, and context setting. Become aware of what influences the way colleagues think about what is going on, and the meaning they are left with. The way you shape and craft conversations creates the images that others take away, the memories they recall, and the feelings they experience.

Imagine that you have the power to influence others dramatically by how you communicate. If you believe that you are in competition, you will speak competitively. If you believe you are in collaboration, you will speak collaboratively.

Below are some examples of the difference between I-centric and WE-centric conversations. Each is about the same situation; however, the impact of each response has a dramatically different influence on the outcomes of a situation and a relationship.

Example 1: Giving and Receiving Feedback

Feedback is vital for us to know how to navigate with each other. Feedback helps us shift our direction and adjust our course of action. Too often leaders use "criticism" rather than feedback to adjust behavior or to shift a conversation.

PROTECT: Criticism	PARTNER: Feedback
"What's wrong with you? You never get your reports in on time. I don't think you get it!"	"When your report got to me at 5:30, I did not have the time to review it before it had to go to the client. In the future, you need to give me at least two hours to review the report so I can read and understand your ideas and suggestions. Then we can talk about it and we can make any necessary changes before the client sees it. What are your suggestions about this?"
(High level of protect; very candid with a lack of sensitivity for the impact on the person.)	*(Low level of protect; some candor with positive intent; midlevel curiosity and high partnering with a sensitivity for the impact on the person.)*
Possible Impact?	Possible Impact?

Example 2: Conversations That Open or Close Space

In the workplace, people sometimes spend more time defending suggestions and ideas than developing bigger and better ideas together. When the leader operates defensively, she reinforces more territorial behaviors in others. How can you open the space for discovery?

PROTECT: Close Space	PARTNER: Open Space
"You need to improve the customer service process. I'm not happy with what you've been doing so I've developed an approach that everyone has to use. Here it is."	"Let's take the idea Charlie came up with as a start for redesigning the customer service process. His approach is a good start for improving our overall approach. Harry suggested we increase the time we spend on specific types of customer issues. What else do you think would make this process become more responsive to the customer? What would happen if we took Karen's idea, and merged it with Peter's suggestion? What if we did nothing? What if . . . . . ."
Possible Impact?	Possible Impact?

Example 3: Conversations That Create Fear or Build Trust

What is the end result you want to create—fear or trust?

PROTECT: Causes Fear	PARTNER: Builds Trust
"The word is out on the street that we're on the chopping block. None of our leaders are addressing the issues and we all know we're in trouble. They keep saying it's just a sign of the times. I wonder how bad it really is?"	"The Town Meeting we had was the best I've ever been to. When the CEO presented the state of the business, he gave us clear examples of the challenges we are facing and how they impact our future revenues. He didn't pretend it would all go away. He was honest and tried to paint a picture of the truth. I'm more confident in our future because it means we can all talk openly about what we need to do to change the picture."
Possible Impact?	Possible Impact?

Example 4: Conversations for Creating Expectations of the Future

What message are you sending your employees?

What is the subtext?

PROTECT: Creates Defensiveness	PARTNER: Builds Support and Trust
"You were late with the report. I expect you to be better prepared than you are. I'm disappointed in you for not delivering."	"The deadline for this report is next Friday, close of business. I expect you to get your part of it to me by Thursday at noon so that I can give it the final touches. Is there anything you need from me to support you? Is there anything preventing you from making that commitment firm?"
Possible Impact?	Possible Impact?

Example 5: Conversations for Having Difficult Discussions Easily

We all like to succeed. Rarely does someone fail on purpose. Yet when the business is in a downturn and old strategies have failed to achieve the desired results, it is not unusual for people to look to blame someone else. Facing a difficult situation head-on with those involved requires a healthy acceptance of personal responsibility and the ability to have tough conversations with others.

PROTECT: Blame	PARTNER: Accountability
"Our business is eroding. I'm sure if our salespeople were better at their jobs, we'd have the cash flow we need to invest in new projects. Go talk to marketing and see if they are having the same problems with the sales force. Then let me know."	"Our business is eroding. Let's take a look at what's happening in the marketplace and see how we stack up. Then let's get together with our sales and marketing teams and strategize on how we can approach the market differently."
Possible Impact?	Possible Impact?

WE-aving It All Together

Words can serve as swords to fight others or as gifts to celebrate our shared success. Conversations contain words that can be seeds for growth and development. We bring to our conversations all the meanings we've collected from our past interactions with people. We transfer meanings from each situation to the next and from person to person. And we label them as friend or foe sometimes without much history to back it up. By carrying baggage into relationships, we often exacerbate issues—far beyond reason. Turning to colleagues for coaching conversations enables us to learn to Let Go of and release emotions that may be getting in the way of Creating WE.

We can change how our minds, hearts, and bodies react to situations around us by creating a feedback-rich culture in which we surround ourselves with opportunities to talk with others about what's on our minds. Living in a feedback-rich culture, we are constantly surrounded by people who we can turn to as colleagues to help us learn and grow, help us check out our strategies, and help us become broader, more expansive leaders and thinkers.

Having feedback-rich conversations with peers enables us to adjust and readjust our course of action so we ultimately hit our targets. Feedback provides us with a control mechanism to check out where we are "really" and to navigate our world successfully. Some people use the word *cybernetic* to describe it; it's a back and forth of information used to guide us to our targets. When the cybernetic loop is broken, we can be like a boat in rough seas without a way to find our way home.

Without that rich feedback we lose our way, we get stressed, we lose confidence, and we miss our targets. Feedback helps us adjust ourselves and our sights and is part of our navigational process for achieving our goals.

Coaching conversations enable us to inspire growth and learning and develop colleagues. They are a form of rich feedback for those involved in the process—and for the coach. Learning to coach colleagues is more than essential. It is the missing link in creating cultures in which colleagues are in sync with each other and are able to bring their best wisdom to work every day.

Are You Up for the Challenge?

Empowering your team to achieve goals and strategies requires flexibility of thought, agility of mind, and speed of response. Most of all, it requires you to break out of old conversational habits and negative patterns of communicating and view the impact you can have on your business in totally new ways. Use conversations as a way to break from the past and create the future. Rather than thinking about situations as problems, think of them as challenges and opportunities, and communicate this point of view in your conversations with others. Until you challenge yourself to change old thinking and old conversational habits, you will see little change from yesterday to today. Without changing how you approach your challenges, no new corporate strategy will ever achieve the desired results or hit the expected targets.

Constructing Your Future

In the chart on the following page, you'll find examples of constructive and destructive conversations. Understanding which you are having at any moment with a colleague gives you a heightened ability to create WE in the moment. As you become more conscious of the language you choose, you will find yourself choosing words that have a positive impact. Coaching each other on how we communicate enables us to remove potential blind spots. Contracting with others for that relationship gives you the permission and the ability to learn, grow, and nourish each other on an ongoing basis.

Vital Conversations

Conversations Are Limiting or Expanding!

Dimension	Protect	Partner
Co-creating *BE ON A WINNING TEAM*	Conversations about how we compete against one another; when we have issues with each other, we hold on to grudges and don't forgive, reinforcing negative perceptions.	Conversations about how we work together to support each other in our growth and challenging activities; we strive to compete against our own last success; we Let Go of grudges quickly. *Attention:* Pay attention to sharing and creating success stories.
Humanizing *VALUED AND RESPECTED*	Conversations that limit how much we give and receive from one another; shallow levels of listening; complaining about being let down and others not coming through.	Conversations that focus on appreciation of one another; expanding how much we can contribute to each other's success; conversations about value, respect, and the power of relationships. *Attention:* Pay attention to the quality of your relationships.
Optimizing *DREAM*	Conversations about fear and obstacles and limitations that focus on what is not possible and why, justifying a limited view of reality.	Conversations that focus on making the impossible possible; how to remove any impediments to success; how to accomplish the unimaginable. *Attention:* Pay attention to how to open up "possibility thinking."
Interacting *EXPLORE AND LEARN*	Conversations about how we can never find the people we need with the talent we need; "if we only had" conversations, focusing on recurring unsolved problems.	Conversations that focus on appreciation of one another; expanding how much we can contribute to each other's success; conversations about value, respect, and the power of relationships. *Attention:* Pay attention to boundaries you may be setting; be open to unlocking them.

(continued)

Vital Conversations (continued)

Conversations Are Limiting or Expanding!

Dimension	Protect	Partner
Catalyzing *CREATE AND INNOVATE*	Conversations about how we can't seem to come up with new ideas, products, or services; conversations about how the competition has the edge.	Conversations that focus on catalyzing one another's best ideas, turning bad ideas into good ideas, stimulating our best thinking. *Attention:* Pay attention to harvesting ideas from seed-thinking to implementation.
Expressing *HAVE A LEADERSHIP VOICE*	Conversations about titles, hierarchy, who has power and why; shallow focus on "superficial qualities" rather than deep insight; positional power.	Conversations that focus on tapping each person's unique voice and wisdom; conversations that level the playing field so everyone's voice counts. *Attention:* Pay attention to how you reinforce contributions and nurture unique points of view.
Synchronizing *PURPOSE AND MEANING*	Conversations about compliance and avoidance of change.	Conversations that focus on continual transformation and growth. *Attention:* Pay attention to how you help people see and connect to the broader meaning and purpose.

8.

Friend or Foe?

Transforming the Culture

*Handle them carefully, for words have more
power than atom bombs.*
PEARL STRACHAN, AUTHOR

STORYTELLING, LIKE THE WORDS WE USE, comes naturally to human beings. It's how we share with others what we are seeing, feeling, and sensing inside. Storytelling is, in essence, our view of reality. Storytelling begins as an I-centric capability enabling us to state and often defend our point of view. In organizational life, storytelling shapes the way we view the world individually and collectively, and it can have positive or negative consequences for the health of the enterprise. Learning how to shift from an I to a WE perspective in the stories we tell is essential to organizational health and growth.

We create stories based on our point of view—based on our function, our title, our respective level in the hierarchy. "Where we sit" can determine "where we stand." Because we each see the world through our respective lenses of experience and beliefs, it's not hard to understand how colleagues engaged in different functions or operating within different environments—even within the same organization—can come to tell their stories about the enterprise from the vantage points of their own separate silos.

Stories have villains and heroes. Stories are designed to protect our egos from harm. If someone else causes me to feel bad, then it wasn't *my* fault—it was *theirs*. If someone judges me unfairly, he is a bad boss, and I'm the good employee. When we get criticized, we criticize back.

This chapter helps you see how our *stories* determine the relationship we have with others—friend or foe. It will, most importantly, give you insights and skills for transforming a relationship, a team, or potentially the future of your business by how you tell the story. This chapter enables you to break old storytelling habits and learn new ways to use this essentially human skill to create a WE-centric organization.

Telling Stories

Power is established through our conversations—and mostly our storytelling with others. Stories shape our sense of the world, our relationships, and our future. Stories communicate our aspirations, our hopes, our intentions, and our beliefs. Most importantly, stories convey the hopes and dreams we hold in our minds about the reality we believe we are living in or want to live in.

We tell our stories all day long. We tell them to customers, to colleagues, and to our friends and family. But the person we tell our stories to most of all is ourself.

Stories You Tell Yourself

All day long, you have the most incredible ability to self-talk. You can be your own best supporter and you can be your own best critic. You can coach yourself through a tough situation, or in the same conversation you can beat yourself up and sabotage yourself so badly that you dive into deep depression or take it out on unsuspecting others.

In your self-talk, you subconsciously interpret what is going on around you by using stored beliefs to draw conclusions about your life at any given moment. That is how your mind works. Your stories are self-referential "home movies" about how well you are making out in life, who is doing what to you, and how you feel about it. You are also your own casting director—you can cast yourself as hero or villain.

Human beings have the power and ability to make up dramatic stories with any conceivable ending. Our stories can portray a future full of promise and accomplishment or one that is dark and empty. It's all stuff we first make up and then come to believe. Once we believe our story, we live it out the way we visualize it in our minds. Like it or not, we are storytellers. Our main audience is us, and our life develops from the stories we create. In other words, if we wake up one morning to discover that our finances have been wiped out because we purchased a bad stock, our story could become that we are a loser and stupid, or we could tell a story of our ability to take risks and go after the Big One. Our stories influence how we see ourselves and how we approach the life challenges that come next. Stories can empower or disempower our life journey.

From a business point of view, if not properly recognized and managed for its impact, I-centric storytelling can:

- Pollute the reality of what is really going on.
- Create bad office drama, played out as paranoia and gossip.
- Become a form of deadly self-sabotage for people who believe their own self-inflicted negative dramas.
- Create a false reality in which coworkers learn to seriously doubt your judgment and their own.

Stories consist of actors and actions. We give our stories drama, built around characters that we take from real life or we make up. Stories have bad guys and good guys.

When we think of others as adversaries—as bad guys—we label them in our minds as such and act toward them accordingly. Even if we have little experience with a person, labeling her or him an adversary gives us the ability to go inside our mental vault, draw out experiences that we have had with other similar adversaries, and project them onto this person. Instantly, the person has a history, a legacy, and a persona—most of which we have made up.

When we think of others as adversaries, we treat them as such. When we think of others as failures, we treat them as such. When we think of someone as a failure, we create a negative aura around that person and the aura is all we see when we interact with her. When we think of someone as successful, we create a positive aura around her and treat her as if she could do no wrong, overlooking every mistake she makes or rationalizing it away. Words define how we will react toward others even before we, or they, open our mouths.

The Story of Sara and Dave

Dave Shipley, a senior consultant in a large consulting firm, had a reputation for ranking out other consultants in public, and he did so quite severely one day to Sara, who was a newer senior consultant of lower rank. Sara brought in a report they were working on together to go over some data. The minute she walked into his office, he started to complain and caustically criticize her for her "poor" work habits. Sara was mortified. Rather than handle Dave by assertively confronting him about his inappropriate behavior, she withdrew and acquiesced. To Sara, who was wounded by Dave's caustic aggressive language, Dave was now a bad guy and Sara was a victim. "Sara the Victim" and "Dave the Bad Guy" are the kinds of labels that we attach to people and see every time we observe them, hear them, and think of them.

And, of course, our labels get in the way of our understanding why a person acts the way she or he does. Labels are permanent filters for the truth. They block new data from our consciousness and keep us locked in our mental closets. Dave may be coming from a territorial mode—feeling threatened by the loss of something he expected to achieve. Sara may be coming from her own survival mode—feeling threatened and scared by the incident. She may even go to others to seek healing for her wounds. In both cases, they are creating new, emotionally charged meanings to fuel the drama in their stories.

They are storing up new memories with interpretations that may, in the near future, negatively impact the success that each of them will have with each other, or with others on their teams. Both Dave and Sara are building up negative interpretations about each other. They are storing up "stuff" that will come out in their environment in unexpected forms, making it toxic not just for themselves, but for others. It's like secondary smoke; the smoker is not intending to cause cancer in others, yet that is the unintended consequence.

Meaning develops through our conversations with others, and at the heart of most conversations are stories. Stories are a primary "currency" for entering each other's space of intimacy. We exchange stories about who did what to us and, in so doing, invite others into our story. We recount how we received our wounds and we hope for a compassionate response. By contrast, if we use transformational stories, we are able to free ourselves of the past and embrace the future. Letting Go of old stories releases energy that is bound up in feelings of the past and creates new patterns of behavior that positively impacts relationships in our environment—it transforms culture.

Diva Is Spelled with an *I*

Dana was a diva. She began her own real estate company with the help of investors who believed she had a great idea. They funded part of her company because they were convinced it would be worth millions someday and they wanted part of the action. They also contributed a few hundred acres of land for her to sell. Within a short time, she had not only sold the land but had also established a ten-person company. Thanks to her feel for real estate, Dana could accurately predict which parts of town would be the next hot areas. She knew how to create excitement for a construction project, and she was able to get sellers their asking prices. In short order, Dana's business had grown considerably and so had her reputation.

Dana was also extremely attractive and wore beautiful designer clothing. She got invited onto boards, which attracted lots of famous people to her door. Women came to her office asking to work with her and train with her. She could pick whomever she wanted, and she chose carefully. Her first office was such a success that she opened a second one on the other side of town. She bought a full-size Mercedes and required her people to lease them as well. From among her best salespeople, she chose the three she wanted to manage her offices. They were off and running—until the fifth year.

By then, Dana had become restless and wanted to change the focus of her business. She wanted to attract the rich and famous to her real estate offices and mix with them socially. She gave big parties for her customers, some of whom became her friends. In return, she would get the opportunity to sell their houses when they wanted to move.

She looked down on customers who couldn't afford multimillion-dollar houses. Since she spent all her time with her customers, they were the people she wanted to be like—and she wanted them to like her. But not all of her brokers could keep up with her. As her career evolved, she scorned the brokers who couldn't sell successfully to the rich and famous. This scorn did not always manifest as overt criticism, but her staff could tell when she didn't like them. She would "forget" to send someone an e-mail to join her at an important meeting or to let that employee know where to go for a special showing.

When a broker took a long time to close a deal, she asked her to take a lower commission, and she would lash out, telling the broker that she didn't have it in her to sell houses. She decided to pit one of her offices against the other to win a big vacation prize for selling the most houses. Because she favored some brokers over others and funneled the business to them, this was not a fair contest and she clearly revealed her double standard.

Her offices started to manifest internal problems, which were made even more serious because Dana was never around to provide direction and guidance. She delegated many responsibilities and, when people did things differently from what she wanted, she criticized them in front of others. At first, people didn't want to criticize her because of her incredible reputation and her ability to attract such important people. Others, even though less impressed, were afraid to be the ones to initiate conversation about office problems. It reached a point where Dana cared more about whomever she was going out with that week than if her payroll was covered, and her employees were afraid to speak up because she always overreacted.

Dana's Story

"I'm so disappointed with my people. I am trying to build this business and they just don't have what it takes. Don't people see the opportunities I see? Don't they understand that you have to keep pushing and networking to make it happen? I keep challenging them to produce. They just don't have it."

Her Staff's Story

"Dana is a social climber. When she starts a relationship, she loves you and she thinks you walk on water. Then you fall from heaven and you are treated like you are worthless. She is so self-centered—she doesn't really care about the office. I used to think she was a mover and shaker and I used to admire her, but she is self-absorbed and treats us like we are invisible."

A Blind Spot in Dana's Foggy Rearview Mirror

Dana looked in the mirror and loved herself in public and in private. She didn't recognize that the problems in her offices were connected to her lack of leadership. She was so busy thinking about her own interests, so caught up in telling her I-centric story again and again, that she failed to see the impact she was having on others. She didn't see that the competition she set up among her employees caused people to backstab and attempt to steal one another's listings. It reached this point because she didn't bring her separate offices together and the employees never had a chance to work out their conflicts in a civil, face-to-face manner. Focused as she was on her own prestige and social status rather than on the survival of her business, she did not realize that the business was in jeopardy.

Brokers began to leave her office. The exodus began when she asked a few of them not to discuss details on a specific land listing.

She didn't want the new buyers to know about some "loopholes" in the negotiation that would favor the seller down the road. Her brokers were appalled by this behavior. The land was sold. Soon, her brokers talked to one another behind her back and learned a lot more about her than she wanted people to know. Of the thirty brokers she had, twenty departed for other agencies within a three-month period. By the end of the year, she had to close up shop!

So, What's Your Story?

If you were Dana, how would you have handled the growth challenges? How would you have communicated about the situation, after the fact, to others? How would you have synopsized the details? Would you have described the dynamics? Given "life" to the characters involved? Interpreted the motivations of others? Related the outcomes? Created a call to action? These are the elements that make up a story. We "make up" or "choose to tell" most of the stories we tell based on our view of what happened. What story would you have told? If you were one of her agents, how would you have handled Dana, other than leave the company? What story would you have told?

Our stories either build or break down relationships with others. At work, we interact with others and we hope create networks and build alliances. Dana understood that to be successful, she needed to build networks. But once she created those networks, she also had to cultivate, manage, and harvest them. She had to realize that her offices were connected and everything she or her brokers said or did was visible—even if it was supposedly done or said in a vacuum. There is no vacuum in business. Once we break trust, we create a ripple effect in our network that can quickly turn into a fatal spiral, as Dana discovered.

Every day in any business, there are a million interactions that will create either a positive or a negative dynamic among people. While these interactions may seem small, they begin to add up to a larger pattern. We are either spiraling up or down. We are either building a stronger sense of I or a stronger sense of WE. Dana had been strengthening her positional power (it was all about her) and had been failing to strengthen and harvest relationships with others—most importantly, her staff. Thus, she failed to put the growth of her business center stage. The kind of stories she believed and told were a reflection of her I-centric point of view.

As executives and leaders, we must continually face these two fundamental dynamics throughout our careers—the pull to protect I and the pull to create WE. Regardless of the challenge, the change, the size of your company, or your geography, these dynamics will be ever-present and will determine whether the real-world story of your business endeavors ends in success or failure.

The Leader as Storyteller-in-Chief

The true leader is one who steps down from the throne and, in so doing, puts the enterprise center stage, opening up the space for the birth of a WE-centric mindset that everyone participates in creating.

If the old I-centric leadership model is about power and con-trol—directing and delegating, power from the top—the WE-centric leadership model is about inclusiveness and solving organizational problems together.

On the surface it's easy to gravitate to a leadership style in which we wield *power over* others. Yet, as we take on a leadership role, we invariably discover that those who transform the world have sophis-ticated skills that empower others without giving away control. This is not an impossible feat. It is the challenge you face every day.

Think of yourself as the Storyteller-in-Chief with a special responsibility to tell the WE story of your team *to* your team. Keep in mind that, at a deep, cellular level, the act of storytelling is an expression of your Vital Instincts to Partner. The conversations that convey your stories and the words that fuel them can either tilt toward I in the form of a self-protective myth (the toxic territorial response) or toward WE in the form of a positive tale of collective success—a story that imparts energy and inspires innovation. As the leader, it's up to you to choose and shape the kind of story you will tell and the kind of future you will make possible.

A Story Gains Power As It's Passed Along

Michael was an executive vice president and a reflective leader. Most of his business career focused on strategy and operations in consumer goods companies. Big and strong, he looked like he could pin down anyone on the mat. By his appearance alone he conjured up fear in his staff. Those who were fearful of him made up stories about what he was like as a person. When he was on a mission he looked stern, although he didn't realize that. He was intense about reaching his goals, and people assumed he was angry with them.

Whenever Michael took on a new project or position, he always began in high control and projected decisiveness. His rationale was that he wanted his team to start out on the right track. The reality was that he had clear ideas about where he wanted to go, and he wanted to make sure people got there. In the beginning, his approach was so fierce that people were afraid to try new things or do things another way, lest he become angry.

My job as his coach and consultant was to help him understand the impact he was having on his colleagues and direct reports. With his challenging way of communicating, Michael engendered fear. He was a micromanager and, in response, people became angry at being so overcontrolled. To be a Vital Leader, one who understood how to create healthy environments, Michael needed to learn to connect his intention with his impact.

Once his team was up and running—and with some periodic coaching about how to shift from creating "follower-ship" to "fellow-ship"—Michael discovered how to let go of control, thereby making room for his people room to grow. Most importantly, he learned how to shift his focus from I-Centric to WE-centric in the stories he told. Just as his behavior had an impact on how others felt, so did his stories, and Michael was about to learn to make that distinction. Michael wanted to drive his team to breakthroughs so they could achieve the corporate goals and become a highly interdependent team. The business expected a lot from the team, and Michael did, too. In order to shoot for and achieve extraordinary results, he had to ensure that his communication, and his storytelling, motivated his team to stretch and reach well beyond what they envisioned they could do. If his storytelling only moved the team to compliance, Michael would get average performance at best. He needed to create a mental shift in what everyone thought was possible.

Example:

I-centric Approach: "I want you to make sure you achieve your numbers. Last month you were underperforming. This month I want you to do better." (This is pure punishment for perceived failure; it's de-motivating and smacks of "please the boss, please.")

WE-centric Approach: "We have such big challenges ahead. We've climbed mountains together in the past, and we'll do it again."

(Michael framed his story in a WE-centric way, rallying his team to achieve great heights and letting them know "we are all in this together.")

Sometimes situations get us upset, challenges seem too big, and we can't get our mind around a WE-centric approach to our communications. One such day came along for Michael. He was upset by an e-mail from a direct report, in which he complained that his team was not able to produce the projected increase of 1 million units of a product. This was a major problem, since the company's reputation was built on its ability to respond to customer demand as rapidly as possible. Jack, the direct report, had shifted into a victim posture by venting and complaining. He was defensive and self-protective.

And, as senior employee, he was in a position to influence the thoughts, feelings, and beliefs of many other employees. Michael recognized that Jack was on the edge. There were several different ways Michael could have responded to Jack. He could have used a punishing style and told Jack that he was failing to meet his standards. Or, he could have responded aggressively and simply taken control. Instead, Michael decided to let go of his usual controlling nature and tell a different story to Jack. He sent the following e-mail to his troubled senior employee: "I am so proud of you and your team. Every time we face another challenge to the business, you figure out a way to deliver. This last-minute order came from the fact that our strategy is really working and customers are responding. Your team's ability to make this happen again is what will help us beat the competition head-on. I am so proud of what you are doing and I trust you will motivate your team to figure this one out."

The next day, Jack called his team together. Michael was in the back of the room listening and had no idea of how it would go. Jack sat everyone down for an emergency meeting. He took his place in the front of the room, and everyone became silent. They looked at his face to see whether they should be upset, afraid, or ready.

Jack told the story Michael told him. He let the team know they had made incredible strides that year and achieved amazing results. Business was up and customers were happy. In fact, customers were so happy with the products that demand was out of sight! He told them that they had a great challenge in front of them, one that would require the team to think through new ways to get more products to market quickly. He told them he had complete faith that they could do it.

In that one moment, the team shifted from reactive to proactive, from angry to challenged, from fearful to empowered, from status quo to raising the bar. A dramatic, visible shift had taken place—the shift from I-centric to WE-centric.

Whenever we are faced with the challenge of change, whether they are good challenges such as the ones Michael and Jack faced, or those that appear more daunting and impossible such as losing huge market share to a competitor, we are actually facing the biggest challenge of all—how to talk to ourselves and others about what's happening.

The stories we tell shape the way we respond. How you frame the challenge determines whether or not your team will feel empowered and believe they can climb any mountain, or instead feel they will be crushed and unable to fight back. You are the leader. You influence others by your thoughts, your beliefs, and the stories you tell.

Stay on Track: Don't Get Derailed!

Michael successfully resisted the impulse to respond to Jack from the I-centric place that had become his Comfort Zone. He was able to tell a WE-centric story and was dramatically rewarded. In the earlier story, however, Dana never did change her story and her business collapsed. Dana was derailed. How can you navigate your Leadership Journey to a WE-centric future without derailing?

Leaders derail for three reasons that relate back to one of our Instincts:

1. They fail to manage their own reactive behaviors, become overly aggressive and controlling.
2. They fail to build mutual relationships with others, make others wrong, and trigger WE/THEY behaviors.
3. They place themselves rather than the company's future in the center, and appear to be out for their own self-interest.

Derailer Number One: Authority

Leaders fail when they do not manage their own reactive behaviors. We all react to emotional triggers and that is part of what makes us human. But to succeed we need to learn how to transform our own reactive behavior into proactive behavior and lead from a place of positive power, not negative power. Without control over our own reactions, we become carriers of potentially lethal negativity.

Examples:

- Leaders who react to conflict by avoiding it instead of learning to deal with it properly.
- Leaders who react to fear with aggression rather than by being assertive.
- Leaders who react to power struggles by acquiescing, rather than by direct confrontation.

Question: Are you a leader who fails to manage your own reactive behaviors?

Answer: Make challenges visible and encourage colleagues to work on them together.

Imagine what it would be like if you learned how to make challenges more visible and explicit. Instead of simply reacting to protect yourself, you would send up the "red flags" of concern, alerting the "immune system" of your culture to come in to play and quell the potential threat and preserve organizational health. You would be focusing your energy, and everyone else's, on what it would take to succeed. You would be creating signals that everyone could use to manage reactivity and quell threats before they created havoc.

Derailer Number Two: Territorialism

Leaders who fail to build mutual relationships will not succeed. Leaders who appear to be manipulating others to serve their own ends—to abet their own growth at the expense of others—will create a backlash and lose both trust and respect. When you are cut off from others, you fail to grow. You become more self-centered, potentially arrogant, and mindless of others' needs.

Examples:

- Leaders who exhort employees to work hard and then take all the credit.
- Leaders who promise promotions to get employees to work harder and conveniently forget the promise.
- Leaders who fall into self-deception, lie, cheat, steal, and deny their role in negative business results.

Question: Are you a leader who fails to build mutual relationships with others?

Answer: Create a feedback-rich culture.

Imagine what it would be like if you learned how to create a culture in which relationships were mutually supportive based on giving and receiving rich feedback for growth and development. Instead of growing at the expense of others, you and they would all grow together.

Derailer Three: Self-Interest

Sometimes leaders become incredibly focused on their own agendas and on creating their own success. When it becomes clear to others that these leaders are looking out only for themselves, they lose the support of the very people who can help get them to their next leadership level, not to mention help them succeed. Eventually, their failure to consider the organization's goals and objectives, not just their own, will eventually become obvious to their boss and that will usually precipitate their downfall. Most of all, focusing on past successes keeps us in the past and dries up the pools of nourishment—the new ideas and the energy so critical for business success.

Examples:

- Leaders who encourage employees to hide information from other departments because it makes their department look better.
- Leaders who promote their own division's work to gain attention from the top brass, knowing it will make others look bad.
- Leaders who are constantly acting or speaking in a self-serving way in public.

Question: Are you a leader who places yourself rather than the company's future in the center?
Answer: Reach out and create a nourishing, expansive environment.

Imagine what it would be like if you learned to shift from an I-centric to a WE-centric point of view. Rather than turning inside and only recognizing your success, you would reach outside and focus on bringing nourishment from and to others. Through this focus on outward and forward thinking, you and others would share Best Practices, wisdom, and insight. You would engage in learning and growing, and you could harvest growth and prosperity.

Managing these three potential derailers is the key to your success. Too often executive coaches are called in to work with senior executives who do not get along with others, are out to achieve their own agendas, and are so reactive that they create harm. By the time the coaches arrive, these executives have already created great havoc in their wake.

If you, as an executive and leader, learn to manage your own reactions, learn how to put your ego behind you, and learn how to build healthy, open relationships with others, your ability to drive your organization to success will increase exponentially.

Try This!

Ask yourself:

1. What are the top three leadership challenges facing our organization/team now?

   _____

   _____

   _____

   _____

2. What is the most vital issue?

   _____

3. What is the impact on me and others?
   - Of not doing anything? _____
   - Of doing something? _____

4. What are the future implications?
   - If it is not addressed? _____
   - If it is addressed? _____

5. What is the desired outcome? When it's complete, how will it look and feel?

_____

6. How will I engage colleagues in working on this challenge?

- Our Engagement Strategy for including colleagues in the challenge:

_____

- Our Communication Strategy for informing everyone of the progress:

_____

- Our Accountability Matrix for creating shared responsibilities:

_____

- Our Benchmarks to ensure we are mutually defining success:

_____

- Our Tracking Process to ensure we achieve and celebrate our milestones:

_____

7. What is the mind shift we need to make to ensure we achieve our outcome?

_____

8. Most importantly, what are the stories we want to share with others about our challenges and how we are achieving our outcomes?

_____

As you reflect on the challenges you face at work every day, remember that you not only have an impact on situations by how you behave, but you also have an impact in how you "talk about the situations with others." Remember the stories of Dana and Michael. Remember how each of them told their stories to others. Choose your words carefully. Be mindful of your impact. Think about how you can use your Storytelling abilities to help transform an experience into one which you and others can thrive.

Here are some exercises that you can use to more clearly understand how you "create stories." There are three exercises:

- **Venting:** Learn how to get things off your chest. You can use venting in a positive way to help you release emotions. Be cautious in how you use this one. Learn to use venting in a healthy way so you can arrive at a healthy story.
- **Accountability:** Learn to notice when you are putting yourself in the victim role in your stories. Learn to step into the "I am accountable" role in your story.
- **Reframing:** Learn how to shape a story for positive impact.

Exercise 1: Venting

We all experience frustrating interactions with others that trigger emotional responses, which then linger on and infect other relationships. It's like striking a guitar chord—after your hand leaves the strings, the chord you've played continues to reverberate. Sour notes create music we don't like to hear, so we complain—or vent.

Healthy venting means giving yourself and others permission to vent—within limits. The point is not to let it go on forever. You can choose to vent for seven seconds, seven minutes, or seven hours. Here are the steps:

- Establish a time frame for venting.
- Ask your partner to help you "get over it" by playing a role as you vent (or vice versa). Be specific—you might ask your partner to:
  1. Listen.
  2. Listen for something specific.
  3. Listen with the intention of helping you create a strategy for re-entering the relationship or situation with a fresh point of view—to reconnect.

4. Listen so he or she can give you third-person coaching, or a new perspective on the situation.
5. Listen to help you interrupt a negative cycle you may be stuck in.

■ Ask your colleague to try different roles to see which one helps you the most.

■ Take turns if you both need to vent.

Exercise 2: Accountability

In some relationship scenarios, we choose to become victims. We allow ourselves to give our power away to others, and then we blame them for taking it. Of course, this only keeps us stuck in a self-defeating cycle. If you have a tendency toward victimhood, try this exercise to help you lift yourself to a new level of accountability.

1. Choose a person to be your coach. Make sure it is someone you trust.
2. Identify a situation in which you felt like a victim.
3. On a piece of paper, write down an objective account of the situation. Then describe it as it would appear from a victim's point of view.
4. Set up three chairs. One chair is for your coach, one chair is for you to speak from the "victim" space, and the third chair is for you to speak from the "accountable" space.
5. Victim: Sit in the victim chair, and tell the story to your coach. Be as explicit as possible and recount the details of the experience that made you feel like a victim. When you're done, ask your coach if you communicated the experience fully from the victim space.
6. Accountable: Now sit in the accountable chair, and tell the story to your coach. Let Go of victim thinking and assume accountable thinking. Own responsibility for creating the situation that occurred. Shift your thinking from "it was done to me" to "I participated in creating the situation by doing,

or not doing, X, Y, and Z." When you're done, ask your coach if you were convincing in assuming accountability for the situation.

7. With your coach, share the feelings each of you experienced when you were speaking from the victim space (i.e., anger, frustration, irritation, pity). Then, share the feelings you and your coach had when you were speaking from the accountable space (i.e., powerful, in control, respect, admiration).

8. What about the accountable space attracts you? Carry this model with you. When you are feeling like a victim, call upon this memory to shift your relationship to the situation and the person. Call upon your accountable behaviors to help you out.

Exercise 3: Reframing

It's easy to be frustrated with others. People rarely live up to our expectations or our standards. They bother us—period. Whatever the situation, when we are frustrated with someone, we claim they "always do this" or "never do that." In other words, we judge them and construct negative stories about them. Sometimes our judgment is valid, sometimes it's not; but that's not the point. The point is that once we begin to see others' behavior in terms of "always and never," we reinforce that perception and believe it. We don't cut people slack. It's helpful to surface these patterns of thought so that we can clear them. In doing so, we release the person to behave more positively, and we release ourselves from being nasty and judgmental.

1. Draw up a list of team members with whom you are having difficulty.

2. On a clean sheet of paper, write down their names and, under each name, make a list of the "always" and "nevers" that are ever-present for you. These are the ways you are judging them critically. These are the patterns that you are creating in your mind, getting upset over, and reinforcing in the real world.

3. Look at what you have written down and identify where and how you may be harboring "stuff" with that person in your team.

4. When you are with these people, try listening with an open heart, mind, and soul, and watch how magnificent they become.

WE-aving It All Together

In this chapter, you have discovered an advanced leadership skill—how to have transformative conversations by shaping stories that infuse energy and commitment into relationships, teams, and organizations. This is, in many ways, the advanced skill to which you as a leader have been building up to in your journey through Part 2, Learning WE.

The first skill, *understanding the culture,* is the ability to see and understand the culture in which you work, and to see how you can play a role in transforming it into a healthier, more inspiring, and thriving culture. When coming from an I-centric point of view, it is easy to interpret the culture as adversarial. However, coming from WE-centric thinking, we can transform the culture through our attitudes—in other words, because we create the culture, we can transform the culture. Culture begins with a state of mind and ripples out into the workplace. Understanding our own mindset helps us understand the culture.

The second skill, *embracing the possibilities,* is the ability to step out of our Comfort Zone and rather than fear the unknown, embrace it with excitement and enthusiasm for the future opportunity of learning and growing. Your shift in focus will create a positive ripple effect for those you influence and with whom you work. When coming from an I-centric point of view, we can easily get stuck in grooves in the present, and find stepping out fearful, challenging, and uncomfortable. Coming from WE-centric thinking, we know that the future is filled with many perspectives, depending on where we stand at any time. When we embrace the future, with all its fascinating possibilities, we free ourselves from fear, from the status quo, and from a holding pattern, and open ourselves to opportunities for growth.

The third skill, *opening the space,* is the ability to intentionally open up dialogue opportunities for feedback-rich communication one-on-one, within teams, and across the organization. When we do this, we also open the space for innovation and creativity. When coming from an I-centric point of view, it's easy to assume that the space is for you alone, but it's not. Coming from WE-centric thinking, we know that the space is free. By opening up space, we create an environment where we all have room to learn, grow, and be nourished by energy, ideas, and outside influences that trigger creativity.

The fourth skill, *shaping the conversations,* helps you let go of old baggage from the past as you embark on your Leadership Journey. When coming from an I-centric point of view, we create territorial sense of meaning. Coming from WE-centric thinking, we learn to develop a shared responsibility for creating the future together—a WE-centric sense of meaning. We learn to recognize and release old baggage filled with toxic experiences that undermine and denigrate relationships, and replace them with new meanings that uplift and inspire relationships, empowering them with a new sense of optimism and effectiveness. As a leader, you can begin to have conversations that interrupt old patterns, and engage in conversations that have the power to create new meanings for companies, businesses, and even entire industries. *Shaping the conversations* is a call to action, inspiring leaders to take action every day to release old emotions that are no longer helpful, and replace them with new, uplifting experiences that generate new energy for mutual success.

And, finally, there is the fifth skill: *transforming the culture.* Having moved from a place of understanding, to stepping out, to opening space for Vital Conversations, you are now ready to master one of the most proactive and powerful skills: *transforming the culture* to promote collective success. When coming from an I-centric point of view, we create territorial relationships. Coming from WE-centric thinking, we create a shared opportunity for mutual success. This is what a visionary leader does—not on your own in isolation—but together, with others. And what you create together are the stories that envision and enable the fulfillment of WE. Through WE-centric conversations, we have the ability to reframe our view of the world, have hope for the future, and see the best outcomes for everyone.

Empowering your team to achieve audacious goals and strategies requires flexibility of thought, agility of mind, and speed of response. Most of all, it requires you to break out of old storytelling habits and negative patterns of communication, and view the impact you can have on your business in totally new ways. Use storytelling as a way to break from the past and envision the future. Rather than thinking about situations as problems, think of them as challenges and opportunities, and communicate this point of view in your conversations with others. Until you challenge yourself to change old thinking and old conversational habits, you will see little change from yesterday to today. Without changing how you approach your challenges, no new corporate strategy will ever achieve the desired results or hit the expected targets.

Are You Up for the Challenge?

Many times you are in a position to intercept negative cycles *before* they occur or to interrupt them when they do occur. In a sense, they enable you to create opportunities to shape new stories of success. This is such a simple tool, yet so powerful. Here are some approaches for using what I refer to as *pattern interrupt:*

- When people are feeling fear about something in your team or organization, open dialogue forums to discuss the situation and provide data that will settle people down.
- Involve the people with fears and concerns in planning and implementing change. From this, they will have a new story to tell.
- Reward and encourage speaking up, by openly acknowledging the value of doing so through storytelling—giving examples of how speaking up can help the organization.
- Involve employees in thinking about the future. From this, you will help them shift their thinking away from "I am a victim" and toward "I am accountable."

- Involve employees in critical decision-making for how to improve the company. This will help them feel included, and from this they will take on a greater role in the company's future success. They will create and communicate a more positive "story" about what is happening.
- Continually share information in a timely fashion. From this people will feel included, not excluded, and as a result, they will feel part of the transition. They will become the supporters.
- Discuss the implications of changes going on in the company with employees at all levels. From this, employees will feel like they are in the know and will tell others how great management is at being strategic leaders.
- Distribute challenges and decision-making deep into the organizations rather than holding them for yourself. This inclusion of others will change how employees feel about change and transformation. They will tell stories of success rather than failure.
- Involve employees in providing feedback about what's going on. This elevates their self-esteem, helps them tap into their instincts, and gives them a platform for speaking up.

Following are guidelines for telling success stories with a WE-centric focus. This is a way to check yourself at the door and see what you are bringing into your work environment every day.

Stories That Shift the Culture: Success Stories

What type of leader are you? How do you set the tone through your storytelling skills? Here are some questions to ask yourself about how to tell stories. Challenge yourself to shift the energy in your culture from "judge to grow," from "fear to possibility," and from "caution to courage."

1. Building a Strong Culture: To what extent and in what ways are you setting a tone for collaboration and ongoing change? How are you using storytelling to help people see that they can contribute and participate in creating a great culture and community?

2. Communicating with Honesty and Trust: To what extent and in what ways are you setting the tone for open, honest communication? How are you using storytelling to help people learn how to express what they are feeling and help the organization move from being politically driven to being respectful, supportive, direct, and open in all communications?

3. Stretching to Achieve New Heights: To what extent and in what ways are you setting the tone for great achievements and phenomenal success? How are you using storytelling to help people move from giving up their dreams, setting small sights, and accepting the status quo to embracing exciting and challenging possibilities for creating outrageous futures?

4. Mining for Best Practices: To what extent and in what ways are you setting the tone for cross-company sharing of information and exchange of Best Practices? How are you using storytelling to help people move away from protecting their turf to breaking down silos, exploring uncharted territory, testing the waters, and pioneering new territories?

5. Generating New Ways of Thinking: To what extent and in what ways are you setting the tone for innovative thinking? How are you using storytelling to help move colleagues from being stuck in the past — their old ways and old grooves — to being innovative, creative, and generative? How are you leading others to find new ways to win new, loyal customers and satisfy current customers?

6. Taking a Leadership Stand: To what extent and in what ways are you setting the tone for the next generation of leaders to be able to emerge and drive the enterprise forward? How are you using storytelling to teach others the way to challenge authority, Groupthink, and consensus, and develop their own ideas, points of view, and leadership instincts to contribute to the growth of the brand?

7. Building Enterprise Spirit: To what extent and in what ways are you setting the tone for enterprise spirit and celebration? How are you using storytelling to help colleagues move from a singular focus on "making the numbers" to seeking a higher purpose in contributing to the ongoing evolution of the enterprise, and more importantly, their own growth and ability to achieve their highest potential.

WE-centric Stories help colleagues achieve their highest aspirations, stretch themselves, and realize they can do more than they expected. Your role is critical. You set the tone by how you use stories to focus others on Creating WE.

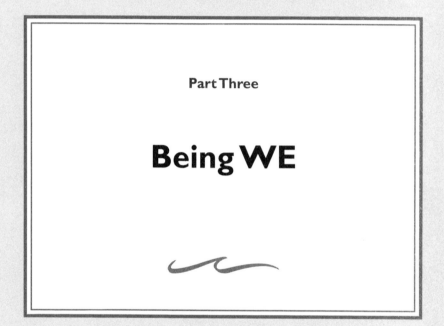

Part Three

Being WE

9.

If They Don't Care, I Don't Care!

Working in Concert

◯‍——

The way a team plays as a whole determines its success. You may have the greatest bunch of individual stars in the world, but if they don't play together, the club won't be worth a dime.

BABE RUTH, HALL OF FAME BASEBALL PLAYER

THE TRUE TEST OF CREATING WE comes with the actual practice of Being WE—of grappling with the many challenging situations in organizational life that undermine your best efforts. Not surprisingly, many of these situations involve coping with change—that ever-present, unavoidable aspect of the human condition that so many of us fear and resist—how to cope not merely in a way that gets everyone safely through change, but actually embraces and sustains change as a positive indicator of health and growth.

Let's begin with an acknowledgment that human beings want to be included and appreciated. When we are not included, we feel left out and reject the system. When we are left out and not appreciated, we turn to others to create our "clan" and become connected again. Human beings need connection to feel safe, loved, validated, and healthy. Through connections, we create healthy environments that trigger our Vital Partnering Instincts; we are healthier and more innovative when we are connected.

So, in order to create WE, we need to value the contributions of others, we need to learn to *include*, not *exclude*. The "old-boy (or -girl) network" mentality is not healthy when its intention is to exclude those who don't fit in. It *is* healthy when it's about including, embracing, appreciating, and valuing. When these essentials are missing, employees feel outside the system and they resist the company direction. They spend more time complaining to others than contributing, and others perceive them as resistors.

This chapter focuses on understanding how to create a culture of inclusion and appreciation. When we create a culture of inclusion, we are creating environments that foster learning, growing, and nourishing, the magic formula for triggering our Vital Partnering Instincts. The absence of these conditions creates territoriality, self-interest, and *power-over* behavior. When we work in concert, we actually stimulate the flow of incredible hormones that act on the brain to enable higher levels of learning—we are more productive, more energetic, more innovative, and achieve higher goals than we would have anticipated.

When teams work in concert, they create an environment for staying in a WE state of mind. In this state you apply all the skills you've acquired in Learning WE; you encourage full engagement, inclusiveness, and mutuality.

What Is Working in Concert?

As your company grows, there is an expansion of potential energy available to work more collaboratively and collegially. Keep in mind the most important principle of our biology that informs true leadership: Colleagues working in concert outperform individuals operating as solo contributors. Working together collaboratively—and in diverse teams—offers the opportunity to learn from one another, gain new skills, perspectives, and experiences. All of these can catalyze new ways of thinking to achieve breakthrough results. In biological terms, all cells recognize they are part of the whole. They synchronize, communicating by signaling when danger is a threat and working together for the common good is paramount.

Study after study shows that when colleagues work in concert, they learn how to communicate more effectively, handle and prevent conflicts, "fight well," and "make up." They are, in short, more apt to achieve the organization's objectives. Working in concert opens up opportunities for accessing a broader mix of skills and know-how, harvesting innovative ideas, and enabling individuals and their teams to respond to complex challenges with a greater chance for success.

We aren't born with all the wisdom it takes to be high performers all the time. Therefore, discovering ways to work more effectively to sustain high levels of performance in the face of uncertainty and change requires the ability to communicate, innovate, and handle the tradeoffs and limitations that often constrain individuals, teams, and organizations.

Breakthroughs in Concert

When people work in concert, they learn from each other and are more apt to develop higher-level skills and the wisdom needed to meet the organization's performance goals.

It's normal for a team of diverse individuals to experience growing pains. In the beginning, unfamiliarity with each other may slow down the "syncing process" until colleagues become familiar with each other and learn how to develop meaningful relationships. Challenges will always arise. Some, such as market competition, a downturn in business, and customer defection, may be external to the team. Others, such as interpersonal conflicts, lack of goals and objectives, unclear roles and responsibilities, and inadequate conversational skills, may be internal. With leadership guidance, teams that "grow together" produce better business results.

Here's how the process works. When colleagues first come together, they are unsure of how the situation will work out. There can be a period of upheaval, internal disagreements, or even fighting before colleagues learn how to communicate and work together synergistically to achieve their collective goals.

Unconventional Wisdom

In Creating WE—we look at the stage that some might call "fighting" or "conflict" as the integral process of "learning" about each other. It's when we are showing our humanness, our vulnerability, and our spirit for inclusion and appreciation. It's a time of "pushing and pulling" and is vital to forming deep relationships. In fact, we don't look at this as fighting at all. This is the most important part of getting to know others. It's about how to speak up when you are disappointed; it's about how to push back and express yourself and, at the same time, strengthen your relationships.

Healthy and Unhealthy Teams

In many teams, conflict may surface and resurface as people sort out the deeper issues of "who's in and who's out," "who does what," and how to balance giving and taking. Some teams can get stuck in challenges and conflicts, and can stay in this conflict state indefinitely. They get stuck when people take the issues underground and create unhealthy practices and norms for handling inclusion, appreciation, and sharing.

Also, conflicts arise any time individuals behave in ways that drive the focus of the team to their personal agendas and interfere with the team's ability to coalesce and accomplish its mission. Such behaviors may be overt and aggressive, or they may be covert and passive.

Conversely, when individuals behave in ways that reduce fears, when turf protection gives way to trust and sharing, individuals behave in ways that are *very* helpful to the team's development— they work in concert with each other. In the same way that healthy cells are more sensitive to each other, individuals on teams develop higher levels of sensitivity to one another. Teams that develop rules of engagement that guide its members toward behaviors that work, and away from behaviors that don't work, gel.

Guidelines for Creating Engagement

Leaders equipped with an understanding of human behavior and what drives us to respond the way we do enable colleagues to gain insight into how to improve performance and reduce conflicts.

It is the wise leader who understands the engagement process, or the behavior of engagement. What enables employees to stay connected and engaged and passionate about creating together, and what causes them to disengage?

This chapter will help you understand why people disengage and what you can do to re-engage them. The material in this chapter will give you a framework to realize when employees are on the ascent or on the descent. Understanding how to use this framework and accompanying guidelines to identify strategies for empowering others to become more engaged allows you to expand your leadership portfolio. When signs of resistance appear, it is a signal—a red flag—that rapport or connectivity is broken, and it's your job as the leader to help restore the connection.

The Arc of Engagement looks like this:

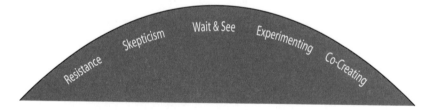

On the far left side of the arc is "Resistance." This is when colleagues are out of sync with the flow of events and have lost confidence in the direction of the company. Employees are unclear on the role they can play in moving the company forward. Resistance is a signal that colleagues are feeling disconnected and may distrust leadership in moving the company to success. They "actively" hold back. Moving slightly to the right, "Skepticism" is when colleagues express doubt or question the leader's rationale for the company's direction. In part, this occurs because they have seen approaches like this fail in the past, or because the approach is contrary to their own sense of direction. They may want to get more involved, but they don't want to experience, yet again, the emotional roller coaster of promise followed by failure.

Next is "Wait-and-See." This is when colleagues are unwilling to act because they are fearful of taking risks and looking foolish. They hold back, expecting others to take the lead. Next is "Experimenting"—an attitude adopted by colleagues who are willing to take risks to create a better way to move forward, who are not afraid to test the waters and step up to a new challenge. And, at the far right, "Co-creating" is when colleagues are partnering and living in a state of mutual trust; they are innovating and pioneering together to create the future. Organic growth is at a high—it becomes a state of being. This is where creativity and risk-taking are aligned and leadership drives transformation. Mistakes are viewed as experiments and there is a strong feeling that "everyone is in this together" and that a higher purpose connects everyone.

Pushback can appear at all transitional points in the arc, helping identify how colleagues move in and out of engagement. Use it to enable yourself and your employees to become shapers of their reality, to become part of the force behind co-creativity—working together innovatively to achieve the organization's audacious goals.

Why Understanding Engagement Is So Important to Innovation

Reading Engagement levels enables you to understand how people are *feeling about* what's happening in the organization. It is like having a real tool that gives you a read on whether people are committed, involved, and engaged in the company strategy or, instead, are likely to disengage and simply stop the process wherever and whenever they choose. Measuring engagement is a way for you to "read" the organizational mood and determine when they are resisting or in protect mode. This helps you know when you need to reconnect with them and how. In both large organizations and small, not everyone will understand your vision or the company's vision at the same time. In fact, you will rarely get the majority to the same place at the same time. We each have our own pace of learning, absorbing, and committing. We each have our own set of inner beliefs about one another. It does take time to digest what's coming at us and to agree to make changes in our lives, especially when we have difficulty addressing those changes immediately and can't readily see how they will benefit us.

Resistance

Our egos are powerful manipulators when we are in a push-push situation with another person. When we feel we are under attack, we naturally try to defend ourselves and openly resist the opposing person's point of view. We also push back to try to convince the other person that we are right and they are wrong.

The harder we push to make our point, the more resistance we engender. We are out to win and don't see the damage we are causing.

Resistance Dialogue Example

Sue: "I think we should buy a copy machine for the office so we can be more productive."

Bob: "That's not what I had in mind. We should send the work out to a subcontractor."

Sue: "You are clearly not aware of the costs of doing that."

Bob: "I think you've forgotten that I've been here for three years and I know what works."

Sue (under her breath): "I'll go talk with Harry, the CFO, and make sure I get what I want."

And so the battle begins.

Many leaders push for "buy-in" and get resistance. Pushing doesn't yield committed and motivated employees. We have an alpha dog in us who wants to show that we can dominate and get our way. We can be so tenacious about it that we sometimes fight to the end at the expense of our relationships and our jobs!

In this self-willed world that tells you to "go for it," you need to watch how your pushing affects other people. Sometimes pushing gets you nowhere but into a holding pattern; sometimes pushing merely creates more resistance.

When you experience more resistance from people and receive less enthusiasm and excitement, you need to stop, look, and listen. *Really listen.* Ask yourself what you may be doing to create this scenario. What are the symptoms? Pay attention to the derailing behaviors.

How Resistors Derail Progress

In a company where resentment, distrust, and oppression rule, people will sabotage your efforts. As a leader in such an organization, you will be faced with employees who push back, rebel, resist, and create bad feelings about management for every critical decision they make.

Derailing behaviors that block transformation occur when people:

1. Act like "they don't get it."
2. Act apathetic by not responding to e-mails and memos.
3. Speak out of turn or make sarcastic remarks.
4. Show up late for meetings.
5. Talk behind your back.

People resist when they don't feel valued, appreciated, and involved in important decisions that affect them. So, they disengage, push back, and don't invest in creating the future. They surround themselves with others who feel as they do. Because they see themselves as out of the loop and disconnected and feel that their leader does not trust or listen to them, they may start to talk with others about their frustration. What was a conversation between two people in private becomes a gripe session with groups of colleagues at the water cooler, in the lunchroom, and during breaks.

Resistance does not just disappear if you ignore it. Resistance builds and ultimately redirects people into survival and territorial modes of behaviors, including when employees dig in their heels and refuse to move with the company strategy and cause other employees to doubt management's sincerity.

Your goal in understanding the Arc of Engagement should be to move people from resisting all the way to co-creating. Make people feel trusted, involved, respected, valued, and listened to and they will go miles for the company. When they are able to experiment and make mistakes, they will undoubtedly uncover ideas that work and that they can combine with other people's ideas to create even better innovative solutions. In time, when you reward employees for stepping out and testing the waters, they will be eager to take the lead.

Of course, we can't expect human beings to "snap to" just because their leaders tell them to. Business is not the military. As a leader of change, you need to understand how to engage people—move them along—to maximize their ability to participate and to feel responsible for and proud of the outcomes they create together.

Resistors sabotage themselves and others by demonstrating protect behaviors:

1. Cutting off communication.
2. Unconsciously forgetting important memos and dates.
3. Pretending they are fine and internalizing their anger.
4. Refusing to be team players.
5. Punishing you with their silence.
6. Lying about their feelings to appear superior and aloof from the problems.

Payoffs for resistors:

1. They don't have to take challenging risks.
2. They can hide from speaking up and putting themselves on the line.
3. They live in a Comfort Zone of inaction.

4. They protect themselves from being vulnerable—and don't need to learn new things.
5. They protect their egos and, by sustaining the status quo, avoid the challenges of growth.

Resistance in Action

Consider the following example from an entrepreneurial software company that I consulted with as they were struggling through change. The two partners running the firm, Daryl and Patricia, had each come from larger companies, and they decided to join forces and start their own business. She was an expert in the field. He was a visionary. Together they had the best of both worlds: operational and marketing experience. Their differing styles, however, often drove them crazy. Patricia was always focused on the present; Daryl was always focused on the future.

As a result, they frequently fought about the direction of the company and how to execute the strategy. Patricia wanted to build the business by making sure that every *i* was dotted, which translated to high-quality products and services. The quality assurance department would not let products out the door until they were tested and retested. Daryl's objective was to get products out the door, stimulate market interest, and eventually be acquired by a larger company.

As their company grew, the partners needed to hire more people to manage technology development and operations. They hired Sharon and Arthur, both of whom came from large companies and had a wealth of prior experience.

As the months passed, the new hires wanted more responsibility. They wanted to do more in the company than implementation of strategy; they wanted influence over product development and customer service. Over time, Patricia and Daryl were so caught up in their own arguments that they didn't pay much attention to the needs of their management team and missed the "include me" signals from these direct reports.

Soon Arthur stopped working hard. He did not seem to care as much about deadlines or follow-ups. Sharon also slowed down, no longer staying late to finish reports needed for client meetings.

Frustrated, she took Arthur to lunch and eventually decided that the problem was that they had unclear roles and responsibilities. They had been hired to be on the management team, yet they had no real decision-making powers.

In the meantime, the two partners pushed these executives to contribute, stay late, and finish their work. Arthur and Sharon became increasingly upset. They refused to acknowledge the urgency expressed by the owners. Quite the opposite—they slowed the process down to a halt. If they were not going to be given the authority and accountability they felt they deserved, they would push back!

They were not, of course, oblivious to the eventual negative impact this attitude could have on the business and on customers; they wanted their management team to respect them so much that all their energy went into pushback rather than on finding a more equitable, mutually beneficial solution. While we made headway on many fronts, and the company moved into a new phase of growth, the resistors were let go from the firm.

> *With this story in mind, ask yourself: What, if anything, might I be doing to create resistance in my relationships and in my organization? How can I shift from resistance to engagement? From protect to partner?*

Skepticism

Skepticism is a lack of trust in the process of transformation and in the relationships with management. Those who operate out of skepticism often believe that people make promises, yet nothing will ultimately change. Many of us have been through change "programs" before, where a lot of energy was expended yet in the end little really changed. When people are skeptical, they do not push back as actively as when they are operating from resistance. They do not generally make efforts to create coalitions to prove that they are right and others are wrong. They broadcast doubt, which causes others to step back from trying new things.

Those who are skeptical have an underlying belief that it's hard to change people, therefore nothing will change. Those operating out of skepticism stop the hands of time to protect "what is." They believe all of the clichés: people are who they are; situations are what they are; you can't teach old dogs new tricks; and no matter how hard you try, you can't influence the future. Anyone who has tried and failed to create change can easily become a skeptic, and sadly, this posture is embraced by a large proportion of the general public. In business, those who are skeptical focus on doubting and even badmouthing the leader's strategy—an attitude that contributes to holding an organization back.

Skeptics sabotage themselves and others by:

1. Talking behind your back and making a joke out of your efforts.
2. Refusing to take risks by saying "I told you so" or "Nothing ever changes here."
3. Refusing to be honest because they think "My feelings don't matter, so why should yours?"
4. Gossiping and backstabbing to protect their turf.
5. Having a destructive frat-house mentality of testing and torturing new leaders as a rite of initiation.
6. Severely damaging group morale by always putting down new ideas, since change terrifies them.
7. Punishing by making fun of people who have trust, hope, and enthusiasm.

Payoffs for skeptics:

1. They have lots to talk to others about—doubting the company line.
2. They build supports around themselves to protect themselves from public exposure.
3. They grow their own authority among their peers.
4. They can "editorialize" about others' ideas—preventing others from attacking them.

5. They become collectors of stories about failure and "why we can't do it here" and therefore become a "proof source" for a status quo culture.

Skepticism in Action

Sarah was a fast-track executive who, by the time she was thirty-six, had run three companies. She was what some called a "turnaround queen." She did this by resizing, reorganizing, and restructuring businesses to make them more customer-responsive.

Sarah, who was incredibly bright herself, had an unfortunate way of making others feel stupid. She often jumped in during conversations and cut people off. Other times, she told people things without listening to what they had to say. She used outside consultants to help her devise strategies and cut out her own middle managers because she felt they were underqualified.

Sarah joined a retail book and music company as chief marketing officer of its Internet division. Her job was to build out the Web site so the company would bring in new customers to shop online and to visit their branded retail stores. Although I had worked with Sarah as a coach while she was in other companies, in this position I did not. Sarah shared her experience with me after she left. She explained that during her first six months, she launched a market research project and discovered that many online customers were substantially different from retail customers. Some people like to touch and feel a product. Others are comfortable shopping online and enjoy comparing the products of several competing companies before making an online purchase.

Sarah presented her findings to her management team: the heads of sales, marketing, operations, human resources, and finance. After this thorough job of research she was convinced that her insights about customer behavior would help her redesign the Web experience to attract a whole new kind of customer, and thus provide the company with a way to radically increase profitability.

The members of the team appeared to listen intently during her presentation. Sarah ended with a request for additional budget to enable her to go after this market. After her presentation, Sarah found some of the team members were hard to contact by phone.

They stopped returning her phone calls and were slow to respond to e-mails. Concerned, Sarah followed up with the CEO to secure the additional funding she needed to move forward. In the meeting with him, she got the sense that her plan might not fly. He did not actually turn her down, but he was elusive in answering her questions. Sarah left the meeting upset, questioning her decision to join the company.

After talking it over with her researchers, she was pleased to find that they supported her point of view. They reassured her that the new markets she wanted to pursue were separate and distinct, and that she had been right to present her case as she did. Six months later, Sarah left the company. She had not received support from corporate for her proposition. Her management team was skeptical of her recommendations and did not want to give her the money she needed to develop her plan, which they didn't feel would produce the promised results.

Where did Sarah go wrong? Why was her management team so skeptical of her proposal? Sarah failed because she did not include any of them in her research. She consulted no one during her initial discovery efforts, nor did she give them a heads-up about her plan. When the time came to vote, they voted against her. Whether her plan was ultimately right or not was not the issue. They doubted her because she failed to bring them along with her. She triggered all their concerns about change, and so they refused her what she needed.

> *In light of Sarah's experience, ask yourself: What, if anything, might I be doing to create skeptics in my relationships and in my organization? How can I shift from creating distrust to creating trusting relationships?*

Wait-and-See

The "Wait-and-See" posture is, of course, more receptive than a skeptical "nothing will change" attitude. However, Wait-and-See people do not want to take the risk and be first.

Those operating out of Wait-and-See want to see where the tide is headed. They want to see what others will do. They are open to change, but they have a low tolerance for risk and need to observe lots of other folks stepping out before they will. Wait-and-See people are afraid of making mistakes. They have scars from trying and failing in the past—we all do. But they see trying and failing as punishment for mistakes rather than as a learning experience. Consider this: If everyone adopted a Wait-and-See posture, no one would ever have the courage to step out, and nothing would ever change!

Wait-and-See people sabotage themselves and others when they:

1. Hold back, driven by an internal perfectionism that prevents them from speaking out spontaneously and honestly.
2. Refuse to confront problems because of their fear-based "what-if" judgments.
3. Become people-pleasers and "good ol' boys" with no capacity to lead in a crisis because they lack the confidence.
4. Are deceptive and base their actions on seeing how people in superior positions react first.
5. Do not know how to resolve conflict. (They keep conflict inside a chronic holding pattern because they are too cowardly to take risks.)
6. Punish others by refusing to take responsibility for being overly cautious.
7. Stagnate a company with their excessive conservatism.

Payoffs for Wait-and-See types:

1. They allow others to take the heat for wrong decisions.
2. They can hide out in a large crowd.
3. Since their point of view is not known, they can change sides either way the wind blows.
4. They avoid potential public conflicts and getting into difficult conversations.
5. They allow others to take the brunt of challenge and change, and ride in the back-draft.

Wait-and-See in Action

One of the divisions of a multibillion-dollar company in the aircraft industry, decided to purchase an ERP (employee resource planning) system. This would help them manage the supply chain more effectively. The system was extremely expensive, at a cost of approximately $350 million. In the meantime, other divisions began to experiment with their own systems, going after the same productivity gains, each with a different vendor and different customization requirements.

The division that had the ERP system knew the project would take eighteen months to complete. The middle executives from other divisions were comparing approaches and found reasons to recommend one system over another. The divisional presidents had a vested interest in their own choice. The larger ERP project seemed to slide, with people continually missing deadlines. The cost to the company for the lost time was $1 million a day.

The CEO put pressure on his presidents to agree on a decision. It was costing the company $1 million a day for indecision. With little tolerance for debate and dialogue, the CEO was enraged that his presidents could not figure out how to make the right decision. What ultimately would be the best way for the company to upgrade its technology? Who was correct?

For fear of the consequences, sixty-five of the top executives adopted a Wait-and-See attitude. No one wanted to make the decision, as each knew it might lead to internal conflict, politicking, and, possibly, forced resignations. People were afraid that if they spoke up and told the truth as they saw it, they would look like resistors. This might also put them at odds with the CEO, who made it obvious that he measured corporate loyalty by who agreed with him.

The real problem lay just below the surface. Because the presidents had invested time and energy in finding their own technology solutions, they thought that transferring over to yet another system would negatively impact their division's productivity. They hoped they could weather this storm and that the problem would resolve itself. They did not want to put their names and reputations on the line. No one wanted to be the one to challenge another's decisions. No one wanted to give up the technology platform he had chosen.

Each felt that if he waited, someone else would step up first and bear the brunt of top management's pushback.

> *Ask yourself: What, if anything, might I be doing to create a Wait-and-See posture in my relationships and in my organization? How can I shift from being in a holding pattern to taking risks?*

Experimenting

Sometimes "living in a box" is just a safer way to live. We get into our Comfort Zone, we do something well, and we like to be able to repeat our success. Experimenting is disruptive, risky, and opens us up to failures. Skeptics remain safe by pushing back on those who want to change—they don't like the experimenters. Experimenters want to make new things happen. They want not only to make something better, but they want to make something new as well.

Experimentation is when colleagues believe that trial and error is good and don't care if everything turns out right. Experimenting is when colleagues have made the fundamental shift from having to do it right every time to believing life is about continually learning to do it better. When people experiment, they step out from the crowd before others do. They are curious and see life as inherently interesting. They believe that change is something you need in your life to make it whole. In business, experimenting is suggesting we try different options to see which will fly. Experimenting is being out on the edge of market research and putting different products in motion to see which ones will produce the best customer response.

Experimenters risk:

1. Looking stupid.
2. Appearing as though they are not on top of things and not "sure."
3. Looking short-sighted, because they honestly do not know the outcome.
4. Being vulnerable because they trust in the unknown.

Payoffs for experimenters:

1. Inspire enthusiasm among staff via spontaneity and trial and error.
2. Allow themselves to be viewed as human, so that when mistakes happen employees don't feel they will be punished.
3. Allow others to take the lead, because they are willing to recognize that there are things they don't know.
4. Depend on team effort to work out the best course of action.
5. Learn, grow, and nourish along with everyone they engage.

Experimenting in Action

Not too long ago, automatic teller machines (ATMs) were unheard of. A few executives from Chase researched the marketplace and found a company that was experimenting with an electronic deposit machine. They reported on it, but no one wanted to listen to these executives.

Their division didn't believe that customers would ever use such a system. The executives tried repeatedly, but the idea was rejected every time. Everyone told them that customers liked to come into the bank and talk with the staff.

Their colleagues felt that a physical bank location was important, and so they invested in real estate to build another branch. The banking industry began to consolidate for various reasons, but some of them wanted to accumulate the real estate—"the territory"—and become the biggest bank in town.

The experimenters wanted to get ahead of the innovation curve and they finally convinced their boss to put money into one test site. This put enormous pressure on them to deliver. In the beginning, customers were not responsive to the new machines. Of course, people immediately said, "We told you so." But they stuck with the test and then asked for another ATM.

In early research, customers did tell them how important it was to have a real person to talk to about their accounts. Yet, these executives continued to experiment with variations of the ATM. Some were independent machines not connected to a retail bank. Others were connected. The key was not allowing the skepticism of customers or colleagues to dissuade them from experimentation.

They stayed with the project, testing and trying all sorts of things and, most of all, learning about resistance to change. Over time, they found the moment of inflection for a larger rollout, and they dove in with a customer-involvement strategy. According to the strategy, the early adopters would bring in the masses, and it worked. Today, we can't imagine banking without ATM machines. Thank goodness for the tenacity and vision of these experimenters!

> *With this story in mind, ask yourself: What, if anything, might I be doing to set the tone for experimentation in my relationships and in my organization? How can I create environments for more engagement and experimenting?*

Co-creating

Co-creating is when we invest in shaping the future, when we are energetically on the forefront of the arc of innovation, sensing the next generation's home base, the next new thing, the breakthrough, or even a disruptive technology. When operating from the co-creating posture, we believe that life is constantly evolving and changing, and therefore we must all look to the future to create it. Co-creators draw upon the past for learning and wisdom to help navigate into the future. For those who co-create, there is no such thing as a mistake, only tests and trials to get where they need to go. They know that from experimentation is born the next fertile idea, the next solution for increased productivity and profit. They believe that without constant change we do not evolve our potential. Life is about taking the next step on our continuous journey. Co-creators know that status quo can be harmful to human beings, and they feel comfortable leading the charge for change.

Co-creators run the risk of:

1. Not having historical data to support their ideas.
2. Venturing out into the unknown with just their instincts.

3. Spending a long time before they see a payoff. (The future cannot be predicted by the past.)
4. Having a hard time building coalitions.
5. Becoming pioneers who must have a personal honor code to see them through to the end.

Payoffs for co-creators:

1. Make invaluable contributions to their organizations, which may create huge impacts on an industry.
2. Learn to trust themselves.
3. Accept that struggle is a part of building one's vision.
4. Accept that we are here to evolve, not just to survive.
5. Inspire others to also create.

Co-creating in Action

Susan was a senior executive. She climbed the ladder of success early in her career in retailing, and with each new career move, had the opportunity of being president of increasingly larger and more visible design manufacturing firms with well-known brands. Sharp and quick-witted, she was extremely candid. Her intuitive merchandising talent plus her leadership capabilities were both her strengths and her weaknesses. At times, these talents gave her more power and influence; at times, they rubbed people the wrong way. Because she was not fearful of authority, she was good at pushing back against resistance and achieving results.

Those who believed in her loved her. She was intuitive and often saw where the business would go before the market did. She was confident in her intuition. She was certain about how to shift strategies and, because of her direct approach, often found that people who had less insight than she did resisted her and slowed her down. This angered her all the more.

She was hired to run a medium-sized retail manufacturing company known for its home-furnishing accessories. The company decided to radically expand its strategy from tabletop accessories to focusing on acquiring unique new products globally. This strategy shift meant an emphasis on designing new products and finding manufacturing partners, and a change from making product to buying product, with a huge thrust on finding new acquisitions.

Susan knew this would be a huge change for her organization and her customers. In fact, it was a radical shift for a manufacturer in the business for sixty years that had barely changed its product line from year to year. For the company, these changes were going to shift the brand dramatically.

This new shift in strategy had a ripple effect in every part of the supply chain, necessitating changes in production, planning, merchandising, design, and delivery.

As the new CEO, Susan was well equipped to become the leader of this company and was prepared to create this dramatic shift. In fact, she brought with her years of experience working in retail, as well as experience running high-end apparel design companies.

Within the first three weeks, however, having completed her internal due diligence of the culture's readiness to change, she realized that the organization she was about to lead in a new direction was mired in the past. Whenever she communicated with the organization about the necessary changes that lay ahead, her team of salespeople, merchandisers, and administrators confronted her with all the reasons they felt change was impossible. Susan was faced with an organization of resistors, skeptics, and Wait-and-See types—and she needed people willing to experiment and co-create.

Susan sadly realized that her team lacked the experience and the skills to transform the business at retail to include these higher-end accessory items. Every team she talked with seemed to be fearful of the changes and wanted to justify why it wouldn't work. She was missing the support that would help her move swiftly toward the strategic goal.

Susan had a big decision to make. She was so frustrated, she considered firing everyone because none of the staff members appeared to be willing to grow into this challenge, nor were they sufficiently experienced and skilled to help drive the strategy forward. Instead, however, she decided to be candid with everyone. She laid tough issues on the table to alert people to the size of the challenge ahead.

Susan put into place key executive workshops for each part of her organization. She used conference calls to connect colleagues located in different parts of the country. She transformed her frustration into education about the business. She learned to provide developmental feedback to get people on track. In four to six months, people started to "get it."

Susan was relentless. She set up critical strategy sessions for her team to discuss key customer accounts and what they needed so they could get on board with the new system. She created clear-cut leadership challenges for her teams to work on and provided them with forums to discuss how to get customers excited.

Susan had choices to make. She was astute to the reality of her business and recognized that she had only a few months to turn everything around. At the same time, she realized that if she allowed herself to function as a reactive leader, allowing the difficulty of her business challenges to trigger negative or controlling behavior, she in turn would trigger reactivity and stress in others.

Sometimes she did mistakenly use her aggressive I-centric candidness; however, when she did, she saw the impact her ranting had on others. When this started to occur, she refocused on turning around her own communication style, rather than operate out of her I-centric mindset. In doing so, she found a new source of energy and skill to turn the organization around.

Susan provided the environment for open communication, learning, growth, and development. She learned how to reduce fear and refocus her team on growth. She stayed committed to the plan, to her team, and helped them keep their eye on the customer by:

- Setting up key account customer teams.
- Including people from sales, merchandising, customer service, and operations on the teams.
- Engaging the teams in focusing on how to "create the future" of profitability for each account by introducing the accounts to the new products and services that were appropriate for each store.
- Running brainstorming sessions with their key accounts to help them gain new insights into the marketplace and the customer needs.

- Running experiments by introducing new products as a test of receptivity to new trends.
- Running more brainstorming sessions within the company to make sure everyone could see the results and regroup with new strategies to continue the growth process.

The end result of her co-creative style was a phenomenal success. While the other companies in the same market suffered from an economic downturn, her company weathered the market challenges and outperformed all other companies in its sector. In fact, she grew her business by more than 50 percent. Most of all, the shift in Susan's leadership style was so amazing that her employees literally "stopped remembering" how she was before her transformation. She became so nurturing, patient, and supportive of learning, growth, and nourishment that employees were hard-pressed to remember the "old Susan."

Her team thrived. Down the road, many were promoted. They remember their time with her as transformational, both for the business as well as for their own personal growth.

Susan discovered that an essential aspect of creating a WE-centric culture is to understand how to create mutually beneficial relationships—co-creating relationships—that are centered on learning, growing, and nourishing. In the face of tough challenges, Susan rallied her colleagues to focus on mutual success, which translated into incredible business success.

Try This!

You probably work on many projects that require you to influence others over whom you do not have direct control. It could be colleagues from other departments or outside customers.

- Use the Arc of Engagement framework of this chapter, and the chart at the end; hand it out at your next team meeting.
- Ask the people on the project team to list all the key stakeholders for the project's success.

- Ask the team members to diagnose where stakeholders are on the continuum from Resisting to Co-creating.
- Ask the team in small groups to decide the desired outcomes they want from each relationship—and to brainstorm a strategy for moving people toward co-create.
- Ask the team members to figure out how they will measure success.

Think about Susan's success story, and ask yourself: What, if anything, might I be doing to set the tone for innovation in my relationships and in my organization? How can I transform environments of fear and reactivity into co-creating environments?

WE-aving It All Together

Understanding the engagement process gives you a new way to gauge the temperature of your teams and the organization. For cells, individuals, teams, and systems to remain healthy, they need to stay connected in healthy ways. When they fall out of connection, they need to re-engage. They need to communicate when things are not going well, and they need to signal each other to move in and close the gap. We become unhealthy when we isolate ourselves, make stuff up about what's going on, and project blame onto others. So, staying engaged in a healthy way is fundamental.

With practice, this is something that you can recognize and influence every day. The principle behind it is simple: When we feel we are controlled and manipulated, we push back and resist change. This is true for you and for the people who work for you. When we are living in mistrust, we exhibit territorial behaviors expressed as self-protection at all costs. We create environments that trigger Territorial Instincts rather than Vital Instincts.

When you don't listen to your employees, they will redirect their energy into finding colleagues who *will* listen to them. The employees you ignore or belittle because they seem unimportant to your agenda will find a coalition of other voices, to create a powerful chorus that can undermine the enterprise's broader goals. On the other hand, when you give your colleagues and direct reports room to experiment and contribute, they will not only go along with change, they will become *leaders* of change.

Too often we think that when people are resisting we need to "push" them into compliance. This is a myth; in fact, it is a way to create more resistance. Instead, when we see resistance, we need to move into a "pull" strategy to engage our colleagues so they become involved and make their valuable contributions.

Rather than tell, we ask! This approach uses *pull energy*. It requires that you listen to employees, acknowledge them, reward them, and encourage their participation. Colleagues living in an atmosphere of trust, support, and acknowledgment drive a WE-centric culture into a state called *breakthrough*!

It is beautiful to hear *a cappella* singers as they each harmonize their parts so perfectly together. The song sounds as though there is a swelling orchestra behind the singers. I sing in an a cappella group as a baritone. The other voices are bass, soprano, tenor, and alto. When we perform, the sound is pure ecstasy. As a leader, you need to listen to conversations as a choral director listens. Each person sings the notes of his or her part. The voices are not the same, yet, when sung together, the combined sound is greater and more beautiful than any individual's vocal vibrations.

An organization working in concert does not imply that everyone sings the same notes. You may expect all employees to buy in to the corporate agenda. Always monitor yourself to be sure that you are not really thinking, "Don't argue with me." There are two sides to any story, and we can get caught up in only one side. As a leader, you want and need people to work together, to move toward a common goal. But, if you start out by "informing" them of the vision and expect that everyone will align behind it, you may be missing the essence of what leadership is about.

Leadership is about engagement and energy management. It's about communication, pushback, listening, and commitment. To get there, you will be involved in dynamics that sometimes look at first like car crashes. Remember, change is about risk, and it's your job—with insight and wisdom—to help colleagues embrace change.

Are You Up for the Challenge?

As a leader of change, you will be faced with the day-to-day collisions and near collisions that come up as colleagues work through the challenges of participation and decision-making. Remember, employees can't make commitments to a company's direction without conversation, without digesting the implications of the changes, and without challenging and pushing back to make sure that, when they leap, they will fly instead of fall. Your job as a colleague and leader is to create dialogue, build understanding, handle implications, and set the stage for full engagement at the co-creating level along with building mutual commitment to organizational success. Use the following chart to guide your journey. Following are guidelines for using the chart:

- Note that the left vertical column on both pages contains the five elements for measuring engagement: Resistors, Skeptics, Wait-and-See, Experimenters, and Co-creators.
- Review the rest of the chart by reading how the world changes from each perspective.
- As you move from Resistor to Co-creator, you will see an increase in energy for action, and an increased ability to create more value for the customer, both internal and external.
- Measure yourself—benchmark yourself against the chart and see where you are now. Then determine where you want to be. Use the chart as your navigational guide.

By now you understand more about your own leadership style—when you are I-centric and when you are WE-centric. You know how to create healthy, thriving organizations. In the next chapter, you will go for the master test, which is how to create a shift in the moment—when you are at "the edge."

| | **Process of Engagement** | | | |
POSTURES	Beliefs	Commitment Level	Impact on Project	Impact on Team
Co-creating	Believes there are no limits to what people can do together	Generative learner; revises systems; sets new standards and directions; fosters commitment to company goals; encourages others' engagement	Inspires others; enables colleagues to contribute; rallies support; inspires others to stretch	Colleagues feel creative alignment, partnership, fulfillment, delight, loyalty, valued, and willingness to commit and engage
Experimenting	Believes people have a lot to contribute and want to contribute; willing to invest to get results	Fulfills roles and responsibilities competently; awareness of and commitment to team goals	Captures opportunities to contribute; tests status quo	Colleagues trust employee and open up; feel that he or she is on their side
Wait-and-See	Believes it's better to wait and see the results of what others do before jumping on the bandwagon; waits to see success; low-level risk-taking	Holding back from making too many commitments; low level of awareness of and commitment to team goals	Captures opportunities to contribute; maintains status quo	Colleagues get mixed signals; feel tensions around trust and confidentiality

(continued)

Process of Engagement (continued)

POSTURES	Beliefs	Commitment Level	Impact on Project	Impact on Team
Skepticism	Believes others are unaware of his or her value	Needs reassurance of value to organization; assumes contributions will be rejected	Misses opportunities to contribute; maintains status quo; stirs the waters for attention; reinforces subcultures, dissension; causes problems; commiserates with complainers	**Colleagues feel distanced and not fully understood; dissatisfied**
Resistance	Believes he or she has no power; defends powerless reality; believes contributions will not be appreciated	Unclear role; often resentful or covertly adversarial; projects judgments onto others; sees no specific way to influence the situation; has no clear purpose and assumes no responsibility	Not effective; avoids interaction and taking action; negative attitude impacts others; gives up without trying; detrimental to projects	**Colleagues feel their needs are being missed; relationship is unproductive; dissatisfied**

(continued)

LEVELS	Listening Orientation	Learning Orientation	How to Advance Self	How to Develop Others
Co-creating	Asks enabling and exploratory questions; flexible dialogue style; accepts and bridges distance between self and others	Willing to modify own ideas and beliefs to include input from others; unbiased and curious; willing to experiment; learns from mistakes and adjusts behavior	Mentor others; focus on challenging and building project capability and strengths; take on responsibility for influencing results and involving others	Ask questions to uncover visions of what great performance looks like; ask questions to uncover obstacles to taking on further responsibility; be strategic
Experimenting	Genuinely interested in listening; knows when to be silent; thinks she or he is a good listener	Willing to examine self and accept others' observations and feedback	Commit to every player winning; rally others around common goals; test beliefs; ask exploring questions; accept feedback; solicit feedback	Ask questions to raise awareness of others' value to team; discuss issues; ask for commitment; ask questions to surface contributions; ask for commitments of time and energy
Wait-and-See	Listens with caution; tends to take words at face value	Is not easily influenced by other people's perceptions of reality; cautions about what is; not interested in investigating what could be	Commit to winning and common goals; test beliefs and challenge assumptions; ask questions and clarify misunderstandings; accept feedback; ask for feedback	Ask exploratory questions to clarify beliefs; listen receptively; transform criticism into contribution; take action

(continued)

Process of Engagement (continued)

LEVELS	Listening Orientation	Learning Orientation	How to Advance Self	How to Develop Others
Skepticism	Tries to listen; self-talk; judges others; asserts own beliefs	Defends perceptions of reality; questions what is; is not interested in what could be; instead of learning from mistakes, falls into self-blame or blames others	Express appreciation of others; support others; accept feedback; tell others what she/he has accomplished; ask how to contribute	Ask exploratory questions to clarify beliefs; listen receptively; transform criticism into contribution; authorize action; take action
Resistance	Listens for why things can't happen; gives advice; misses cues; negative self-talk; blocks out feedback; doesn't hear hope or opportunity	Assumes she or he knows it all; defends knowledge base; repeats mistakes; is not open to learning; struggles with self-worth; victimizes self	Test beliefs; share conflicts and feelings; become open to learning from others; trust yourself; create goals	Listen; ask questions that uncover accomplishments and create goals; request commitment to change

Are You Up for the Challenge?

I-centric leaders are fearful of the worst happening, so they react to the normal ebb and flow by reprimanding people for not performing. Because they become fearful under crisis, they are less supportive, saying, "I told you so." Rather than creating successes and exceeding expectations, they merely produce what is expected and often fail to express support when times are difficult. In business, few things are steady and predictable. Under the flow of business at the most critical of times, the I-centric leader loses the support of his or her team—those most in need of encouragement—and because they retreat, avoid, and share disappointment, they create an atmosphere of discouragement, bringing energy down, dampening desire, and closing down the imagination.

WE-centric leaders believe that co-creativity shifts conversations from breakdown to breakthrough. They are ready to look at new ideas, then share and borrow and test them. They combine the old to get the new—they are energy generators. They are catalyzers. They are agile in their ways, and facilitate idea-sharing and idea-building sessions wherever they go. They think in new ways and inspire others to do so. They seek out new ways to look at problems co-creatively with others; in fact, problems are really opportunities and challenges that bring together colleagues in shared and inspired experiences together, releasing energy and creating excitement along the way. WE-centric leaders think "WE" and create organizational spaces where individuals and teams interconnect to share their wisdom, their experiences, and their insights to expand everyone's horizons and exponentially multiply knowledge and wisdom. Are you up for the challenge?

10.

They Said It Couldn't Be Done!

Sustaining WE

∽

By failing to prepare, you are preparing to fail.
BENJAMIN FRANKLIN

BEING WE, LIKE BEING ALIVE, is not a static condition. Even when you've mastered the ability to work in concert with your colleagues, Being WE can never be taken for granted. As Mark Twain said, "Nothing remains the same." In fact, sameness is an illusion. Sustaining an open mind, and being able to learn, grow, and nourish others is the condition that we must constantly pursue and perfect. The ultimate challenge, then, of Being WE is sustaining WE. Developing a mindset that enables us to innovatively adapt to the changing dynamics of our workplace and our relationships is critical to our success.

Sustaining WE requires leaders to make choices every day that shift the perceptions and direction of decisions in positive, energetic, WE-centric ways, creating a powerful ripple effect of positive, powerful energy, for transforming relationships and the business.

Shift Change into Growth

When things change, and our expectations are not met, we often get upset and angry. Not surprising. Facing unexpected and unmet expectations seems to complicate your well-planned business life—and the resulting challenges can appear daunting, or they can inspire you and others to greater heights.

So much depends on your state of mind and your behavior in the moment. You have choices about how to act, and your choices determine the outcomes you get. In each case, the point at which you make a choice is what I call a Leadershift. It is a decision point that determines the future for you and your organization. The prescriptions for how to handle vital choices are demonstrated in the next set of real-life stories. Each decision the leader was asked to make had the potential to either create an unhealthy or a healthier environment. From each decision comes the potential for incredible energy for Creating WE.

To make a Leadershift, you need to understand the following principles:

- **Beliefs:** First, you need to begin with your own beliefs about the nature of power and how you marshal power in yourself and your organization. Power-over others does not release sustaining energy for change; power-with relationships do empower change.
- **Conversational Choices:** Next, you have to realize the power you have—in the now—to start a conversation moving toward a positive breakthrough for yourself and others. WE-centric leaders have a keen awareness of how their now impacts their future. They realize that, with every decision they make, they not only shape their future, but the future of everyone involved in the experience with them as well. WE-centric leaders value feedback from others and they adjust their approach based on how they affect others.
- **Ripple Effect:** Everything happens in conversations. If you are consciously aware of how your conversations affect others, you can choose to craft them in ways that create uplifting experiences. A series of uplifting experiences creates a ripple effect that drives and supports organizational transformation. They are powerful and uplifting because they inspire everyone involved to new levels of leadership. They inspire us to tackle challenges together that are bigger than we can tackle alone.

Through your positive, uplifting approach, through your inclusive behavior, and your breakthrough conversations, you enable your organization to realize how to achieve results beyond everyone's expectations.

Are you prepared to step up to a new level of influence? Are you prepared to open the space for your organization to thrive? Creating Leadershifts brings a new energy into relationships and organizations. They create a tsunami of energy that raises everyone up to a new level of "being." How does this happen? Whenever you create a Leadershift, you catalyze leadership in yourself and, more interestingly, in others. Along with your act of courage, you encourage and foster growth in others as well as in yourself.

Too often, challenging situations cause us to retreat, attack, or acquiesce. These challenges can appear on the surface to be bigger than what we can handle, and we see ourselves standing at the edge of our ability to be successful.

For example, mergers and acquisitions can seem too daunting when we view the merging entities as separate cultures, with separate norms, separate ways of doing things. Usually the small company is eaten by the larger and loses its persona. Usually people leave the company in droves and, with that loss, goes much of the wisdom and human energy for creating the new entity. What is left is often a demoralized culture, a group of individuals who are riddled with fear over how the new parents will treat them—friend or foe—and who feel abandoned by those who left for "greener pastures." The new entity needs to be shaped and crafted. There need to be ceremonies to bring together the best of the best. Without this, some part of the heart and soul of the surviving companies is lost, and over time, the confusion of who we are—our identity—becomes an organizational malaise.

In spite of my personal, fanatical desire to create inclusive environments, and teach others how to do so, I know there are times when it's better for someone to leave rather than stay. Years ago my husband and I called this person the "point of power." He or she is incredibly disruptive to the new order of things, wants to hold on to the past, creates havoc, draws others in, and causes constant disruption. Today, I see this person as the "unhealthy cell" in an organization moving to a new state of health.

In my studies in social relations at Harvard, I was part of a semester-long experiment in leaderless groups. Thirty students met every day to study the process of groups, leadership, and power. We had no professors. They were observing us through a one-way mirror. Our only task was to be together and manage what happened every day, until the semester was over. We reflected on our group process and wrote our paper on what we thought was going on.

At different times, different self-selected leaders arose to help move the group process forward. During the first three weeks, a few people held the leadership for a while, then the process evolved to other leaders. One person arose who resisted sharing leadership and wanted to sustain his role throughout the summer. He was tough, arrogant, mean, aggressive, and at times caused fear and hate in all of us. He wanted to "own" us and we wanted to get rid of him. It took another four weeks of distress. At times we hoped our professors would step in, but they didn't. In a final surge of group power, we expelled the intimidating leader. Then we spent the rest of the semester talking about what we did and how much force we had to use to get rid of him. We all had mixed emotions about "what was right and what was wrong" and these confusing feelings absorbed us until the last day.

Back then, authoritative, powerful, and controlling leadership figures could get away with their arrogant behavior without fear of losing their power or position. They intimidated others from speaking up, created guilt for pushing back; they made others feel too weak to take the steps to dethrone them. Today we have less tolerance for such miserable, autocratic leadership—thank goodness. Today, in the political realm as well as in companies, we are making it "okay" to speak up and call someone on their behavior sooner rather than later. My coaching practice is full of case studies of leaders who are seeking coaches to help them get over their power addictions. This is the direction we are heading toward: more ethical, more mindful of others, more constructive.

Today we all are much wiser about leadership. The norms for what good leadership looks like are rapidly changing, favoring those leaders who have mastery over their emotions and can uplift themselves and others.

Instead of falling back into I-centric thinking and fear-based behaviors, your goal is to create the space for difficult and challenging conversations to take place. When you recognize that you or your employees are moving into defensive behaviors, your goal is to make the Leadershift and lead colleagues into conversations that can create an uplifting experience that shifts the perspective you hold in the moment. Understanding how you can positively influence the direction that conversations take through Leadershift transforms problems into opportunities for growth, enables everyone to learn in the moment, and nourishes WE-centric thinking.

The Seven Leadershifts

These next sections contain seven Leadershifts—each illustrated by a true story that shows how leaders sustain change by consciously making WE-centric leadership choices. Each approach adds a letter to spell the word C-H-O-I-C-E-S. Anchor these in your mind, and you will know what to do when a leadership challenge arises and you need to make a decision about how to approach it. You will see how these critical pivot points can help you dramatically shift the atmosphere of your teams and organization from territorialism (protect) to vital (partnership).

Ask yourself how you show up at work. Which type of leader are you? Which type of leader are you becoming? Your choices determine your reality.

CHOICES

C = Co-creating: Do you exclude (I) or include (WE)?

H = Humanizing: Do you judge (I) others or appreciate others (WE)?

O = Optimizing: Do you fear change (I) or embrace change (WE)?

I = Interacting: Do you withhold (I) or do you share (WE)?

C = Catalyzing: Do you hold on to the status quo (I) or innovate (WE)?

E = Expressing: Do you dictate (I) or develop others (WE)?

S = Synchronizing: Do you demand compliance (I) or inspire commitment to a higher purpose and value (WE)?

In the beginning of a Leadershift, you may find yourself feeling awkward or self-conscious or you may even feel a desire to withdraw. Once you see the results, however, you will know you have moved to a higher level of leadership and influence. The goal of this method is to provide you with a framework for positive interaction. To reach that objective, you will need to understand the alternative actions you can take at any moment.

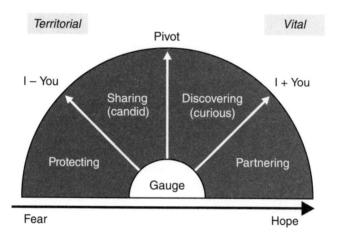

Every day, and in every interaction, forces will be drawing you toward I-centric, protective behaviors. The greatest tension exists at the pivot point where you are clearly conscious you have a choice: either protecting the past or creating the future. When you are in a state of willingness for things to change and to be influenced rather than a state of defending, the Leadershift happens. When you are at this pivot point, you are facing your greatest leadership challenges: understanding how to balance the need for being influential and the need for being open to influence. You are at the same time being pulled toward both protecting and partnering, creating a breakthrough filled with outrageous possibilities.

Co-creating: The Challenge of Setting the Tone

Setting the context or tone is critical for building the spirit of partnering and establishing a positive, inspiring, and collaborative atmosphere for a new community to emerge. It begins with you being inclusive rather than exclusive. It begins with you choosing to elevate people from a territorial I-centric to a vital WE-centric view, and for you to live the change you want to create.

Initiate Change—Beginning with Yourself

When Bayer, a $10 billion multinational health-care company, acquired a smaller $600 million diagnostic company, the CEO, Rolf Classon, chose to call it a "merger." He wanted to immediately establish the relationship he wanted with the new organization. I was part of a consulting team that facilitated a multiday vision, values, and leadership session to help the leadership team create the new direction for their culture and their business.

"We are becoming one company," he told the top 100 people from both companies at their kickoff meeting. He went on to convey that he wanted to set new ground rules for working collaboratively in a new environment in which "together we can create something that never existed before."

The executives discussed changes that needed to be made in the organization to maximize the new partnership. Then they broke into smaller teams to craft the new vision and values, with the intent of reporting their insights to the larger executive team.

When the executives reconvened, a spirit of collaboration had clearly emerged. Rolf once again stood before the group and asked, "How many of you have been through a visioning session before?" Everyone raised his or her hand. "How many of you have left those sessions and returned to the workplace, only to find that nothing had changed?" Mostly everyone raised his or hand. He then declared, "For us to be successful as an organization, we need to realize that we can't create the organization we want without making fundamental changes in ourselves."

As the event unfolded, something magical occurred—Rolf, by his example, taught the executives the true meaning of leadership.

"Change begins inside each person. So I want to let you know that over the past few days I have been looking at what I've been doing to unknowingly prevent change from taking place. I've discovered at least sixteen things I want to change about myself! Here are my top three: my arrogance, my control, and my lack of trust. At lunch I want you each to think about what change means to *you*, and what you can do personally to inspire your own growth. After lunch I want to hear from my top executives—from the podium—expressing their personal insights."

Rolf had allowed himself to be as vulnerable as he had ever been in his life when he acknowledged the personal work he needed to do to make this merger a success. As he left behind his flaws so did the other executives, which made room for cooperation and partnership to grow.

Rolf continued his talk about the future. He engaged others in conversations about the "big challenges" and the "big picture." The key was creating a shared context for change. By setting the stage in this way, he enabled others to find a common ground on which to build the future.

By setting the context, you level the playing field. Thus, power and hierarchy become less important than the results colleagues can create through teamwork. It is a field in which all can put themselves into the context of organizational change and define how they can contribute. When you are on the edge of discovering the context of change, you may find yourself thinking about *how* you can be an inclusive leader.

Shift

Learn to recognize when you are coming from *I* in an unhealthy way. For instance, are you withdrawing and excluding others? Are you defensive and reactive, setting the context for territorialism to emerge? Shift your mindset from I to WE, and set a new context for communication, connectivity, and collaboration, for joining with others for mutual gain.

Humanizing:
The Challenge of Building Positive Relationships

The way you think about people influences how they interact with you. If you think, "We are all in this together," you will behave that way. Appreciate what others bring and leave judgments behind. Rather than see others as competitors, or as lacking what it takes, foster a spirit of partnership. Expect contributions. Help others bring forth their best talents—and they will!

The Importance of Appreciating Others

Stew Leonard created the world's largest dairy store in Norwalk, Connecticut. He called the store Stew Leonard's, and it was an extraordinary store. It began as a small dairy. Through thirty-two expansions, it grew into a $100 million business in a single location. Today, Stew has three stores, all operating at the same level of excellence, and all run by a family member. In 2002, the store was recognized by *Fortune* magazine as one of the "100 Best Companies to Work For," and this honor has been renewed every year since then.

Stew Leonard succeeded in creating a unique and incomparable shopping environment in which the customer's experience was paramount. As customers enter through the large entrance, they are greeted by a three-ton rock on which Stew's Rules (all two of them) are painted in huge letters:

Rule #1: The customer is always right.
Rule #2: If the customer is ever wrong, reread Rule #1.

In the mid-1980s, however, Stew Leonard realized he had done a great job of creating his vision and appreciating his customers. The store was busy with customers who traveled miles for the experience of shopping in this incredible place. Yet there was not a similar *esprit de corps* among a group of employees who seemed disengaged from the vision. Employee interviews and focus groups suggested that, while the vision of "customer first" was critical to the store's success, many employees were unclear as to their role in achieving that vision. In addition, many employees worked in jobs that seemed to have an unclear career path. They couldn't see how to move from cash register to manager—there was no apparent path.

When faced with these insights, Stew immediately took steps to change the situation. With the help of his head of human resources, Stew Leonard's Dairy created a career "Ladder Program," which ensured that each employee could see the steps they needed to take to move up within the company. The Dairy launched an orientation program to help new employees joining the company understand the corporate culture and see the role they could play in the company's success. All new employees were also invited to special training programs to learn about the culture, philosophy, and how they could move up the career ladder. This would not only help them understand the company philosophy, but also realize how they could be part of building and living it every single day. With the same effort he put into developing his "customer first" philosophy, Stew embarked on a mission to enable employees to be fully engaged in creating positive experiences for the customer—for creating Leadershifts every day.

The workplace became vibrant with new practices for educating and including employees in shaping the customer experience. In addition, the management team put into place cross-functional training and employee promotions based on accomplishment and development.

Within a short time, retention levels and morale improved and employees began referring their friends to work at the store. The leadership team started an employee suggestion program and created ways for employees to translate the customer-first philosophy into a living environment of appreciation for everyone.

Today, Stew Leonard's University teaches tens of thousands of corporate executives how to build strong cultures that lead to greater profitability and success. This University is more than a concept. It's a Leadership Program with classes held right at the store, visited regularly by executives worldwide from all types of industries. Executives who attend Stew Leonard's University are given a personal tour of the store by Stew's employees, who are excited to share their personal success stories and talk about their areas of responsibility.

During the program, employees relate how they care about the customer and what they personally have done and intend to do to help grow the business. At Stew Leonard's University, employees teach the courses and share the principles for success. They are not shy when facing executives from IBM and large global companies; they are proud and want to share what they have learned. The teachers are the employees, and their lives have been changed by this experience.

At one time, Stew's culture was a focus primarily on the customer. With the same generous spirit, he transformed it into a culture of appreciation for everyone. Today, employees are the heart and soul of his vision. This transformation took place because their leader, Stew Leonard, realized the power of Creating WE.

Shift

Learn to recognize when you may be unknowingly putting distance between yourself and others by holding grudges or criticizing, or by not sharing your positive feelings toward them, and shift your mindset into a true appreciation of others.

When you are Being WE, you are creating environments full of appreciation. You see people as your equal, which energizes relationships throughout the organization, creating a positive ripple effect of appreciation. You think WE and create organizational spaces in which colleagues and teams work together to support one another's growth and development. You know that the quality of conversations is paramount to building healthy relationships and getting outrageous results. Reflect on how you create environments for employees to share appreciation with others.

Optimizing:
The Challenge of Transforming Fear into Hope

As a child, you fantasized about who and what you might be when you grew up. Companies are created out of the same powerful dreams and the incredibly hard work of people who believe they can turn dreams into reality. Yet when dreams are enormous and the challenges of getting there are great, doubt and fear can erode everyone's power to stay the course. People may give up before they've realized their goals. Or, they may blame others for standing in the way of their success. Rather than optimize, they "pessimize."

Instead of Chapter 11—a New Chapter of Hope

In September 2001, Craig Muhlhauser became the new CEO of Exide Technologies, the 118-year-old battery manufacturer. He replaced Bob Lutz, the previous CEO who had recently been recruited by General Motors. When Bob was CEO of Exide, I worked with him on "Recharging Exide" and transforming the culture from one riddled with fear and apprehension to a collaborative culture in which executives globally learned how to work together toward common goals.

When Craig took over as CEO, I continued to work with him on his organizational challenges. He was immediately faced with the biggest leadership challenge in his business career—the huge lawsuit against Exide that was about to be settled. With the transformation started by Bob, consumer, investor, and retailer confidence in Exide was now slowly turning around. People in the company, however, were afraid of the lawsuit's impact on Exide. The debt was more than $1.6 billion, and they were fearful of the company's ability to stay alive.

Craig was not new to business turnarounds. He had worked as a senior executive at General Electric and as a divisional president at Ford. He understood what it took to create turnarounds and was up for the challenge. Craig saw the sunshine behind the dark clouds. He believed in Exide's products and its people. He brought in new talent to help employees turn the company around. One of those he recruited was Bob Weiner to head up a lean manufacturing effort. Bob succeeded in transforming the process and practices of manufacturing so that Exide soon had a 99 percent on-time, quality delivery performance. Customers saw a new Exide emerging.

Craig pushed the envelope further on transforming the organization. He launched cross-functional teams to focus on cash-flow improvement. These teams were given the task of recovering $50 million in six months. In fact, they delivered $150 million in six months. Craig kept the atmosphere positive. To maintain high morale, he kept everyone focused on achieving the so-called impossible. He turned problems into opportunities for growth and constantly recognized and celebrated milestones and successes.

At the same time, the company was unavoidably facing Chapter 11. Craig saw this as an opportunity to launch the radical business transformation he knew his company needed. As a consummate communicator, he made sure everyone was comfortable talking about the challenges they faced. He engaged everyone in rebuilding Exide. Whenever he sensed people were fearful, he reframed their style of thinking, helping them visualize the positive outcomes that lay ahead. For the first time in Exide's recent history, customer confidence had returned and what followed were straight quarters of better-than-expected earnings.

Craig had an unwavering belief that this turnaround would take place. In spite of the doubt from others who had never seen a company of this size and age restore itself to health, Craig stayed the course. His deliberate, focused, and unwavering belief in the impossible created the space for this dramatic shift to take place.

Shift

Learn to recognize when you are coming from fear, apprehension, despair, aggression, and worst-case scenarios. Learn to notice when you are blaming others for not pulling their weight, or are creating environments that trigger fear of failure rather than aspirations for success. You may be sending people into protect behavior. Shift your mindset from worst-case to best-case scenarios, believe the impossible is possible and—during transitions, transformations, and integrations—inspire hope in yourself and others.

Integrating:
The Challenge of Cross-Divisional Collaboration

You are in a position, as a member of your organization and maybe even a leader, to encourage learning and interacting across boundaries. You have the opportunity to help employees learn how to work together—even in the face of seemingly insurmountable challenges. Rather than fall back on what you know, encourage self-discovery, team discovery, and enterprise discovery. Break down silos; share information, don't withhold it; and also encourage and reward others for doing the same.

Fashioning a Boundary-Free Culture

Donna Karan International Company had a meteoric rise to stardom, as did the founder. Donna's story is fascinating. For Donna, the opportunity to run her own company arose while she was working as head designer at Anne Klein. In 1984, the majority owners of Anne Klein and her husband, Steven Weiss, surprised her with the capital to launch the Donna Karan Fashion Company. The company was incorporated in 1996, and was acquired by its present owner, the French luxury conglomerate LVMH, five years later.

Donna created a lifestyle brand. She revolutionized how women dressed for work with the launch of her DK collection in 1986. Three years later, she revolutionized how women dress on weekends, with the launch of DKNY in 1989.

Within ten years, the company had two strong brands, DK Collection and DKNY, that had expanded its presence at retail in the United States and abroad with divisions in men and women's apparel, shoes, and accessories. The company was a fashion phenomenon. Under the corporate umbrella, Donna Karan International, the company went public. Each division had its own president. Donna herself worked with each design head and the design teams to build the seasonal lines, turning out incredible fashion year after year.

While I was working with the company, we had many conversations about the power of the brand, and developing a strong and consistent brand strategy. We even discussed creating a newsletter to help employees "think brand." Through these discussions, it became clear that if the brand presidents got together to discuss emerging design ideas and their respective brands, they could perhaps make decisions together on how to strengthen the brand at retail. The presidents set up regular monthly meetings and together began to break down barriers and share ideas, working in a unified way to focus on the business side of building DKNY and DK.

The meeting strategy was simple: DK presidents came together in a series of regular brand meetings to discuss how best to work together. With Donna's support, the presidents of men's, women's, and accessories met monthly along with representatives from their divisions. These were valuable meetings that sought synergies across the brand. Through these discussions, similar colors or fabrics for a particular season would emerge, perhaps creating savings across the lines would be possible.

Meetings that began at the presidential level inspired similar meetings on other levels, among designers, sales, and operations. Some meetings mapped out the value chain from concept to market, so that those involved could create better "handshakes" and work more effectively to stay on schedule.

Once companies in all industries learn to break down silos, it becomes easier to create, share ideas, and build internal and external insights across divisions. Once organizations begin to collaborate around brands, it's easier to see "gaps" in the market, and to see where to generate sub-brands based on customer need.

At one of the DKNY brand development meetings, a team of twenty-one executives brainstormed about "who is our customer?" The team also used the meeting to become recommitted to the DKNY tagline: "The energy of NY." This reinvigorated commitment emerged from an intense day of brainstorming to find the brand's essence—a creation of minds working together.

Great collaboration often either opens new untapped market opportunities or validates them, shifting focus and resources toward business growth initiatives. In an effort to create new sub-brands, the Donna Karan team segmented certain lifestyles and product categories, giving brands the opportunity to capture more floor space in department stores. Through a collaborative effort, the Donna Karan team pulled together their facts and insights about emerging market trends and launched into sub-branding DKNY, which led to the creation of a variety of growth sub-brands, including DKNY Jeans, and Junior and Active, which are now licensed to Liz Claiborne. In creating such a powerful series of cross-divisional and cross-functional conversations, the company became stronger, the executives became smarter, and the company's brand became stronger at retail.

Shift

Learn to recognize when you are only focusing on obstacles and feel you can't break through them. Notice when you create false boundaries that separate teams that need to work together for mutual success. Notice when you are creating silos and when your mind is full of toxic beliefs that prevent you from sharing and cause you to withhold. You may be falling into "protect" behavior and may be perpetuating conversations that create barriers, silos, and turf wars. Shift your mindset from withholding and protecting to sharing and giving.

When you are Being WE, you are creating environments that break down silos and encourage sharing across boundaries. Recognize the importance of boundaries to create definition and offer a way to interconnect and amplify the potential of teams and individuals. Rather than being restricted by boundaries, use them to encourage interconnectivity, exploration, and sharing. From sharing with positive intention comes the ability to access Best Practices.

Catalyzing:
The Challenge of Reinvention

You can help employees focus on creating success by encouraging them to challenge conventional thinking, encourage options thinking, and test scenario thinking. You can help them expand their horizons, anticipate the future, and stretch well beyond what is possible today by creating an environment in which employees are not stuck in the past, but instead are able to focus on breakthroughs in every area of their professional and personal lives.

Turning Adversaries into Partners

One of my favorite and longest engagements was with Boehn-ringer Ingelheim Pharmaceutical Company. In our almost ten-year relationship, together we built all the training programs for the sales organization from their first orientation to the company to the programs for fifteen-year veterans. In addition, I was asked to work with the senior management team to create leadership, coaching, and innovation programs for the managers. We called the sales program "BEST," for Boehringer Ingelheim Sales Training, and our goal was to help the sales executives become the best in the industry.

This project brought incredible insights to all of us, and in doing so elevated the BI team to heights they never expected. Early in the project, we learned through an industry study that the BI sales force was rated 39 out of 40—with 40 being the least respected and least known. The sales force, like many, was trained to make presentations and handle objections from physicians. The goal of the sales force was to try to persuade physicians to prescribe BI's drugs to patients.

Upon examination of the typical sales encounter between physi-cian and sales rep, we discovered something about language that helped the BI sales executives create a huge shift in their relationship with phy-sicians, and ultimately in the profitability of their business. When we observed how reps conversed with physicians, it became apparent that they were taught to "handle objections" by trying to persuade the phy-sicians that the objections were not really important. Their approach was to provide a rationale and data to "make the objections go away."

The word *objections,* in and of itself, suggested an adversarial relationship with customers. And so, instead of "handling objec-tions," we asked the reps to eliminate the word *objections* from their vocabulary altogether. They were asked to observe the interaction with the physician from a new point of view—and to find new words to describe what they were seeing.

Once they eliminated the word, they began to think of their relationships with physicians in a new way. Their attention went to how to "create value for the physician." They started to learn how to create engaging and creative ways of having conversations and how to share what they knew in new ways. Rather than looking at their interactions with physicians as adversarial, they began to see the physicians as inquisitive; they were asking legitimate questions, not being resistant. This new way of "languaging" or describing the sales experience catalyzed fundamental shifts in the relationship between sales rep and physician, away from a selling relationship and toward a partnering relationship.

Within a year, the Boehringer Ingelheim sales force was voted—by their peers and customers—as one of the most respected sales organizations in the pharmaceutical business. They not only changed their language, they catalyzed new relationships with physicians, shifting it from I-centric—*I want to sell and persuade you*—to WE-centric—*I am here to serve you.* Along with the BI sales management team, I was asked to speak at pharmaceutical conferences about this powerful approach and to teach other sales organizations about how, by altering language, they could create a fundamental shift in their business relationships and their business results. Furthermore, this experience heightened everyone's desire for success.

Within eighteen months, BI had dramatically increased sales and expanded its market share! And it all started with this simple experiment in reinvention through catalyzing innovative thinking about the use of words. Embracing this single change created an opportunity to trigger Vital Partnering Instincts.

Shift

Learn to recognize when you are stuck in the past, are falling into Groupthink, conventional wisdom, and are accepting outdated definitions. Become open to "creating new meaning" and learn to shift your mindset to discovery by interrupting the conventional patterns of thought and focusing on innovative ways of looking at challenges— redefine your world of words and you will redefine your solutions.

Expressing:
The Challenge of Speaking Up

By now, you have begun to understand the power of language to create meaning and motivation and how words paint pictures that have implications for how people act. You no longer believe you should be an autocratic leader, leading by power over others. Rather you are now actively encouraging others to find their own voices and express their points of view.

The Power of Courageous (and Groovy) Conversations

Dreyer's Grand Ice Cream was founded in 1928 as a premium, naturally flavored ice-cream company by William Dreyer and Joseph Edy. Until 1977, the company served California exclusively. Then, two new leaders, T. Gary Rogers, CEO, and W. F. Cronk, president, expanded the company's distribution system into thirty-four states. By 1989, they were a $400 million company. Today, the company's revenues are in the billions.

Rogers, who came to Dreyer's from the well-known consulting firm McKinsey & Company, wanted to apply the best management principles he knew to build the Dreyer's culture. The two leaders believed in people and in learning. They believed that it was vitally important for every person in the organization to contribute and participate in building the company's future.

The company's management philosophy, summarized in ten principles they call "the Grooves," is taught to everyone at every level in the organization. It serves as the basis for their orientation program, which encompasses weeks of ongoing training on company values, culture, and business.

Their philosophy is so powerful and their integrity and value systems so clear that the company is able to maintain a relatively small management staff for their larger rank-and-file work force.

I started to work with Dreyer's in the late 1980s when the philosophy of the Grooves was already a way of life. The founders are incredible role models of their values and beliefs, and set a tone for others to live the Grooves as well. The founders believe that "when employees are inculcated in the Grooves, the need for training in other areas is dramatically reduced." They are proudly tough-minded about this belief system, and their determination to live the model is apparent in all their communications and training programs.

Each manager is responsible for getting his or her employees into the Grooves' management philosophy derived from the following ten key management principles:

1. Management Is People
2. Hoopla
3. Hire Smart
4. Learn, Learn, Learn
5. Respect for the Individual
6. Face-to-Face Communication
7. People Involvement
8. Upside-Down Organization
9. Ownership
10. Ready, Fire, Aim

What is most important is the way in which "Living the Grooves" is managed and how it shapes the culture. Colleagues meet regularly to discuss the Grooves and how they are living them. The Grooves model is not a backdrop of everyday life; it is the fabric that holds it together.

The Grooves are not a credo laminated onto a plaque that hangs on a manager's wall; they are actualized practices that drive the business from day to day. The Grooves are not something that management gives lip service to at one meeting and forgets at the next. These principles are the oxygen that breathes life into the system and nourishes its people.

At Dreyer's there is no inner circle and outer circle. Doors are open everywhere. An employee can bring an idea to senior executives, and the idea will be considered. There is no screening process based on seniority.

Grooves meetings are different. They are not meetings in which people come to get their marching orders from their bosses. Grooves meetings are times to communicate openly about what works and what doesn't work. They are times for sharing, comparing, and for understanding what's going on in the company. The meetings are opportunities for the CEO and top management to constantly ask employees, "What do you think?" and receive candid responses. Employees are challenged to experiment and collaborate. In fact, the Dreyer's model is based on collaborative learning. The power behind the Grooves is that the culture has embraced these principles as a way of life.

Shift

Learn to recognize when you are coming from ego and authority. In stressful situations, ask yourself, Am I posturing? Am I playing boss rather than developer of others? Am I coming from face-saving behaviors? Rather than thinking I am expected to have all the answers, can I admit I don't and honestly engage with others in conversations about the tough issues to get to the answers? Shift from I to WE.

Synchronizing:
The Challenge of Becoming a Bigger WE

By now you realize that forced compliance and top-down imperatives shrink people's spirit and their drive for achievement. When people are inspired by a higher purpose, they are able to work through tough issues and shift from compliance to commitment.

Finding an Uplifting Purpose—Even in Liquidation

Gordon Brothers Group, a liquidation company, is over 100 years old. From their very beginnings, the company's purpose was to find ways to help retailers liquidate unsold inventory. Every generation stayed with this purpose, adapting it as necessary to changes in the marketplace.

When Michael Frieze took over the company, he brought with him a new spirit. Michael possessed a strong belief that the better the talent he brought into the company, the greater the organization's success would be. He gave these highly skilled executives great latitude to bring their own ideas to the business, encouraging them to move from conventional thinking about liquidation to a broader view of liquidation. Michael did not limit his executives' thinking about liquidation as simply the disposal of waste; he encouraged them to think about the higher value that liquidation can bring to business.

One of the executives he hired, Ward Mooney, whom you read about in a previous chapter, had a particularly great impact on how the organization viewed liquidation. Ward envisioned a Gordon Brothers that could be much more than a liquidation company. He saw Gordon Brothers as a source of capital for retailers. And, within a year of its conception, a retail lending division was fully operational and highly successful.

I had the good fortune of working with Michael Frieze and the senior leadership team to turn the grand visions into reality, and business growth. Michael hired me to be both a coach and an organizational strategist to help each senior leader learn to create WE as a pathway to creating business growth and prosperity.

We worked on many different ways to create growth. Gage, another executive, came up with the idea of building a distribution division via the growing Internet. Michael supported Gage in working through this challenge. Within two years, Gordon Brothers had two new divisions: one for business-to-business liquidation; the second for business-to-consumer liquidation. Both were substantially funded by outside venture capital. Today, one of these businesses, known as SmartBargains, is a highly successful Web-based supplier of branded discount merchandise sold directly to the public.

These successes were possible because Michael, as the company leader, created an environment that rewarded individual contribution *and* teamwork. He set high standards for his employees and attracted extraordinary talent. When someone had an idea on how to grow a new division or expand the business, he supported their research, encouraged them, and challenged them to succeed.

As a result, the business set new standards in its industry. But Michael still didn't accept the status quo. Every few years he looked at how to start a new division. Every time the company seemed to wander into a status quo posture, he sought a way to restart creative thinking. Complacency was not part of the company culture. He was open to feedback and encouraged all executives to participate in a 360-degree feedback process.

Michael knew that living with purpose and passion would engage employees to grow into their highest level of potential. He encouraged people to think about value and how to bring it into the world. Michael encouraged people to think beyond just selling products and services; he taught them the value WE can bring to a business and the customers. Michael discovered the power of Creating WE as he moved the company from a focus on protecting the past to a focus on creating value.

Shift

Learn to recognize when you are pushing people into compliance and when you are inspiring them to take on a larger, bigger commitment to create the future. Colleagues become committed when they feel they are in sync with one another and part of something bigger than they can create alone, and when they feel they are striving for a higher purpose to bring more value into the world. Shift from I to WE.

It's All about Embracing and Sustaining Energy

Change comes from inside; it comes from learning to "transform your thinking" to open the space for new ideas to emerge. Change is about choices, and knowing you have choices in the first place. It's both personal and interpersonal. It's about people wanting to do something great and wanting to be a part of something greater that they can accomplish alone. When people are inspired by seeing a higher purpose, and bringing greater value into the world, they have an appetite to achieve greater things together and are committed to making greater things happen. Change that comes out of such passion and energy is transformational, and it is an irresistible dynamic that can take everyone beyond their highest expectations.

WE-centric leadership enables us to live in a state of dynamic change—a state of ongoing reinvention. WE-centric leadership is a force that inspires interconnectivity and drives individuals and companies forward to realize their mutual aspirations. The WE-centric leader always asks, "What conditions are necessary to kindle and rekindle the spirit every day?" The leader understands that focusing on value creation inspires people to engage so that powerful possibilities will emerge among stakeholders, trading partners, alliances, employees, and customers.

Progress made toward a goal is one of the most reinforcing activities in creating an organizational will for action. Those who change early—the early adopters—help those more cautious to find the initiative to take action. You can fuel change, or bring it to a screeching halt by how you discuss it.

What you notice, and how you describe it, creates the power to uplift people's enthusiasm to unanticipated heights. Positive intention produces positive results. Words can influence people to consider your point of view. They can encourage people who previously "had no time" for you to now set up a meeting with you. Words can forge breakthroughs between two people who were not previously allies. Learning how to positively tell the story of change fuels the progress of change.

These critical elements are keys for successful change to take place and to be sustained over time. Language carries the seeds of transformation, and language must shift for perceptions to shift. Changes in action, coupled with changes in how we talk about the experience, create new momentum that will drive the organization forward.

The CHOICES stories recounted in this chapter are examples of how you can apply the Practices of Partnering every day. You can either dig in your heels around your vested interests, or push through your Comfort Zone to create an infinitely more vital workplace for your team, for your organization, and for yourself.

Try This!

Whether you are a man or a woman—old or young—or a seasoned or new leader, you have choices about how you want to show up at work, and influence and engage with others. From the moment you wake up to the moment you step into your office every day, you influence others and create ripple effects wherever you go.

The Ripple Effect

1. Reflect on relationships, situations, and encounters you have had over the past few weeks. Are there times when you felt like you were at your edge?
2. Are there any experiences you wished you could do over? Are there any where you wanted things to take a different turn? Where you had hoped for a better outcome?
3. List the situations, relationships, and encounters you would like to experiment with.
4. Go through this book and identify a Leadershift that you would like to experiment with—find one that attracts you most.
5. Over the next few weeks remember the shift you want to create and you will see opportunities arise to try new behaviors.
6. Perhaps a time when you were:
   - Wanting to judge your colleague—try appreciating them.
   - Excluding others—try including them.
   - Dictating to others—try asking their opinion.
   - Controlling others—try catalyzing their ideas.

7. Observe the impact you make.
8. Ask for feedback from the people involved to see how you released new energy and created a ripple effect through new experiences and new energy.
9. Continue to experiment with new approaches.
10. Reward your success!

WE-aving It All Together

Being WE is a dynamic state of reinvention in which we feel comfortable challenging the status quo—and each other—to think in new ways.

Health is a natural state of being. Lack of health—or disease—is the absence of the nutrients for health and growth. When we find ourselves embroiled in combative relationships with others, fighting for our own self-interest, and using power plays to get to our goals at the expense of others, we are creating unhealthy environments for everyone. The antidote is to learn to think bigger together, to create things that never existed before, to open the space for innovation, and to tackle our common challenges in ways that define a new, more empowering organization.

Redefining how we work together is fundamental to Creating WE. There are beliefs we have grown up with about power, for example, that are growing old and stale. Healthy environments enable difficult and courageous conversations to take place. Healthy environments are not fear-based; they are aspirational. Healthy environments like the ones in these stories yield greater business results than we could achieve alone.

As a WE-centric leader, to sustain health, you need to realize the role you play in creating shifts from I to WE. This chapter reminds us that we have CHOICES to make every day. When we are conscious of these choices and the impact they have on others, we can choose to engage rather than disengage; we can choose to include others rather than exclude them. And each choice we make does have an impact—a big impact on our own health, as well as on the health of our teams and our organization.

When we were young, some of us were sold a bill of goods—a set of beliefs—that we have carried forward into our adult life. Many of those beliefs center on what will happen "when you become an adult." Many of us were taught to believe that when we became an adult we would be *all-knowing, all-powerful,* and could exercise that power as we saw fit. Many of us were taught that learning stops when we become an adult, and that we can then stop growing.

Along with these beliefs, or rather, myths, is the recommendation to be powerful, dominant, all-knowing, and self-centric. In doing so, we create the very challenge this book is here to address. Once we make ourselves the center of the universe, we stop learning, growing, and nourishing one another. When this state occurs we go into a holding pattern. We make ourselves the most important part of our reality. We become reactive when things change around us and fail to meet our expectations, and we become territorial. We reinforce patterns of interaction that lead to I-centric thinking.

Leadership is not static—we don't really stop growing, yet we can protect ourselves from learning, growing, and nourishing if we buy into the myths we were sold long ago when we obediently followed authority figures whose power intimidated us and kept us in our place. "I'll be an adult someday and won't have to take that crap." Instead, we can dish it out.

Most of my coaching career has included example after example of a fallen hero—a leader who rose to the top, brought along an incredible set of skills that the company paid a fortune for, and yet who also brought along an outdated view of what leadership is all about. Sometimes, without clear consciousness, they have fallen into the alpha male or female trap of intimidating others to compliance, or closing down conversations because their opinions are *the* opinions. Many of the C-level executives whom I have coached to become more WE-centric have realized along the coaching journey that they have brought the intimidating style as a survival approach to a very competitive environment. Many of the executives have worked through their illusions and have found that living in a more collaborative, supportive environment is really better for everyone.

Sometimes we get stuck with a boss who has not been given the fortunate gift of coaching. Sometimes, we try to bring enlightenment to this boss, and we get shut down in front of our colleagues. As a result, no one has the courage to speak up. My hope is that once you share this book with your boss or colleagues, they will see the light, abandon their unhealthy ways, and choose to transform themselves even without a coach.

Are WE Up for the Challenge?

My greatest hope is that within a few years, there will be a huge revolution in business that shifts the norms from I- to WE-centric leadership, and that this movement will have the power that the "nonsmoking norm" has had in businesses, airplanes, restaurants, and living spaces. I also hope that WE-centric leadership will spread like a good virus throughout the world and help create healthy, thriving organizations of all sizes from the smallest to the largest.

When we remind ourselves that partnering is as easy as learning, growing, and nourishing—and when we encourage one another to create environments that allow our individual Vital Instincts to thrive—we will have environments that transform I-centric cultures into WE-centric cultures, and we all will thrive.

The Heart of Leadership

In the following chart, "The Heart of Leadership," you will see a summary of the principles discussed in this chapter. Creating WE takes a consciousness about the choices you make every day to bring either I-centric or WE-centric energy into the world. The choice is yours.

Creating WE requires that you understand how you affect others. It's only when you see the link and adjust your leadership from the eyes of the receiver that you truly integrate and reach your full leadership potential.

The Heart of Leadership

Monitoring Leadership Behaviors: "I-We"

Dimension	I-Centric View	WE-Centric View
Co-creating *The Context We Set*	**Knowing How to Win** *Being a competitive player* **Potential Negative Consequences:** Creating an internal win/lose environment where divisions compete with each other	Taking charge *and* balancing competition *and* collaboration; competing for market share; collaborating with colleagues; creating win/win
Humanizing *The Relationships We Build*	**Providing Clear Direction** *Letting people know where they stand* **Potential Negative Consequences:** Blaming others if they fail; focusing on weaknesses rather than strengths	Being assertive, providing clear direction, *and* challenging employees to develop their own ideas; listening with an open mind while suspending judgment and criticism; supporting risk-taking; giving people space to make mistakes and learn
Optimizing *The Dreams We Hold*	**Driving for Results** *Getting people to make commitments* **Potential Negative Consequences:** Coming across as aggressive; appearing too bossy; creating a fear-based environment; giving too much negative feedback	Holding people accountable *and* providing encouragement, feedback, and support; being able to forgive and make up, and Let Go of grudges; coach people for commitment
Interacting *The Actions We Take*	**Establishing Boundaries** *Guiding where energy is focused* **Potential Negative Consequences:** Saying "no" too often; using positional power and hierarchy to limit sharing, cross-pollination, and unknowingly reinforce silos	Being able to set boundaries *and* break down walls, promoting cross-pollination and sharing; expanding horizons; bringing the outside in; freeing the spirit for learning; harvesting collective Best Practices *(continued)*

The Heart of Leadership (continued)

Monitoring Leadership Behaviors: "I-We"

Dimension	I-Centric View	WE-Centric View
Catalyzing *The Ideas We Evolve*	**Working Swiftly and Agilely** *Being incredibly productive* **Potential Negative Consequences:** Doing most of it yourself; believing others don't have the stuff; limiting the organizational accountability; working through a "to-do" list; failing to tap original thinking	Being able to get stuff done *and* get others engaged in the process, unleashing the spirit and imagination of others to be accountable for creating the future; inspire out-of-the-box thinking, testing, and experimenting; building scenarios
Expressing *The Words We Choose*	**Having a Leadership Point of View** *Inspiring others to become committed to a common goal* **Potential Negative Consequences:** Coming across as dictatorial and inflexible; pushing your ideas on others; taking pride in your own ideas and not listening to others' ideas	Having a leadership point of view *and* inspiring employees to discover their own voice; harvesting the leadership talent in the organization; expanding the leadership potential; sponsoring individual and team challenges; building bench strength; creating mentoring; coaching initiatives
Synchronizing *The Purpose and Passions We Live*	**Being a Charismatic Leader** *Providing direction for achieving results* **Potential Negative Consequences:** Creating compliance to your vision; assuming "telling" leads to aligned action and commitment to a common goal; can create compliance	Being a charismatic leader *and* engaging in strategic conversations about the future; sustaining management and employee dialogue; stimulating continual reassessment of the business; creating the space from ongoing dialogue

Throughout this book we have been exploring the dimensions of your mind—how you think, the assumptions you make, the choices you make, and your impact on others. I hope you are developing greater self-awareness and a keener sense of how you affect others in the *now*, and how that impact ripples into the future. Central to the story of WE-centric leadership is becoming comfortable with three things: making your beliefs transparent, accepting rich feedback, and experimenting with that feedback to shape and craft the leader that you are able to become.

Whether you are working in an organization with 10, 100, or 100,000 people, your beliefs, behavior, and attitude have an impact on others. Some ripples you create will be bigger than others, and I hope they will result in a healthier, more robust organization.

Vital Leadership takes time. It's an evolution of deep awareness of how you create experiences for others that have the profound ability to enable your organization to thrive and explode with potential.

Regardless of the type of business you're in, you are a leader and you have power and influence. Learning how to use that influence in positive ways is critical to your success. You can use your power effectively and help your organization thrive and sustain change, or you can use your power ineffectively and shrink the potential and aspirations of everyone you touch.

To be successful, you need to reflect on how you want to lead, then artfully adjust your approach as you learn more and more about what creates health, growth, and expansion for yourself and others. You will succeed by understanding your own leadership, and when your approach doesn't produce the results you desire, you must be willing and able to transform it.

Afterword

Standing at the Edge
of a New Beginning

Better keep yourself clean and bright;
you are the window through which
you must see the world.

George Bernard Shaw, playwright

Congratulations! You have now arrived at an important milestone in your Leadership Journey to Creating WE. You now understand the interplay among Believing, Learning, and Being WE. You clearly see that your beliefs act as filters that influence what you see, learn, and do, and now you see that you can create new experiences for yourself and others through conversations. You know that you can change your culture by how you show up every day and influence conversations, which ultimately influence your organizational norms—your culture.

Now you understand that you have the power, at any moment, to shift a situation that is in a downward spiral into one that is vital and fulfilling by shifting your mindscape—your view of reality and the role you play in it. You now have the skills to interrupt your own patterns of negative thoughts and beliefs and turn them into positive thoughts and actions that can create breakthroughs with others. You now have the tools to create something bigger than you ever imagined—as well as a future for your company or enterprise, as it deserves to be created.

Living in the NOW

As you go into the world to experiment with the New You, you will find that some people will be extremely supportive and will resonate with your new leadership skills. Others will look at you in confusion, wondering why you are acting so differently. Still others may think you must be ill. Stay the course! Work your edges! Keep giving yourself permission to feel good about the commitment you are making to your personal and professional growth and health.

At times you will find the work atmosphere oppressive and impossible to transform. You will feel as if you are "falling down the steps" as conflicts arise. People's reactive behaviors will begin to show up everywhere. People will be in conflict over who had which resource, who gets to go to which meetings, who are the favorite children, and basically who is losing and who is winning.

You now have the conversational skills to turn these situations around. You are a master at Courageous Conversations, and of Vital Conversations. You know how to handle conflict and complexity by making a Leadershift.

Keep in mind that a positive, open conversation can help shift the discussions from territorial, where people fight for their own vested interests, to vital, where they strive for a mutually satisfying outcome. If you are not communicating and working through the tough stuff, don't expect it to go away; it only gets worse. That patch of crabgrass in your garden will infect the whole lawn faster than you can keep up with it if you don't do something about it.

Master Yourself

You can't lead others until you know yourself. Vital Leaders have a keen sense of how their *NOW* impacts their *FUTURE*. Learning to stay in the NOW is vital. When you receive pushback and it sends you into your protect behaviors, you are operating out of your less-effective leadership behaviors. Master yourself first.

Create the Signals for Health

In healthy workplaces, there are universal signals that everyone shares. These act as an immune system, giving health to the whole enterprise. Start with this list, then build your own. Realize you play a role in creating health.

- Always look for the nonverbal responses to what you are saying. Check reactions.
- After you tell, ask if there are any questions for clarification.
- Ask questions such as, "Is there anything that is unclear or confusing?" and "Are there any implications that we need to discuss?"

You are now at the edge of a new beginning for your organization but, more importantly, for yourself as a leader and human being. The next steps you make are critical to moving from the understanding you've gained in this book to creating a new reality in the world in which you live.

Remember Your Elemental Wisdom

When we learn to develop greater awareness of the principles that underlie growth and health, we can create environments that foster health. So much has to do with the way we use words and language when we communicate, and the underlying mindset we hold as we interact with others. Keep in mind the following as you continue on your journey:

- **Transformation is linguistic:** Become astutely aware of the role language plays in shaping your thoughts, feelings, and actions, as well as those of others. Language defines how you communicate the rules of engagement, the norms, and the practices of your culture—your "habit patterns." Language expresses your codes of conduct, your protocol, and the road signs that tell you to go or not to go at an intersection. By becoming aware of how you use language to shift your patterns of interaction with others, you become a master of personal and cultural transformation.

- **Move with—not against—others:** When you believe others are your adversaries, you move against them. This turns them into adversaries. By moving with them, and with the intention of creating something wonderful, you do create something wonderful. Your beliefs drive your intentions, your intentions drive your actions, and your actions drive the results you achieve.

- **Speak from the I; listen from the WE:** When speaking face-to-face with people with whom you need to "work out issues," speak from your authentic "I." Share feelings in a candid, not judgmental, way. Be candid and open but not blameful. Difficult conversations are challenging, yet when one I meets another I in candor, they form a perfect WE. Bringing in a third person to work it out for you is not a substitute. When you speak, speak from the "Heartful I." This is the first step to creating open and honest conversations. Listen with the idea of trying to partner and create synergies with others.

- **Be willing to change your beliefs:** We all subconsciously create stories about others and make assumptions and inferences about their motivations. When we are upset and territorial, we assume that their intentions are negative. These beliefs stand in the way of building a shared vision. When you are able to Let Go of old, faulty assumptions, beliefs, and stories, and learn through open dialogue what is really driving motivations, you create powerful transformations in your life and workplace.

- **Come from abundance, not from lack:** When you are feeling that there is not enough to go around, or you believe that people don't have what it takes, you come from a mindset of "lack or inadequacy," and you build your beliefs about people and situations from that perspective. This paradigm turns the world into a place where something vital is missing. No one is good enough, no one is smart enough, and no one is who or what we want them to be. When you come from the perspective of abundance, however, you seek to find the greatness inside. And when you seek it, you find it!

■ **Create uplifting transformational experiences:** When everyone is pulling in the same direction, the weight each individual has to pull is reduced. When you join with other leaders to open a space where you can think together about what each wants your company to become, the team can accomplish incredible results. When you decide you want to involve and encourage employees to become part of a shared vision and involve them in realizing that vision, more often than not they will exceed your expectations.

WE-centric leadership is a mindset. Being WE is the result of learning and practicing WE—what you do every day. If you didn't begin with Believing WE, you certainly will when you see the spectacular results you will achieve!

Where Are You Now?

To many people, business is about financial success. True, financial gain is one of the outcomes of business success. However, the bigger business we've been talking about in this book is the business of your life, how you shape and craft your life to achieve your desired financial and business goals. You will gain financial success by the way in which you live your life. In that arena, there are two dimensions: your inner life and your outer life. How the two come together is what creates your actual result.

As you interact with your own life and with the lives of others, you will trigger new possibilities or you will feel the pain of old wounds. As you go through your life, you may also conjure up dramas that can get in the way of your success. If you consciously recognize that you are in control of your reactions, you will be able to step into your personal power with confidence and gusto.

The mandate of the WE-centric organization is to create a future that honors life, honors relationships, and honors accountability for the results we all can create together. When we are willing to enter a relationship with others that is designed to *influence and alter our experience of reality*, we enter into a transformational experience that will change our lives far beyond our wildest imagination. If you accept this responsibility, you have become a member of the new generation of leaders who are transforming themselves, transforming the world of business, and also transforming the fabric of humanity.

When my daughter Becky was twelve, she wrote a poem that I read all the time. It inspires me. I offer it as a gift from me to you, so that when you feel off-center and want to give up, it can help you recharge your battery and get back into the mission of Creating WE. Today, Becky is a mother in her own right. Here is her poem:

There once was a boy with a dream all his own,
To fly to the moon and invent his own phone.
He had such big dreams that spread far and wide,
That nothing could stop them 'cause they came from inside.
Then one day the boy's thoughts started to stray.
All he wanted was a job with high pay.
And all those dreams that he had collected
Were no good now and simply rejected.
As time passed, the man got older,
He sat for long whiles getting much less bolder,
He didn't walk much for because when he did
His bones creaked loudly, not much like a kid.
Then one day while sitting in his chair,
The Man remembered the very, very rare
Dream that he had known while around the age of ten
And suddenly the man became a young boy again.

Vital Instincts Tool Kit

You have come this far because in your heart and soul you know that you have powerful leadership instincts just waiting to emerge. Remember to trust your Vital Instincts and to respect yourself. Remember to take time to celebrate your successes—even the small ones. If people push back on you, don't let their implied negativity stop you from staying the course. Here are some additional exercises for you to take along your Vital Instincts Journey. Use these to refresh your mind when you need inspiration and to refresh your soul when you need an uplift.

Daily Touchstones for Health

Here are seven touchstones to guide you as you enter what may appear to be a challenging leadership experience. Use each as a touchstone to remind you how to create environments that foster Vital Instincts. Use the touchstones as daily prescriptions—take one a day to keep you moving forward and to remind yourself of the wisdom you already possess. Return to them when you feel your energy depleted, when you feel you are sliding back, or when you just need to refresh your mind and spirit.

Touchstone I:
The Questions for Opening New Pathways

Leadershifts begin with *questions*. When we ask questions for which we know the answers, we are merely validating what we know. The priceless gems are the questions for which we have no answers. These higher-level questions enable us to move from a stagnant view of the world to a new view filled with energy and opportunity.

Answer these questions and see what pathways they open for you:

1. What is—or what could be—your role in Creating WE in your company?

_____

_____

_____

2. What beliefs will you need to discard?

_____

_____

_____

3. What kind of WE-centric leader do you aspire to become?

_____

_____

_____

4. From what do you draw your greatest strengths and energy as a leader?

_____

_____

_____

5. What passions drive you forward every day?

_____

_____

_____

6. How can you create a culture in which colleagues can coach and support one another beyond whatever negativity shows up?

_____

_____

_____

7. How can you create an atmosphere that encourages experimentation?

_____

_____

_____

8. How can you create an environment that allows colleagues to discuss their intuitive feelings about the business and where it's going?

_____

_____

_____

9. How can you create a forum in which colleagues can ask "what-if" questions for which there are no obvious answers?

_____

_____

_____

10. When will you be ready to begin the journey?

_____

_____

_____

Touchstone 2:
The Images for Turning Visions into Reality

Images are the next touchstone. Envisioning our success as a leader anchors our success to the present. Visions of the future pull us forward to define the future. We need to create images of the future that are robust, outrageous, and full of new and challenging possibilities, so that they motivate us to break from the past and step up to our next level of greatness.

What visual images can you imagine or surround yourself with that will help you become the WE-centric leader you want to be?

Touchstone 3:
The Relationships for Catalyzing New Possibilities

Relationships are the third touchstone. There is nothing more important than building strong relationships, where conflict is viewed as a way to expand and grow. Relationships depend on starting from a place of appreciation and understanding. We shape our relationships by the words we choose. Words are not neutral. They are the golden threads that connect one heart to another heart. Examine where you are standing in your relationships, as in the following:

- Do you enter each business relationship with an open mind, with an open heart, and with the desire to discover and create wonderful outcomes with each person?
- What old business relationships do you need to Let Go of that may be dragging you down?
- How can you catalyze new possibilities in all of your business relationships?
- Think of people you need to connect with who can support your growth as a leader. Who are they?

Touchstone 4:
The Conversations for Unleashing
a New Spirit of Co-creation

Conversations are the fourth touchstone. As we connect through conversation, we release energy and create new possibilities. Conversations set the tone and allow us to either feel we can move mountains or make us feel trapped. Although it may seem on the surface that conversations are purely an exchange of information, that is not the case. Conversations link us to others at a deep level. After a conversation we either feel good about the other person and ourselves, or not. We enter each other's lives through our dialogue, and join together to become part of each other's thinking as we catalyze new ideas, connections, and possibilities—or we don't. We are connected through conversations—those we have in person, through e-mail, through others, through words spoken, through subtext unspoken. Conversations have the ability to transform us and our work and our world.

Think of conversations you want to have with people in your life who can help you become a vital WE-centric leader. What are the conversations you need to have, and with whom?

Touchstone 5:
The Lift for Harvesting New Powerful Connections

The *Lift* is the fifth touchstone. Lifts are life-changing experiences that have so much impact on the lives of those involved that they reconfigure how we think about the present and the future. They help us elevate to a new level of insight and feeling about ourselves and about life. Harvesting new connections is one way that we release ourselves from old patterns and old behaviors. Some people are convinced that it takes forever to transform a person entrenched in the past, or a company that is set in its old ways of doing business. This is not true. It does not take forever. Uplifting experiences create instantaneous transformation, and learning how to create uplifting experiences will catapult you forward on your Leadership Journey.

- What old patterns of behavior do you want to leave behind on your journey?
- What behaviors are holding you back from becoming the most effective and dynamic leader you could possibly be?
- What experiences would you need to have that will help you undergo a transformational lift and create lifts for others?

Touchstone 6:
The Stories for Creating Outrageous Futures

Stories are the sixth touchstone. The way we talk about our experiences after the fact creates the foundation for our future. Experiences happen and we construct a story by creating characters with personalities. We give our characters "destiny" and we choose the good guys and the bad guys. We give our characters lives with relationships, and we put ourselves inside the story as either the winner or the loser. We select words to describe people in our story

LEARNed Responses

If you are in a tough situation where you feel a conflict coming up, use the simple mnemonic LEARN to remind you of specific things you can ask:

L — What did you LIKE (about what we are discussing)?
E — What has set up new EXPECTATIONS we need to deal with?
A — What causes you ANXIETY?
R — What creates new REQUIREMENTS, will take new RESOURCES, could feel uncomfortable, or could cause RESISTANCE?
N — What are the NEXT steps to handle this? Anticipate the concerns and plan the company's or your own next steps.

and we overlay our feelings, our beliefs, and our perceptions. Our stories frame our experiences in the way a picture frame frames a picture. Stories are what we give to others—hopefully, the gifts they open every day. Think about the stories you tell others.

Ask yourself the following questions:

- What stories are motivating and life-affirming calls to action?
- What stories drive your passion and success?
- What stories can you leave behind?

Touchstone 7:
The Transformations for Living the Vision

Transformations are the final touchstones in our journey to success. Transformation occurs the moment you realize you are not the same person you were yesterday. Transformation occurs inside you first, then outside. Inside, you now hold new beliefs about who you are and who you can become. You have a new awareness of your purpose and a new set of exercises and ambitions, joy-producing goals for your future. Your personal transformation catalyzes new energy that you can bring into your life and the lives of others you care about.

Imagine yourself stepping into your new WE-centric leadership role and ask yourself the following:

- What is different now? What has changed? What are your new aspirations as a leader?
- What are the beliefs that will transform your self-image and propel you forward?
- What new awareness do you have for your future?

Return to the NOW!

If you find yourself living in the past, bring yourself back into the NOW! Of course, some people do that more easily than others. The secret is to deal with the now even if it feels uncomfortable—such as facing conflicts and other difficult situations, telling the truth in a tactful way, and making up. And, speaking of making up, here are a few tips that will help you maintain your stamina for the work of Creating WE.

Fix It Immediately

Anytime you make a mistake with a customer and fix it—they love it! "Service Recovery" is the term used when you accept the problem and agree to fix it. This is also true when you apologize for the inconvenience. Customers appreciate it when we, as vendors, take responsibility for our actions. They do not like it when we defend ourselves and try to explain why we did whatever got them upset. They don't care why; they just want the problem resolved. The same is true in all of our relationships. If we step on someone's toes, we can usually make up by saying we are sorry—i.e., apologizing—and promise not to do it again.

My husband taught our children a game when they were little. It was called the "Make-Up Game." When they got into fights and couldn't stop, he taught them the steps to work it out, and made a game out of it to take the sting out of having to apologize. The Make-Up Game works with adults, too. This may sound childish at first, but I've taught this to executives, including multistore managers from Coach, and they have told me how much it helps.

Ask: Are we in a fight (or having issues)? Let's talk. What do you need to get off your chest? Then, listen. Appreciate the other person's point of view. (Don't judge them.)

Ask: What can I do for you (change, stop doing, start doing) to make it better? What do you need from me? This is what I need from you. (This is where you help each other turn emotions into positive requests for what to do differently in the future. You learn to verbalize what you need and want—this is really healthy.)

Ask: How much more time do we need to work it out? (This sounds silly; it has a touch of humor in it, and sometimes creates a great pattern breaker—meaning you see that you sometimes carry anger for a long time and fail to get over it yourself.)

When you are finished discussing the conflict, one person says, "You say Make!" The other says, "You say Up!" (This is what kids do. Adults may want to shake hands, to say thanks for the talk, or say something really great like, "This was really helpful to me. How was it for you?") Then both parties shake hands. If you can't, you are not finished talking. You'll know when you've reached the destination.

Index